Penguin Books
Screen Test

Peter Bowen is a Canadian who attended Carleton University and the University of Western Ontario before coming to England in 1964 to study. He studied at New College and holds a doctorate in zoology from the University of Oxford. He has been Producer at the University of London's Audio-Visual Centre, and is now Director of film and television services at the University of Warwick.

Martin Hayden is a graduate of the University of Sussex and of the Royal College of Art. He spent a brief period doing odd jobs in commercial film-making before being appointed Producer at the Audio-Visual Centre of the University of London.

Frank Riess was born in Santiago, read modern languages at Wadham College, Oxford, and did postgraduate studies at Oxford and Berkeley. He has published several articles on different aspects of Latin America and a book on the poetry of Pablo Neruda. He is a Lecturer in Latin American literature in the University of Nottingham.

Peter Bowen, Martin Hayden and Frank Riess

SCREEN TEST

A Quiz Book about Movies

Penguin Books

Penguin Books Ltd, Harmondsworth,
Middlesex, England
Penguin Books Inc., 7110 Ambassador Road,
Baltimore, Maryland 21207, U.S.A.
Penguin Books Australia Ltd, Ringwood,
Victoria, Australia
Penguin Books Canada Ltd,
41 Steelcase Road West,
Markham, Ontario, Canada

First published 1974

Filmset in Photon Times 10 on 11 pt by
Richard Clay (The Chaucer Press) Ltd, Bungay, Suffolk
and printed in Great Britain by
Fletcher & Son, Ltd, Norwich

Contents

Contents

Preface

This book is for people who like movies. In reading and answering its questions, we hope you will enjoy remembering films you have seen, and discovering just how much you know about the cinema.

We think that the quiz format will be an entertaining way of reviving memories and acquiring new information, and we have tried to devise questions about all the major types of films, the outstanding names and the best-known titles. Of course there are many less well-known entries, providing a mixture which all kinds of moviegoers, from the casual to the compulsive, should find stimulating.

It has been necessary to place films into more or less well-defined categories. Our classification is by no means definitive, and overlap is not only inevitable but often desirable. *Gone with the Wind* (1939), for example, is a romantic drama, an epic, a war movie and in most countries a foreign film.

Dates of films have been a problem. Different references often quote conflicting dates; indeed, one book may give two dates for one film. Some sources quote the year in which a film was made, others the year of release in the country of its making, still others its release date in their own countries. Some standardization is necessary, and we have opted for internal consistency and a reasonable approximation of the year of release in the United States or in Britain. In any case, we are using dates as reference points, to locate a film in its period. The precise date is not vital in a book of this type.

Films are sometimes released under different titles in different countries. We have tried to list all the alternative titles, giving the generally better-known title first.

We finished this book in mid-1972; films released later than this are therefore not included.

We used a number of books as sources of information and as

check lists, and they are acknowledged elsewhere. But it would be churlish not to mention here Leslie Halliwell's *The Filmgoer's Companion* (3rd edition), the most useful reference book about movies. We are also grateful for the expert and friendly assistance we received from the staffs of the Information and Stills Departments of the British Film Institute, to the various studios, listed elsewhere, for permission to reproduce the pictures, and to Joel W. Finler who supplied us with some stills from his collection. Finally, our thanks to our wives, friends and colleagues for their interest and forbearance during the preparation and writing of this book.

PETER BOWEN
MARTIN HAYDEN

London, 1972   FRANK RIESS

1   The Silents

Looking back, we tend to think of the first thirty years of film-making as a single unit – the Silent era – although the term itself had no meaning before the advent of sound; such a reference clouds perception of the period in which the major film genres were established. Silent films feature frequently in this book, but the silent era, which laid down the patterns of subsequent aesthetic and industrial development, is important enough to warrant a chapter of its own.*

1   ——— ——— invented the phonograph in 1876. Soon afterwards, he was exploiting a new invention, the kinetoscope, in penny arcades and peep shows. The first *projected* kinetoscope was shown at the Koster and Bials Music Hall, New York, in the year ———.

2   Before the star system, production companies didn't publicize the names of actors. Instead, they were labelled with the companies' names. One such was 'The Biograph Girl': what was her real name?

Later, stars became the main draw, and new labels and words were introduced into the language. With whom do you associate the following?

The Vamp
America's Sweetheart
The 'It' Girl

3   True or false?

1. 1915 saw Thomas Ince, Mack Sennett, D. W. Griffith,

---

* Answers on page 18.

Douglas Fairbanks, the Gish sisters, Billie Burke and William S. Hart *all* working for the same company.

2. Charlie Chaplin started at Keystone in 1913 for $150 a week. By 1917, he had been offered more than a million dollars, by Thomas L. Tally, a west coast showman, to make eight two-reelers.

3. In 1924, Warner Brothers had on their payroll Ernst Lubitsch, Rin Tin Tin, John Barrymore and Sacha Guitry. They all appeared together in a film in the following year.

4. David Wark Griffith, working with Mutual, directed a patriotic film, *Hearts of the World*, in France in 1918. Noel Coward appeared briefly in it, with Lillian Gish.

4 1. Jesse Lasky, of the Jesse Lasky Feature Play Company, was joined by actor-writer Cecil B. de Mille and one Samuel Goldfish in 1914. Everyone remembers de Mille, but who was Goldfish?

2. Samuel Goldfish, Edgar Selwyn (an actor and theatre producer) and playwright Margaret Mayo formed another company in 1917. What was its name?

3. In 1924, this company merged with another. What was the new company called?
Within a year, Goldfish had gone independent, and someone else took over control of the company. Who was he, and what was the company's next (and final) name?

5 By 1919, the studios were finding it difficult to pay the astronomical salaries demanded by some of the stars. The stars, for their part, felt that they were being exploited by the studios. In response to this impasse, the Big Four formed the United Artists Corporation, to allow them to produce and distribute their own pictures. Who were the Big Four?

6 Pre-eminent in the smouldering Latin Look of the twenties was, of course, Rudolph Valentino. Although he had no serious competitors, there were others who adopted the same style: Ramon Novarro, Ricardo Cortez and Antonio Moreno, for example. All four are pictured above: which is which?

7 But not all the heroes were so glamorous. Many were
ordinary types, full of virtue, good looks and clean living –
like Thomas Meighan, Richard Dix, Richard Barthelmess
and Rod La Rocque. Which names match these pictures?

8 Many silent superstars had brothers or sisters who, although not as well remembered as their siblings, were regularly in work, and occasionally made a name for themselves too. Can you match the following stars with their lesser-known brother or sister?

1. John Barrymore   Noah ——
2. Charles Chaplin   Dustin ——
3. Norma Talmadge   Jack ——
4. Lillian Gish   Constance ——
5. Mary Pickford   Dorothy ——
6. Wallace Beery   Syd ——
7. Wiliam Farnum   Lionel ——

9 Some actors became famous by capitalizing on arbitrary or unique characteristics. Here are the leading characters from *The Cheat* (1915), *Disraeli* (1921), *A Woman of Paris* (1923) and *Don Juan* (1926). Who are they?

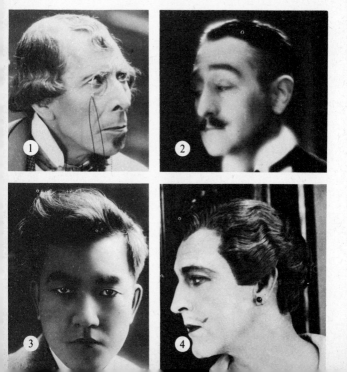

10 The three films in each of the following groups have something in common. What is it?

1. *Cabiria* (1913)
   Quo Vadis (1913)
   The Last Days of Pompeii (1914)

2. *Male and Female* (1919)
   Don't Change Your Husband (1918)
   The Affairs of Anatol (1921)

3. *The Wonder Man* (1920)
   Headin' Home (1920)
   Daredevil Jack (1920)

4. *The Covered Wagon* (1923)
   The Ten Commandments (1923)
   Greed (1923)

5. *His Majesty the American* (1919)
   The Thief of Baghdad (1924)
   Don Q, Son of Zorro (1924)

6. *Pretty Ladies* (1925)
   The Only Thing (1925)
   Old Clothes (1925)

7. *The Little American* (1917)
   Lest We Forget (1918)
   Shoulder Arms (1918)

11 1925 was a critical year for the movies, since they were threatened by the rising popularity of 'Broadcast Radio'. In spite of, or perhaps because of, this competition, *The Big Parade*, *Phantom of the Opera*, *The Gold Rush*, *The Last Laugh* and *Stella Dallas* were all made that year. Who was the principal male star in each picture?

12 English director William Desmond Taylor was murdered, and Mabel Normand and Mary Miles Minter were said to be involved.

Starlet Virginia Rappé died as a result of injuries sustained at one of Fatty Arbuckle's drinking parties; Arbuckle was arraigned on (and later acquitted of) charges of rape and murder.

Matinee idol Wallace Reid died in an asylum while on a cure for his drug addiction.

Scandals like these caused the formation of, and supposedly proved the need for the Motion Picture Producers and Distributors of America Inc., set up in 1922 to impose a 'dictatorship of virtue' on the industry. It enforced strict controls of what happened on the screen, and put morality clauses in everyone's contracts. The MPPDA became better known under the name of its first president.

Who was he?

Where was he recruited from?

How long did he stay in office?

What was the Production Code?

When was it first published?

13 The American Academy of Motion Picture Arts and Sciences introduced its awards system in 1927. The first award as Best Actress went to a comparative newcomer whose star was very much on the rise. Who was she?

Was it her appearance in *Seventh Heaven*, *Sunrise* or *Street Angel* (all 1927) which won her the award?

14 An early development in the movies was the serial – guaranteed to bring the fans back next week to see the heroine (always the heroine) escape from death (or worse) in the nick of time, by the skin of her teeth. Can you complete the following serial titles, and say who played each heroine?

1. The Perils of —— (1914)
2. The Hazards of —— (1915)
3. —— of the Dailies (1914)
4. The Exploits of —— (1915)
5. The —— of Kathlyn (1913)

15 One of the hallmarks of silent films was the exotic lady, emphasizing her allure with sensational costumes, blatant sex appeal and some astounding names. Here are Pola Negri, Vilma Banky, Dolores del Rio, Louise Brooks and Alice White. Which is which?

16 The alternative school of heroines was altogether nicer and not half so colourful. Here are some examples: Bessie Love, Marion Davies, Mary Astor, Alice Terry and Norma Shearer. Again, which is which?

The Silents — Answers

1 Thomas Alva Edison never realized the possibilities of the medium he invented. He exploited his kinetoscope as a cheap catchpenny device for mass entertainment of the uneducated poor. His efforts to maintain a monopoly in film production were eventually thwarted by the energetic and independent ideas of men like Carl Laemmle of Universal. The Koster and Bials show was in 1896.

2 Florence Lawrence was 'The Biograph Girl'. When she moved to Imp Productions, Biograph circulated a rumour that the new 'Imp Girl' had been run over and killed by a tram in Kansas City.*

Theda Bara was the original Vamp, although the term was later to embrace a whole style of acting and of dress (and a popular dance of the twenties).

America's Sweetheart was, of course, Canadian Mary Pickford.

'It' was sex appeal under a different (and more genteel) name. Romantic novelist Elinor Glyn dubbed Clara Bow the 'It' Girl.

3 1. True. They all worked for Triangle films. The studio was at Culver City, named after the man who donated the land to the company.

2. True, although Tally is said not to have found Chaplin funny.

3. False. They were all working for the Warner brothers,

* Florence Lawrence first appeared in vaudeville at the age of four. She was billed as 'Baby Flo, the Child Wonder Whistler'.

but it is hard to imagine a film that could successfully combine the talents of so disparate a group.

4. True. Coward was eighteen at the time.

4

1. He changed his name to Sam Goldwyn, and became one of the top producers. He was noted for his 'family' films, and was famous as a star-maker. The company later merged with Jesse Lasky's Famous Players, which eventually became Paramount.

2. The Goldwyn Picture Corporation.

3. Goldwyn merged with Marcus Loew and his Metro Company. The Wall Street backers felt that this would place some control on Goldwyn, whose judgement was suspect: he was so unconventional that he had even imported a foreign film (*The Cabinet of Dr Caligari*, 1919).
The final overlord of this mélange was Louis B. Mayer, who controlled Metro-Goldwyn-Mayer until he was forced to resign in 1951.

5

They were Mary Pickford, Charles Chaplin, D. W. Griffith and Douglas Fairbanks. Pickford and Fairbanks were married the following year, and they lived happily at 'Pickfair'. They were divorced in 1935.

6

1. Ramon Novarro (1899–1968), who was really Ramon Samaniegos, from Mexico, was Metro's Latin lover. In the picture he is uncharacteristically dressed: he was usually in Sheik gear or as semi-nude as they could manage, as in *The Arab* (1924) or *Ben Hur* (1926). His other notable films included *The Prisoner of Zenda* (1922), *Scaramouche* (1922) and *Mata Hari* (1932). His big Arab comeback, *The Sheik Steps Out* (1937), was a failure.

2. Antonio Moreno (1886–1967) was a Spaniard who began in Hollywood in 1912. His most successful films were in the twenties: *The Trail of the Lonesome Pine* (1923), *It* (1927) and *Synthetic Sin* (1928) are good

examples. The coming of sound revealed his heavy accent, however, and he was forced to move to character parts, in films like *Storm over the Andes* (1938), *Captain from Castille* (1947) and *The Creature from the Black Lagoon* (1954).

3.   Rudolph Valentino (1895–1926), former gardener, dishwasher and gigolo, became such a big star on the basis of the tango sequence in *The Four Horsemen of the Apocalypse* (1921) and *The Sheik* (1921) that there were suicides on his death, and his funeral was the biggest thing since the Great War. In 1938, *The Sheik* was re-released by Paramount and earned a fortune. He made at least thirty-three other films in his ten-year career, and there are at least four published biographies.

4.   Ricardo Cortez (1899–   ), Jack Kranz from Vienna, began his career as an ersatz Valentino in films like *The Torrent* (1926, from which this still is taken, and in which he co-starred with Greta Garbo), *Behind Office Doors* (1928) and *The Sorrows of Satan* (1927). He later diversified, achieved something of a reputation as a heavy in the thirties, and even turned his hand to directing before he finally quit the movies in 1940.

7   1.   Rod La Rocque (1896–1971), or Roderick La Rocque de la Rour, was built up by de Mille when he entered the movies from the circus. His first movie was *Efficiency Edgar's Courtship* (1917), which established his popularity, and he continued with a solid following through the twenties with films like *The Ten Commandments* (1923), *Forbidden Paradise* (1925) and *Our Modern Maidens* (1928). He married exotic star Vilma Banky and their wedding reception, produced by Sam Goldwyn, was one of Hollywood's most elaborate.

2.   Richard Barthelmess (1895–1963) was at his best in his films for Griffith: *Broken Blossoms* (1919) and *Way Down East* (1920); the latter was his only United Artists'

film to make money. His *Tol'able David* (1921) has become something of a classic, but his popularity was founded more on films like *The Fighting Blade* (1923), *The Amateur Gentleman* (1927) and *Dawn Patrol* (1930). He maintained his innocence through the thirties (*Heroes for Sale*, 1933, for example), and made his last screen appearance in *The Spoilers* in 1942.

3.   Thomas Meighan (1879–1936) was another de Mille creation. He wasn't always the nice guy: in *Why Change Your Wife?* (1920), he played the unfaithful husband caught between Gloria Swanson and Bebe Daniels. But in most of his films he typified the twenties hero: mature, with experience, resourcefulness and a reputation for straight dealing, in films like *Male and Female* (1919), *The Miracle Man* (1919), *The New Klondike* (1921) and *Tin Gods* (1926). One of his best-remembered films is *The Alaskan* (1924).

4.   Richard Dix (1894–1949) was the good brother in the modern part of *The Ten Commandments* (1923). His stern features and good heart were also featured in *The Christian* (1923), *Manhattan* (1924), *The Vanishing American* (1924) and *The Quarterback* (1926). He had a flying start in the talkies with *Cimarron* (1931), but quickly faded into lesser roles such as *The Whistler* series of B-features.

8   1.   Lionel Barrymore (1878–1954), brother of John and Ethel, the best-known screen actor of the family. He acted in films from 1909 until 1953, as well as directing a few in the thirties. From 1938, he had to give all his performances from a wheelchair. He is best remembered for his character roles, especially as Dr Gillespie in the fifteen *Dr Kildare* films.

2.   Syd Chaplin (1885–1965), brother of Charles, made many two-reelers, and a few features in the twenties, then retired when sound came in. Charles also has an actor son Sydney.

3.   Constance Talmadge (1900–   ), sister of Norma, comedienne and heroine of silent films (*Intolerance*, 1915),

whose last screen appearance was in 1929. There was also another sister, Natalie, who made a few silent comedies, and then retired to marry Buster Keaton.

4.   Dorothy Gish (1898–1968), sister of Lillian, both of whom were famous leading ladies for Griffith. Dorothy left films in 1928 for the stage, although she made a few movies after the mid-forties.

5.   Jack Pickford (1896–1932), brother of Mary, another member of the Griffith stable, made many silents (including a *Tom Sawyer* in 1917), but didn't make it into the talkies. There was also a sister, Lotte, who made a few early silents.

6.   Noah Beery (1884–1946), brother of Wallace, one of the silents' most famous villains, continued in films until 1945. His son Noah Jr is still active in pictures.

7.   Dustin Farnum (1874–1929), brother of William, star of many western (*The Squaw Man*, 1913) and action (*The Scarlet Pimpernel*, 1917) films.

9   1.   George Arliss (1868–1946), British stage actor who was middle-aged before making his first screen appearance in 1921 as *Disraeli*, the first of his series of highly theatrical portraits of great men. He won an Academy Award for his 1930 *Disraeli* sound re-make, and continued with films like *The Man Who Played God* (1931), *Alexander Hamilton* (1931), *Voltaire* (1933), *Cardinal Richelieu* (1934), *The House of Rothschild* (1934) and *The Iron Duke* (1935).

2.   Adolphe Menjou (1890–1963) became a star as a result of *A Woman of Paris*, directed by Charles Chaplin. He gradually evolved a reputation as *the* immaculately-dressed seducer: *The Kiss* (1916), *Gold Diggers of 1935*. Latterly, he was playing mostly character parts: *The Hucksters* (1947) and *Paths of Glory* (1958).

3.   Sessue Hayakawa (1899–   ), one of the screen's most durable actors, as *The Cheat*. He was educated for the navy,

trained in Shakespearean theatre and ended up bringing the exotic mysteries of the East to Hollywood, in films like *Forbidden Paths* (1917), *The Tong Man* (1919) and *Daughter of the Dragon* (1921). His appearance in *The Bridge on the River Kwai* (1957) was misleadingly billed as a comeback. He'd never been away.

4. John Barrymore (1882–1942). The Great Profile, with his bravura style, always managed to introduce some bizarre or grotesque vignette into his films to demonstrate his stupendous abilities. He played in all sorts of films: crime (*Sherlock Holmes*, 1920), horror (*Dr Jekyll and Mr Hyde*, 1920), adventure (*The Sea Beast*, 1925) and romance (*Don Juan*, 1926). His great voice was a real asset in the talkies, but after his triumphs (*Grand Hotel*, 1932), he slipped into B-features (like his three *Bulldog Drummond* movies).

10 1. All were early epics, made in Italy and imported into the United States by George Kleine of the Motion Picture Patents Company.

2. Gloria Swanson starred in these films; all were directed by Cecil B. de Mille.

3. These were three attempts to make movie stars of contemporary sports heroes: Georges Carpentier, Babe Ruth and Jack Dempsey, respectively. Another, made in the same year, was *The Heart Punch*, starring Jess Willard.

4. All were lavish blockbusters for their time. *The Covered Wagon* was the first real American epic not directed by Griffith. The leads were Lois Wilson and J. Warren Kerrigan, and it was directed by James Cruze. *Greed* was Erich von Stroheim's masterpiece which, cut to the bone, ran more than eight hours. He finally agreed to reduce it to four hours, but producers Mayer and Thalberg cut it to two. Von Stroheim repudiated it, but it remains one of the outstanding movies of any time. *The Ten Commandments* was de Mille's first epic, and it set him on the road to becoming

the king of the epics. This version was really two stories: the first was the story of Moses, but the second, a modern one, was something of an anticlimax. It had no particular parallel with the biblical story, although it did have the typical de Mille mixture of sex and religion.

5. All were star vehicles for Douglas Fairbanks, from United Artists, of course.

6. The first three films to feature Hollywood's longest reigning star: in the first two she appeared under her own name, Lucille Le Sueur, in the third, she appeared for the first time as Joan Crawford.

7. These are examples of Hollywood's 'war effort' which starred, respectively, Mary Pickford, Rita Jolivet and Charles Chaplin.

11 They were respectively: John Gilbert, Lon Chaney, Charles Chaplin, Emil Jannings and Ronald Colman.

12 The MPPDA became known as 'The Hays Office' after its first president, Will H. Hays ('The Czar'). He was lured (with $100,000 a year, rising to $150,000) from his job as Postmaster General in President Harding's ill-fated cabinet. The Production Code ('The Hays Office Code', although Hays himself did not devise it) wasn't published until 1930. It was immediately adopted as law by the Vatican and the Province of Quebec, but in Hollywood was largely ignored until the formation of the National Legion of Decency in 1934, a Roman Catholic censorship body. Its pressure on Hollywood brought about the formation of the Production Code Administration, with attendant certificates and Seal of Approval, whose job it was to enforce the Production Code. Hays retired in 1945; the Code remained for thirty-six years, but its gradual erosion began in the early fifties, encouraged by challengers like Otto Preminger (*The Moon is Blue*, 1953). It had become less effective by the time the final modifications were made by Jack Valenti in 1966.

13 She was Janet Gaynor, and she won her award for *Seventh Heaven*, in which her co-star was Charles Farrell, with whom she made many successful romantic films.

14 1. *The Perils of Pauline*, starring Pearl White, certainly the most memorable (and most parodied) of all the serials.
2. *The Hazards of Helen*, with Helen Holmes.
3. *Dolly of the Dailies*, starring Mary Fuller.
4. *The Exploits of Elaine*, with Pearl White again in the title role.
5. *The Adventures of Kathlyn*, with Kathlyn Williams.

15 1. Polish actress Pola Negri (1897–) came to Hollywood with German director Ernst Lubitsch after early successes as *Carmen* (1918) and *Madame du Barry* (1918). Most of her silent career was a running battle with Gloria Swanson, Paramount's number one female star; box office receipts kept her in second place. She had an affair with Valentino shortly before his death.

2. Dolores del Rio (1905–), a wealthy and aristocratic Mexican actress, was kept in the public eye in the late twenties and early thirties by an elaborate publicity campaign which played up her society heiress background. This was as much responsible for her popularity as her appearance in films like *What Price Glory?* (1926), *High Stepper* (1927), *The Loves of Carmen* (1927), *Gateway to the Moon* (1928) and other exotic romantic movies.

3. Louise Brooks (1906–). Although she enjoyed a tremendous vogue, on the basis of films like *The American Venus* (1926) and *Rolled Stockings* (1927), she was never really given adequate roles in Hollywood, and her best-remembered work was done in Germany: *Pandora's Box* (1929), for Pabst, and *Diary of a Lost Girl* (1930).

4. Vilma Banky (1903–) was discovered by Sam Goldwyn while he was holidaying in Budapest, and her brief career included many lush, escapist romantic dramas like

The Dark Angel (1926), *Son of the Sheik* (1926) and *Night of Love* (1927). She married Rod La Rocque, and their judicious investment in real estate has maintained them since the advent of sound.

5. Alice White (1907–42) was for a few years Clara Bow's only serious rival in the late twenties razzmatazz scene. She was often featured in 'wild party' movies such as *Mad Hour* (1928), but she just didn't have as much 'It', nor did she have the exotic appeal of stars like Nita Naldi or the outrageous reputation of Joan Crawford (with her 'lingerie party' on her yacht in *Dance Fools Dance* in 1931). She quickly faded from the movies.

16   1. Alice Terry (1899–   ). Her success was more critical than commercial, for she was frequently overshadowed by her leading men: Valentino in *The Four Horsemen of the Apocalypse* (1921) and Novarro in *The Prisoner of Zenda* (1923). She married handsome but not too successful director Rex Ingram and retired in the late twenties.

2. Norma Shearer (1900–   ), one of the major stars of the silents and of the first decade of the talkies. Her success was due as much to her determination and hard work as to her marriage to MGM's Irving Thalberg. Her notable silent pictures included *He Who Gets Slapped* (1924), with Lon Chaney, and Lubitsch's *The Student Prince* (1927), with Ramon Novarro.

3. Marion Davies (1897–1961). She left a convent to join a touring company of *Chu-Chin-Chow*, and ended up a star at MGM, largely through the sponsorship of William Randolph Hearst. Her long-forgotten films include Ruritanian dramas (*Beverly of Gaustark*, 1926) and period pieces (*When Knighthood was in Flower*, 1927), but her best work was as a comedienne, especially in King Vidor's *Show People* (1928).

4. Bessie Love (1898–   ). Her real name was Juanita

Horton, but her screen name expressed her under-age appeal as she softened Bill Hart's bitter westerner in *The Aryan* (1916), and played Richard Barthelmess's Pacific island girl somewhere south of Pago Pago in *Soul Fire* (1925). She was upstaged by the dinosaurs in *The Lost World* (1925). Her big hit was in the first of *The Broadway Melody* series (1929), which won an Academy Award. She is still active in films, and was recently seen in *Sunday, Bloody Sunday* (1971).

5.   Mary Astor (1906–   ). Although Lucille Langehanke first appeared in films in 1920 (*The Beggar Maid*), and was later teamed with John Barrymore (*Beau Brummel*, 1923), she didn't really hit her stride until *Don Juan* (1926), in which she displayed splendid helplessness in all kinds of distress, including the torture chamber. She went on to become one of the major stars of the thirties and forties, and still appears in occasional films and on TV.

2 Westerns

The opening of the American west created the most enduring form of popular art, the western. It was one of the first categories identified as good box-office, and although generations of film-makers have enriched the style, the basic pattern endures: however complex the issues, the only possible resolution is the shoot-out, the formal ritual of triumph and death.*

1   'Bronco' Billy Anderson was the first western series hero. He appeared in several hundred short westerns between 1910 and 1916, but his career in westerns began much earlier, in 1903, when he had a small part in the first western ever made. What was the title of this historic film?

2   Series westerns are now produced solely for television, and their characters are presented as fallible human beings. The original western hero was a simpler and nobler type. Who are the cowboys in the pictures opposite?

3   Many westerns are based on historical figures and incidents, although some reconstructions are more accurate than others:

1.   Annie Oakley (1859–1926) was a sharpshooting back-woods girl who ended up as one of the stars of Buffalo Bill's Wild West Show. Her best-known reincarnation was by Betty Hutton in *Annie Get Your Gun* (1950).
But who was the actress who played her in a more accurate biography in 1935?

* Answers on page 39.

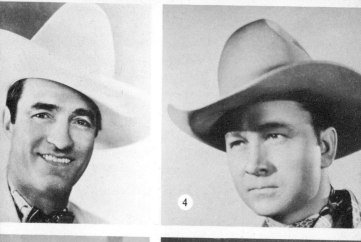

2. Wyatt Earp (1848–1928) was the most famous quick-draw lawman. Stuart N. Lake's book *Wyatt Earp, Frontier Marshall* was filmed as *Frontier Marshall* in 1939, with Jon Hall as Earp. John Ford re-made it in 1946 as *My Darling Clementine*, this time with Henry Fonda.
John Sturges has featured Earp and his almost equally-famous sidekick Doc Holliday in two films: can you name them, and the actors who played Earp and Holliday?

3. Killer Billy the Kid was shot by lawman Pat Garrett in 1881, at the tender age of twenty-one.
    a. What was Billy's real name?
    b. Was he ever played by Roy Rogers?
    c. Did he really tangle with vampires?
    d. Who played him in the first talkie biography in 1930?
    e. What was the 1958 biography called, and who played Billy?

4. Major General George Armstrong Custer achieved immortality of a kind when he and his entire company were massacred by the Sioux at Little Big Horn in 1876. His eccentric character has inspired a number of biographies ranging from deification to damnation.
How many Custers can you remember?

5. Outlaw Jesse James (1847–82) had an undeserved reputation as a kind of western Robin Hood, and there are many screen versions of the tales of plunder and revenge which surround him. He was played by Tyrone Power in 1939 in *Jesse James*, and by Jeffrey Hunter in *The True Story of Jesse James* (1957).
What was Jesse's brother's name, and who played him in these two films?

6. The first *Wild Bill Hickok* (1921) was William S. Hart. Gary Cooper later played him in *The Plainsman* in 1937.
Who played him in the only musical featuring this gun-fighter?
Who was his girlfriend, and who played her?

7. For years, Indians were the traditional western villains; lately they have received more sympathetic treatment, although they are rarely elevated to the heroic class.
Which actors have been the best-known impersonators of these heroic chiefs?
   a. Sitting Bull
   b. Cochise
   c. Geronimo

8. Davy Crockett (1786–1836), trapper and scout, beat the Indians but was finally killed by the Mexicans.
   a. Who played him in the Disney version (the one with the song)?
   b. Who played him in the film in which he was supported by Richard Widmark as Jim Bowie, the well-known knife-fighter?

4 The alienated figure of the professional gunfighter – introspective, weary and doubtful of his own morality – has become a favourite tragic theme. Who really began it all, and in what film?

5 1939 was a good year for Thomas Mitchell. He played Scarlett O'Hara's father in *Gone With the Wind* and also appeared in a classic western, for which he won an Academy Award (Best Supporting Actor). What was the film?
Who directed it?
What character did Mitchell play?
Can you remember any of the other characters, and the actors who played them?

6 Although the western is a great American tradition, many European stars have felt the lure of the frontier, and have been imported to bring an unusual flavour to the wide open spaces, such as Marlene Dietrich in *Destry Rides Again* (1939).

31

Here are some famous European ladies who have appeared in westerns: can you name them, and the films in which they are shown?

7 What do the films in each of the following groups have in common?

1. *Union Pacific* (1939)
    The Violent Men (1956)
    Forty Guns (1957)

2. *Broken Arrow* (1950)
    Cheyenne Autumn (1964)
    Apache (1954)

3. *The Gold Rush* (1924)
    Where the River Bends [*Bend of the River*] (1952)
    North to Alaska (1959)

4. *The Big Sky* (1952)
    Man Without a Star (1955)
    The War Wagon (1970)

5. *Warlock* (1959)
    Viva Zapata (1952)
    The Ride Back (1957)

6. *Nevada Smith* (1965)
    Chato's Land (1972)
    Ride Beyond Vengeance [*Night of the Tiger*] (1965)

7. *Rio Conchos* (1964)
    The Wild Bunch (1969)
    Butch Cassidy and the Sundance Kid (1970)

8 James Stewart, Henry Fonda and Glenn Ford are three actors who have been closely associated with westerns since their film careers began. Each seems to have the right mixture of originality and familiarity to be a successful western star.

Below is a list of western titles: which of these three starred in each?

1. *The Trail of the Lonesome Pine* (1936)
2. *Destry Rides Again* (1939)
3. *Texas* (1941)

4. *The Ox-Bow Incident* (1942)
5. *The Man from Colorado* (1948)
6. *Fort Apache* (1948)
7. *Winchester 73* (1950)
8. *The Redhead and the Cowboy* (1951)
9. *Carbine Williams* (1952)
10. *The Far Country* (1954)
11. *3:10 to Yuma* (1957)
12. *The Tin Star* (1957)
13. *The Sheepman* (1958)
14. *How the West Was Won* (1962)
15. *Big Hand for a Little Lady* [*Big Deal at Dodge City*] (1966)
16. *Pistolero* [*of Red River*] (1967)
17. *Welcome to Hard Times* (1967)
18. *The Cheyenne Social Club* (1970)

9 The Big Ones:

1. The United States Cavalry has often featured in the myth of the west. Probably the actor who has appeared in Blue most is John Wayne: can you name at least three films in which he has sported this uniform?

2. *Shane* was written by Jack Schaefer and directed by George Stevens in 1953. Alan Ladd was the regretful, misfit gunfighter; but can you name the five other principal players?

3. *High Noon* (1952), directed by Fred Zinneman, gave us Gary Cooper's definitive portrayal of the man alone. Who were the two women who further complicated his life?

4. *The Magnificent Seven* (1960) was a re-make in a western setting of *The Seven Samurai* (1954). Who were the Seven? (None of the actors from the rotten sequels will do.) Which ones were left alive at the end of the picture?
Yojimbo (1961) and *Rashomon* (1951) are Japanese classics which have been re-made as westerns. What are the titles of the re-makes?

5.   *The Big Country* (1958) was a large-scale western with Gregory Peck and Charlton Heston as the chief protagonists. Who played the two patriarchs?
Who were the two women in Peck's life?

10   Pictured below are the stars (one for each film) of *Escape from Fort Bravo* (1953), *Guns in the Afternoon* [*Ride the High Country*] (1962), *Comanche Station* (1960) and *The Professionals* (1966). Which title matches which picture, and who are the actors?

11 Supporting actors in westerns are often familiar faces, but how many of these eight bad guys can you actually name?

12 True or False?

1. All four Marx Brothers followed Horace Greeley's advice in [*The Marx Brothers*] *Go West* (1940).

2. So did Harold Lloyd.

3. Bob Hope sold life insurance to Jesse James in *Alias Jesse James* (1959).

4. In *The Paleface* (1948) and *Son of Paleface* (1952) Bob Hope's leading ladies were Jane Russell and Dorothy Lamour respectively.

5. English actor Kenneth More played a gunman in *The Sheriff of Broken Neck* (1958).

6. Dean Martin and Frank Sinatra were *Pardners* (1956).

13 So far, the New West has not produced any legends, although several fine films in recent years have had modern western settings. The following are good examples:

Bad Day at Black Rock (1955)
Giant (1956)
The Misfits (1961)
Lonely Are the Brave (1962)
Hud (1963)
The Chase (1966)

1.   Which of these had the heaviest irony?
2.   Which one had the hero who was most physically unique?
3.   Which one featured an actor who had appeared in *Shane* (1953)?
4.   Which actors made their final screen appearances in which of these films?
5.   Which one used the most automobiles?
The most guns?
Which one featured a helicopter?

14 Fill in the blanks:
1.   —— —— was *The Man Who Shot Liberty Valance* (1962).
2.   Charlton Heston shot —— —— in *Will Penny* (1967).
3.   —— —— broke —— ——'s gun hand with a rifle butt in *One-Eyed Jacks* (1960).
4.   Richard Boone shot —— —— in *Hombre* (1967).
5.   —— —— shot Yul Brynner in *Invitation to a Gunfighter* (1964).
6.   Lee Marvin shot —— —— in *Cat Ballou* (1965).

Westerns — Answers

1 *The Great Train Robbery*, directed by Edwin S. Porter, told the story of a gang of desperadoes in the old west, of pursuit and eventual retribution. This eleven-minute film was not only the first western, but also pioneered the use of matched, edited shots to tell a story.

2 1. William Surrey Hart (1870–1946) grew up in the real west, spoke Sioux at the age of six, began his acting career in Shakespeare, and hit Hollywood in 1914 with a completely new style of western. He was the first sympathetic villain, a gritty mixture of outlawry, sex and sentimentality, in films like *The Return of Draw Egan* (1915), *Hell's Hinges* (1916), *Wagon Tracks* (1919) and *Wild Bill Hickok* (1923). When his brand of realism lost favour and his contract with Paramount lapsed, he went independent and created the classic *Tumbleweeds* (1925), unhappily not well received at the time.

2. Hoot Gibson (1892–1962). Originally a cowpuncher, he had a long, mostly featureless, career, extending from *The Cactus Kid* (1919) through *The Spirit of the West* (1932) to *The Horse Soldiers* (1959).

3. Tom Mix (1881–1940), the boy from Mix Run, Pennsylvania, served in the Spanish-American War, the Boer War and the Boxer Rebellion. He spent a few years as a frontier marshall in Oklahoma and as a Texas Ranger before becoming a minor Hollywood star in 1912, three years before Hart's first film. Mix's movies were the ones which primarily undermined Hart's popularity in the twenties. His gargantuan collection of boots and his penchant for turning up at formal dinners in full cowboy gear

(Hollywood style) are as memorable as his boyish, action-packed movies such as *Cupid's Round-Up* (1918), *North of Hudson Bay* (1924), *The Lucky Horseshoe* (1925) and *Destry Rides Again* (1927). He had made more than 400 films before he was killed in a car crash.

4. Tex Ritter (1907–) began in radio, and is remembered more for the number of second-raters he made in the thirties and forties than for their quality: films like *Song of the Gringo* (1936), *Sing, Cowboy, Sing* (1938) and *Marshall of Gunsmoke* (1946). He is best remembered as the singer of the ballad in *High Noon* (1952); he has been living off it ever since.

5. William Boyd (1898–1972), the world-famous Hopalong Cassidy, featured in scores of good clean western dramas from 1935. His early, pre-western career was more promising: *Why Change Your Wife* (1919), *King of Kings* (1927), *The Volga Boatmen* (1927) and *Yankee Clipper* (1928).

6. Gene Autry (1907–) came to the rescue of the ailing western in the thirties, and won back the rural audiences who had been lost to radio. He created the singing cowboy, complete with trusty guitar and faithful horse, Champion. He rode for some twenty years from 1934, through films like *Carolina Moon* (1940), *Range War* (1946), *Guns and Saddles* (1949) and *Goldtown Ghost Riders* (1953).

3

1. Barbara Stanwyck. Although this version did not have the musical's excesses, it did concentrate on a heavy love affair between Annie and the star of the Wild West Show (Preston Foster). Buffalo Bill was played by Melvyn Douglas.

2. *Gunfight at the OK Corral* (1957) had Burt Lancaster as Earp and Kirk Douglas as Holliday.
Hour of the Gun (1967) had James Garner and Jason Robards Jr in the two roles.

3.   a. William Bonney
    b. Yes, in *Billy the Kid Returns* (1939)
    c. Yes, in *Billy the Kid Meets Dracula* (1966)
    d. Johnny Mack Brown
    e. *The Left Handed Gun*, the first film of director Arthur Penn, starred Paul Newman as Billy.

4.   The chronological Custers (eleven in all) are:
      Dustin Farnum — *Flaming Frontier* (1926)
      Frank McGlynn — *Custer's Last Stand* (1936)
      Ronald Reagan — *Santa Fe Trail* (1940)
      Addison Richards — *Badlands of Dakota* (1941)
      Errol Flynn — *They Died with Their Boots On* (1941)
      James Millican — *Warpath* (1951)
      Sheb Wooley — *Bugles in the Afternoon* (1952)
      Britt Lomand — *Tonka* (1958)
      Phil Carey — *The Great Sioux Massacre* (1965)
      Robert Shaw — *Custer of the West* (1967)
      Richard Mulligan — *Little Big Man* (1970)

5.   Frank James was played by Henry Fonda in 1939 and by Robert Wagner in 1957. Fonda also starred in *The Return of Frank James* (1941).

6.   Howard Keel played Hickok to Doris Day's *Calamity Jane* (1953).

7.   a. J. Carrol Naish was *Sitting Bull* (1954).
    b. Jeff Chandler was a notable Cochise in *Broken Arrow* (1950), *Battle at Apache Pass* (1952) and *Taza, Son of Cochise* (1953).
    c. Chief Thundercloud was *Geronimo* in 1938; Jay Silverheels (remember Tonto?) was Geronimo in *Battle at Apache Pass* (1952) and Chuck Connors played him in *Geronimo!* (1962).

8.   a. Fess Parker, who set the fifties trend in coonskin hats.
    b. John Wayne, in *The Alamo* (1960).

4   Gregory Peck (in a moustache) gave a moving performance as *The Gunfighter* in 1950.

5   Mitchell played the drunken doctor on John Ford's *Stagecoach*, which also carried: John Wayne as the Ringo Kid; Donald Meek as the whisky salesman; George Bancroft as the sheriff; Andy Devine as the driver; Claire Trevor as the good-hearted whore; Louise Platt as the pregnant wife of the cavalry officer; John Carradine as the Confederate gentleman/gambler and Berton Churchill as the crooked banker.

6

1.   Jean Simmons, holding her own in *Rough Night in Jericho* (1967). She began as a child actress in Britain (*Give Us the Moon*, 1943), but since 1952 has lived in the United States, where she has done most of her best work, though not always in westerns (*The Robe*, 1953; *Spartacus*, 1960).

2.   Claudia Cardinale as the millionaire's wife whom *The Professionals* (1966) have been hired to rescue. Her early work in Italy (*Rocco and His Brothers*, 1960; *The Leopard*, 1962; *8½*, 1963) was certainly her best; she is now thoroughly enmeshed in the Hollywood machine (*The Pink Panther*, 1963; *A Fine Pair*, 1969).

3.   Audrey Hepburn in *The Unforgiven* (1960), as the girl brought up to believe that she is the natural daughter of the family who snatched her from the Indians. Born in Belgium, of Irish-Dutch parents (Edda Hepburn van Heemstra), her early films, such as *The Lavender Hill Mob* (1951), were British, but she was soon snatched by Hollywood and has never looked back.

4.   Brigitte Bardot, as a member of the European hunting party mixed up with hostile Indians (and Sean Connery) in the British-financed *Shalako* (1968). She is one of the few actresses to achieve global success without the Hollywood machine behind her, though her stardom is due more to her sex appeal than her acting abilities: the former was on

spectacular display in several indifferent pictures like *And God Created Woman* (1956), *Babette Goes to War* (1959) and *Vie Privée* (1962).

5.   Jeanne Moreau as Lee Marvin's worldly lady friend in *Monte Walsh* (1970). Apart from one or two mistakes (*The Sailor from Gibraltar*, 1966), her films are usually interesting and she has always brought something special to her roles in films like *Lift to the Scaffold* (1957), *Les Liaisons Dangereuses* (1960), *Jules et Jim* (1963), *Viva Maria* (1965) and *Chimes at Midnight* (1966).

7   1.   All feature the uncompromising Barbara Stanwyck.
2.   All are notable for the sympathetic treatment they gave the Indians.
3.   All were gold-rush westerns, a variation on the cowboy theme.
4.   Kirk Douglas starred in all three.
5.   The star of these was Anthony Quinn (as a club-footed gunman, revolutionary Mexican and outlaw, respectively).
6.   Revenge was the principal theme in each: in *Nevada Smith*, Steve McQueen hunted down the men who murdered his mother; in *Chato's Land*, Charles Bronson gunned down the men who tortured his wife and burned his farm; in the third, Chuck Connors revenged himself on the villains who branded him, and on the town boss who had stolen his fiancée.
7.   The main characters were wiped out at the end of all three: Richard Boone and Jim Browne by a load of dynamite, William Holden and his buddies by the Mexican Army, and Paul Newman and Robert Redford by Bolivian soldiers, respectively.

8   1.   *The Trail of the Lonesome Pine* – Fonda
2.   *Destry Rides Again* – Stewart
3.   *Texas* – Ford
4.   *The Ox-Bow Incident* – Fonda
5.   *The Man from Colorado* – Ford

6. *Fort Apache* — Fonda
7. *Winchester 73* — Stewart
8. *The Redhead and the Cowboy* — Ford
9. *Carbine Williams* — Stewart
10. *The Far Country* — Stewart
11. *3:10 to Yuma* — Ford
12. *The Tin Star* — Fonda
13. *The Sheepman* — Ford
14. *How the West Was Won* — Stewart
15. *Big Hand for a Little Lady* [*Big Deal at Dodge City*] — Fonda
16. *Pistolero* [*of Red River*] — Ford
17. *Welcome to Hard Times* — Fonda
18. *The Cheyenne Social Club* — Stewart *and* Fonda

9

1.   John Wayne was saddle-sore in:
The Dark Command (1940)
Fort Apache (1948)
She Wore a Yellow Ribbon (1949)
Rio Grande (1950)
The Horse Soldiers (1959)
The Alamo (1960)
How the West Was Won (1962)

2.   Van Heflin — the threatened farmer; Jean Arthur — his wife; Brandon de Wilde — their son; Jack Palance — the villainous hired gun; Elisha Cook Jr — the plucky-but-doomed farmer (who else?).

3.   Grace Kelly played Cooper's new wife who was forsaking him, while Katy Jurado was his old flame (also leaving town).

4.   They were Yul Brynner, Steve McQueen, Horst Buchholz, Charles Bronson, Robert Vaughn, Brad Dexter and James Coburn. Brynner and McQueen survive and leave, while it is implied that Buchholz will settle down with a village girl.

Yojimbo became *A Fistful of Dollars* (1966).
Rashomon became *The Outrage* (1964).

5.   Burl Ives and Charles Bickford were the two old men who finally shot each other. Jean Simmons got Peck; Carroll Baker lost him.

10 Durable outdoor types, these four fall into the 'leading actor' rather than 'star' category.

1.   William Holden, in *Escape from Fort Bravo*, whose début was in *Golden Boy* (1939), and whose other solid pictures include *Sunset Boulevard* (1950), *Stalag 17* (1953), *Bridge on the River Kwai* (1957), *The Horse Soldiers* (1959), *Alvarez Kelly* (1966) and *The Wild Bunch* (1969).

2.   Joel McCrea, in *Guns in the Afternoon*, whose first good role was in *The Jazz Age* (1929), and who went on to make films like *Wells Fargo* (1937), *Union Pacific* (1938), *Sullivan's Travels* (1941), *The Virginian* (1946), *Saddle Tramp* (1951) and *Gunfight at Dodge City* (1959).

3.   Randolph Scott, in *Comanche Station*, first appeared in *Sky Bridge* (1931), and moved on to *Go West Young Man* (1936), *The Last of the Mohicans* (1936), *The Spoilers* (1942), *The Stranger Wore a Gun* (1953), *Ride Lonesome* (1958) and *Guns in the Afternoon* [*Ride the High Country*] (1962), the last with Joel McCrea.

4.   Robert Ryan, in *The Professionals*, the most varied actor of this lot, began with *Golden Gloves* (1940), and has made many other films, including *The Boy with Green Hair* (1948), *The Naked Spur* (1953), *The Tall Men* (1955), *The Proud Ones* (1956), *Hour of the Gun* (1967) and *The Wild Bunch* (1969).

11 1.   Richard Jaeckel, in *3:10 to Yuma* (1957), graduated from frightened youths in war movies to mean punks in westerns. Best remembered as the guy who died proving that Gregory Peck was still the fastest in *The Gunfighter* (1950).

2.   Juan Garcia, one of cattle baron Robert Ryan's hands in *The Tall Men* (1955). He also featured in the all-Mexican production *The Pearl* (1948) before his Hollywood career of standard Mexican heavies in films like *Plunder of the Sun* (1953) and *Vera Cruz* (1954).

3.   Ben Johnson, an ex-stunt rider, here as one of Marlon Brando's rough companions in *One-Eyed Jacks* (1960). Has played many supporting roles, in films like *She Wore a Yellow Ribbon* (1949), *Shane* (1953) and *Major Dundee* (1965), and has at last been seriously recognized in *The Last Picture Show* (1971).

4.   Jay C. Flippen was on the stage and in vaudeville before going into the movies in 1949. This still is from *Where the River Bends* [*Bend of the River*] (1952) in which he played a good guy, companion of James Stewart, but his roles have been various, frequently heavy, such as the corrupt sheriff in *Cat Ballou* (1965).

5.   Walter Brennan won three Academy Awards as Best Supporting Actor with a fabulous array of character parts in a career which began in 1923. Here he is the rancorous Old Man Clayton in *My Darling Clementine* (1946), and his many other films have included westerns such as *Rio Bravo* (1958) and *Support Your Local Sheriff* (1969). He died in 1971.

6.   Jack Lambert's scowling heavy has been equally at home in gangster and western movies, always recognizable as bad in films as diverse as *The Killers* (1946), *Dakota Lil* (1950), *Murder Inc.* [*The Enforcer*] (1951) and *How the West Was Won* (1962). This still is from *Day of the Outlaw* (1959).

7.   Mickey Shaunessey as the town thug who tries to beat off Glenn Ford after Ford has stirred his chicken chop suey

with a cigar butt in *The Sheepman* (1958). His first film was *The Last of the Comancheros* (1952), and he has been in a variety of films: *The Conquest of Space* (1955), *Jailhouse Rock* (1957) and *North to Alaska* (1960).

8.   Arthur Kennedy, whose neutral features and controlled playing have taken on either pleasant characters or reasonable villains. In *Rancho Notorious* (1952) and *The Lusty Men* (1952) he was a rather nice guy, but quite the reverse in *The Man from Laramie* (1953) and *Nevada Smith* (1966), not to mention *Peyton Place* (1957).

12 1.   False. Only three of them (Harpo, Groucho and Chico) went.

2.   False. He didn't, but Buster Keaton did (*Go West*, 1925).

3.   True. Only Bob Hope could do it.

4.   False. It was Jane Russell in both (as Calamity Jane).

5.   False. He sold guns in *The Sheriff of Fractured Jaw* (1958).

6.   False. It was Dean Martin and Jerry Lewis.

13 1.   Although ironies abound in these films, the most outstanding one is in *Lonely Are the Brave* when Kirk Douglas, as the anachronistic cowboy, is knocked off his horse by a truck loaded with toilets.

2.   Spencer Tracy was the formidable one-armed karate expert in *Bad Day at Black Rock*.

3.   Brandon de Wilde, who played Paul Newman's kid brother in *Hud*.

4.   James Dean's last film was *Giant*; Clark Gable and Marilyn Monroe were last seen in *The Misfits*.

5.   *The Chase* featured a horrific siege in a car dump, and certainly had more shooting than any of the others. In *Lonely Are the Brave*, a helicopter was used to pursue Kirk Douglas.

14 1. Everyone thought it was James Stewart with his '38, but it was really John Wayne with his Winchester.

2. Principally Donald Pleasence, as Preacher Quint, but he also got Quint's three sons ('The Rawhiders'): Bruce Dern, Matt Clark and Gene Rutherford.

3. Karl Malden did it to Marlon Brando, but Brando shot him in the end.

4. Paul Newman.

5. George Segal didn't really mean to, but he got confused.

6. He shot himself, in his dual role as Kid Sheleen and his twin brother. He also shot John Marley (Cat's father) and probably a few others.

3 Mystery and Suspense

An element of mystery is an essential of any good story, and is a major factor in keeping audiences watching. The films below, however, are those which depend almost entirely on mystery and suspense for their impact. Most have contemporary settings and reflect the influence of the undoubted master of the genre, Alfred Hitchcock.*

1. Hitchcock tends to use actresses in phases, using a particular lady for a time and then dropping her in favour of a new face. He has even described his actors and actresses as 'cattle', unimportant in comparison with his central cinematic idea. Look at this list of titles:

Marnie (1964)
North by Northwest (1959)
Vertigo (1958)
Dial M for Murder (1954)

a. Who were the leading ladies in each of them?
b. What do they all have in common?
c. Which ones appeared in *other* Hitchcock films?

2. Which film has Hitchcock made twice, and who were the leads in each version?

3. Ingrid Bergman has starred in two of Hitchcock's films. Which ones, and who were her leading men?

4. Hitchcock quickies:
a. Who played the title role in *Rebecca* (1940)?
b. What play by Patrick Hamilton became a Hitchcock film?

* Answers on page 54.

c. Who played Anthony Perkins's mother in *Psycho* (1960), the only film she made for Hitchcock?

d. What colour bothered *Marnie* (1964), and why?

e. Who were the leads in *The Wrong Man* (1956)?

f. In which Hitchcock film did Sybil Thorndyke make one of her rare screen appearances, and who played her husband?

5. What plot details can you remember from some Hitchcock films?

a. How many murders were there in *Marnie* (1964), how were they committed, and by whom?

b. How was the victim murdered in *Rope* (1948), and where was the body hidden?

c. What was *The Trouble with Harry* (1955)?

d. Who murders whom in *Dial M for Murder* (1954), and what is the twist?

e. Who were the *Strangers on a Train* (1951), what bargain did they discuss, and what did it lead to?

f. In *North by Northwest* (1959), Cary Grant was made to look like a murderer. How was he supposed to have done it, and where?

2   Surprisingly, Agatha Christie has not had much of her work adapted for the screen, although her famous French detective Hercule Poirot appeared in several minor films in the thirties (played by Austin Trevor), reappearing again in 1965, in a loose adaptation of *The Alphabet Murders*.

1. What other leading Christie character has appeared in four films (not all of them based on original Christie works), and who played this character?

2. Who was the murderer in *Ten Little Indians* [*Ten Little Niggers*] (1945)?

3. In *Witness For the Prosecution* (1958), lawyer Charles Laughton defended a man on a charge of murder.

Who was he?

Whom was he accused of murdering?

Who was the *Witness For the Prosecution*?

What was the witness's relationship to the defendant?
What was the outcome of the trial?

3 Body disposal is a frequent problem for characters in mystery and suspense films. How did they get rid of:
1. Johnnie Solo in *Goldfinger* (1964)?
2. The body in *Rear Window* (1954)?
3. The poisoned gentlemen in *Arsenic and Old Lace* (1944)?
4. Each other in *The Ladykillers* (1955)?
5. The victims in *Psycho* (1960)?
6. Anna Massey in *Frenzy* (1972)?

4 What details can you remember about these mysteries?
1. What was the central mystery in *Blow-Up* (1967)?
2. In *Les Diaboliques* (1954), what does the drowned man in the bath do?
3. In *Charade* (1963), where was the money hidden?
4. In *Bad Day at Black Rock* (1955), who was the missing man, and what had happened to him?

5 The deaths of victims can be horrific, surprising or, occasionally, funny. What do you remember about the deaths of:
1. Sebastian Venables?
2. Olivia de Havilland and Joseph Cotten in *Hush, Hush, Sweet Charlotte* (1964)?
3. Kirk Douglas in *The List of Adrian Messenger* (1963)?
4. Oddjob?
5. Ayesha?
6. Stapleton in *The Hound of the Baskervilles* (1959)?
7. Shirley Eaton in *Goldfinger* (1964)?
8. Alec Guinness in *The Ladykillers* (1955)?

6 Do you recall:
1. What they were after in *Wait Until Dark* (1967)?
2. Where they hid the gold in *The Lavender Hill Mob* (1951)?

3. Who was Floyd Thursby?
4. Anything about 'Rosebud'?
5. What they were after in *Topkapi* (1964)?
6. What everyone was worried about in *The Wages of Fear* (1953)?
7. Who was Carson Dyall?
8. What they were after in *How To Steal a Million* (1966)?

7 It is impossible to know how many films there have been about Sherlock Holmes, either based on the original works of Conan Doyle or based on the characters he created. Who played Holmes and Watson in:
1. *Sherlock Holmes* (1922)?
2. *The Hound of the Baskervilles* (1939 and 1959)?
3. *The Private Life of Sherlock Holmes* (1969)?
4. *The Return of Sherlock Holmes* (1929)?
5. *The Speckled Band* (1931)?
6. *Silver Blaze* (1936)?
7. *A Study in Terror* (1965)?
8. *They Might be Giants* (1971)?

8 Here are some tense moments from mystery and suspense movies. Can you name the people in the pictures, the films they are taken from, and any plot details that might relate to each picture?

Mystery and Suspense – Answers

1. a. The leading ladies were, respectively, Tippi Hedren, Eva Marie Saint, Kim Novak and Grace Kelly.
    b. All of them are 'Hitchcock blondes'.
    c. Tippi Hedren was also in *The Birds* (1963).
    Grace Kelly was in *Rear Window* (1954) and *To Catch a Thief* (1955).

2. *The Man Who Knew Too Much.*
In 1934: Leslie Banks and Edna Best.
In 1955: James Stewart and Doris Day.

3. *Notorious* (1946), with Cary Grant.
Under Capricorn (1949), with Joseph Cotten and Michael Wilding.

4. a. No one. She is dead before the film begins, although her presence haunts the entire story, and is kept alive in everyone's minds by Judith Anderson.
    b. *Rope* (1948).
    c. Again, no one. She was dead, but still hanging about, mummified. She was impersonated by Perkins.
    d. Red. It reminded her (surprise!) of blood.
    e. Henry Fonda and Vera Miles.
    f. *Stage Fright* (1950), married to Alastair Sim.

5. a. One only. Marnie, as a little girl, beats to death with a poker a sailor who is threatening her prostitute mother.
    b. He was strangled, and his body put in a chest in the living-room.
    c. He was a body, and no one knew what to do with it.
    d. Ray Milland hires Anthony Dawson to murder his wife, Grace Kelly. While she is being strangled, she

desperately grabs for something to defend herself with, gets hold of a pair of scissors and stabs him. Milland manages to twist things to look as though she has killed Dawson for personal reasons, and almost gets away with it.

e. They were Farley Granger and Robert Walker. Walker proposes that, as each of them is plagued by another, they swap murders. Granger doesn't take him seriously until his wife is murdered; then Walker starts putting pressure on him to carry out his part of the 'bargain'. For more details see Horror 9. 3. d.

f. He was thought to have stabbed a man in the United Nations building in New York.

2 1. Miss Marple, played by Margaret Rutherford. A critic once remarked that the only other person who could possibly have played Miss Marple was Miss Christie herself. The films were *Murder, She Said* (1962), *Murder at the Gallop* (1963), *Murder Most Foul* (1964) and *Murder Ahoy* (1965).

2. Barry Fitzgerald. There was also a 1965 re-make.

3. Tyrone Power had been accused of murdering a rich widow. His only alibi was provided by his wife, Marlene Dietrich. When she took the witness stand she told the truth, but so manipulated things that, when she was re-called to the stand, her testimony was made to look like perjury. Power got off, and as he left the court was joined by another woman, his mistress. Dietrich, having sacrificed herself for nothing, grabbed a knife which had been introduced as evidence and stabbed him.

3 1. His body was placed in the trunk of a car which was then put through an automobile junk yard compressor.

2. It was cut up into small bits, and removed from the apartment a few pieces at a time.

3. Mad nephew Teddy was told that they were all yellow fever victims; as he was digging the Panama canal in the

cellar, he accepted this, and buried them in the locks of his canal.

4. The bodies were dumped into empty coal carriages from the bridge at a railway junction.

5. They were placed in their cars and sunk in a swamp.

6. She was placed in a sack of potatoes on a truck about to leave Covent Garden market.

4

1. A casual photograph taken by David Hemmings indicates that there may have been a murder committed, but when he returns to the scene, he can find nothing.

2. Although his wife had drowned him in a bath, he wasn't really dead at all. At the end, he rose out of the bath, causing his wife to have a heart attack, thereby killing her as had been his intention from the beginning.

3. The money – $250,000 – had been converted into three rare stamps, which were found on a letter on the dead man's body, but which no one recognized.

4. He was a Japanese-American farmer, who was murdered by the ignorant and prejudiced locals during the Second World War. The mystery was solved by mysterious one-armed Spencer Tracy, who had come to Black Rock to look for the farmer, to give him news of his son, who had been killed in action with the American army in Europe.

5

1. In *Suddenly Last Summer* (1959), he was overpowered by a group of Spanish street urchins, who proceeded to eat him alive, much to Elizabeth Taylor's surprise.

2. Bette Davis pushed a large potted plant off a balcony, which got them as they stood beneath, plotting.

3. In an attempt to escape, his shying horse threw him over a wall, and he was impaled on a hay rake on the other side.

4. He was electrocuted in *Goldfinger* (1964) in an attempt to retrieve his lethal bowler hat, which was wedged between the bars of a vault in Fort Knox.

5. *She* (1964) went back into the eternal flame, not realizing that this broke the spell which gave her eternal life. She aged 10,000 years in seconds.

6. He was drowned in a bog on the moor, clutching a boot.

7. Her body was completely covered with gold paint, causing (so the explanation went) auto-poisoning.

8. Having disposed of the last of the gang (Herbert Lom) into a coal car, he waited for the train to pull away. The signal changed, hitting him on the head and tipping him into another coal car. He was never seen again.

6
1. Heroin, hidden in a doll, which Audrey Hepburn had (but she didn't realize its contents).

2. In what were supposed to be lead paperweights, models of the Eiffel Tower.

3. Though he never appears, he is Mary Astor's criminal lover; he gets shot early in *The Maltese Falcon* (1941).

4. It was the sled that Orson Welles had as a boy in *Citizen Kane* (1941), and he speaks the name just before he dies. Throughout the film, it is constantly referred to, but is not revealed until the closing shot.

5. A jewelled dagger, incredibly well guarded (electronically) in the Topkapi Museum in Istanbul.

6. The trucks they were driving were carrying nitroglycerine.

7. He is alternatively said to be dead, alive (Cary Grant) or in disguise as any number of others in *Charade* (1963). It finally turns out that he is Walter Matthau.

8. A forged Cellini 'Venus' which, if it had been the real thing, would have been worth a million.

7
1. John Barrymore and Roland Young.

2. In 1939 Basil Rathbone and Nigel Bruce, certainly the most famous pair, who made a series of a dozen or more films, mostly in modern settings, such as coping with spies during the Second World War (*Sherlock Holmes in Washington*, 1942).

In 1959 Peter Cushing and André Morell.

3.   Robert Stephens and Colin Blakeley.

4.   Clive Brook and H. Reeves-Smith.

5.   Raymond Massey and Athole Stewart.

6.   Arthur Wontner and Ian Fleming (not the Fleming of James Bond fame).

7.   John Neville and Donald Houston. In this one, they were involved with Jack the Ripper.

8.   A fantasy, in which the characters were acted out by George C. Scott and Joanne Woodward.

8   1.   Rock Hudson as the man trying to regain his lost youth in John Frankenheimer's *Seconds* (1966).

2.   Gregory Peck, in deep trouble, as the hero on the run in Edward Dmytryk's *Mirage* (1965).

3.   Robert Ryan, the suspected anti-semitic murderer, under interrogation in Dmytryk's *Crossfire* (1947).

4.   Vivien Merchant in Hitchcock's *Frenzy* (1972), the Cordon Bleu housewife who drives her Scotland Yard husband (Alec McCowan) up the wall with her way-out cooking.

5.   Orson Welles and Loretta Young in *The Stranger* (1946). He is a clock-fixated Nazi hiding out in a small American town, and she suspects him of murder. He begins to terrorize her, but he is eventually tracked down and caught by detective Edward G. Robinson.

4 Spies

Spy films are not a major movie genre, although the spy theme recurs frequently in thriller-melodramas. Secrecy is the essential plot device, in war-time cloak-and-dagger adventures, psychological dramas of love and loyalty, and the gadget-ridden parodies of the sixties. Recently, there has been too much of the last, and this section seeks to redress the balance.*

1   Exotic foreign locations are usually important in spy movies. They are tense because they are strange and full of untrustworthy foreigners. Can you fill in the missing locations?

    1. Clive Brook was the British officer bound for —— aboard the *Shanghai Express* (1932).

    2. Humphrey Bogart ran the Vichy gauntlet in *To Have and Have Not* (1945), smuggling French Resistance leaders into —— on his boat.

    3. In *Five Fingers* (1952), James Mason was valet to the British Ambassador in ——, meanwhile passing diplomatic secrets to the Germans.

    4. As *Big Jim McLain* (1953), John Wayne hunted down communists in ——.

    5. At the end of *The Man Between* (1953), James Mason, concealed in a laundry van, failed to escape from ——.

    6. Wealthy German pacifist Marlon Brando was blackmailed (by Trevor Howard) into leaving the safety of his nest in —— to sabotage a shipload of rubber bound for the Fatherland, in *Saboteur, Code Name Morituri* (1965).

* Answers on page 63.

7.   Michael Redgrave and the communist guerrillas collaborated to knock off Audie Murphy, *The Quiet American* (1958), in ——.

2   What do the films in each of the following groups have in common?

1.   *Ministry of Fear* (1943)
     Confidential Agent (1945)
     The Third Man (1949)

2.   *The Man Who Knew Too Much* (1934)
     The Thirty-Nine Steps (1935)
     Foreign Correspondent (1940)

3.   *The House on 92nd Street* (1945)
     Walk East On Beacon (1952)
     The F.B.I. Story (1959)

4.   *Mission to Moscow* (1943)
     North Star (1943)
     Days of Glory (1944)

5.   *Iron Curtain* (1948)
     Diplomatic Courier (1952)
     My Son John (1952)

6.   *Man Hunt* (1941)
     Hangmen Also Die (1943)
     Cloak and Dagger (1946)

7.   *They Got Me Covered* (1942)
     Knock On Wood (1953)
     The Intelligence Men (1964)

3   There have been only a few 'real-life' spies portrayed on screen. One non-fiction spy film is *Man On a String* (1 based on film producer Boris Morros's autobiography, *Years as a Counterspy*, in which the title role was playe Ernest Borgnine. Most of the other spy biographies been of women.

Who were the actresses who played the spies in these films?
1. *Nurse Edith Cavell* (1939)
2. *Odette* (1950)
3. *Carve Her Name With Pride* (1958)
4. *Mata Hari* (1932 and 1964)
5. *I Was an American Spy* (1951)

4   In the sixties came the spy spoof boom, but precedents had been set a long time before, in films such as *Comrade X* (1940), with Clark Gable rescuing ex-communist bus-driver Hedy Lamarr in a hijacked Russian tank. The Bond movies began and sustained this burgeoning new style of super-secret-agent films. Sex, technology, fantasy and black humour were legitimate ingredients in this new form of escapism.

Many stars attempted to climb on Sean Connery's band-wagon: can you match these actors with their screen spy names and the film in which the character appeared?

Michael Caine	Nicholas Whistler	*In Like Flint* (1967)
David McCallum	James Bond	*Where the Spies Are* (1966)
Terence Stamp	Boysie Oakes	*The Wrecking Crew* (1968)
Dirk Bogarde	Matt Helm	*The Billion Dollar Brain* (1967)
James Coburn	Harry Palmer	*Casino Royale* (1966)
Dean Martin	Dr Jason Love	*The Liquidator* (1965)
Rod Taylor	Illya Kuryakin	*Hot Enough for June* [*Agent $8\frac{3}{4}$*] (1964)
Ursula Andress	Derek Flint	*Modesty Blaise* (1966)
David Niven	Willie Garvin	*The Spy With My Face* (1965)

5   Not surprisingly, perhaps, the Bond-type films have given rise to an alternative movement to de-glamorize spies, showing them as unwilling protagonists, trapped in constantly shifting situations in which there is no truth, trust or friend. To which films do the following statements refer?

1.   Unruly Sergeant Michael Caine is almost brainwashed, nearly shooting his boss Guy Doleman rather than evil operator Nigel Green.

2.   Laurence Harvey is the double agent who is instructed to assassinate himself.

3.   Mathematician Paul Newman fakes defection to East Germany in an attempt to trick an elusive (and vital-to-security) equation from a rival professor.

4.   Ageing and disillusioned agent Richard Burton pretends to go to pieces in order to get taken on as a defector by the other side, so that he can eliminate the East German counter-espionage chief.

5.   No one believes Nobel laureate Paul Newman when he uncovers an involved plot to kidnap fellow-winner Edward G. Robinson.

Spies – Answers

1   1.   He was going to Peiping (*from* Shanghai), and he made it, thanks to Marlene Dietrich.
2.   Martinique. But most of it was shot on the back lot at Warner Brothers.
3.   Ankara. The book on which it was based, a true story, was by L. C. Moyzich.
4.   Hawaii. One of Hollywood's more hysterical responses to the 'communist conspiracy to enslave humanity'.
5.   East Berlin. He saved the girl by distracting the guards and getting shot.
6.   Bombay. A very cool pacifist, he masquerades as a senior SS officer and outsmarts the Gestapo agents on board.
7.   Saigon. Although both parties wanted him out of the way, they had different motives.

2   1.   All were written by Graham Greene, who has probably been responsible for more spy movies than any other writer. His originals and adaptations (of his own novels) include *Stamboul Train* [*Orient Express*] (1934), *The Man Within* (1946), *The Fugitive* [*The Power and the Glory*] (1948), *Our Man in Havana* (1959) and *The Comedians* (1967).

2.   All are films directed by Alfred Hitchcock, for whom international espionage has had a special fascination. The first two were made in England and relied on menacing European spy rings to provide the tension. The third, made in the United States, was concerned with Nazi spies, and was Hitchcock's plea to America to enter the war.

3.   All were closely concerned with the operations of the Federal Bureau of Investigation. The first was a semi-docu-

mentary about the FBI, the second was based on a book by Bureau Chief J. Edgar Hoover, and the third '. . . managed to suggest that going out for a walk on Sunday morning, without going to church, is an un-American activity'.*

4. All three, made during the Second World War, extolled the virtues (and ignored the necessities) of US–Soviet collaboration. They subsequently became an embarrassment and a threat to the careers of their makers.

5. These are post-war reactions to the Soviet menace, when the film industry was also feeling threatened. *Iron Curtain* began the trend. *Diplomatic Courier* Tyrone Power single-handedly thwarted Russian plans to occupy Yugoslavia. *My Son John* was evidence of how low the Reds would stoop, corrupting all-American boy Robert Walker.

6. All three are films by Fritz Lang, in which he gave full rein to his anti-fascist sentiments, using his fellow exiles to portray the Nazis whom they had escaped.

7. All are spy-filled comedies: Bob Hope in 1942, Danny Kaye in 1953 and Eric Morecambe and Ernie Wise in 1964.

3 1. Anna Neagle, supported by May Robson, Edna May Oliver and Zasu Pitts.
2. Anna Neagle again, this time with Trevor Howard, Marius Goring and Peter Ustinov.
3. Virginia McKenna, as Second World War heroine Violette Szabo.
4. The original was, of course, Greta Garbo. The virtually unknown re-make starred Jeanne Moreau.
5. Ann Dvorak played real-life heroine Claire Phillips, underground activist during the Philippine occupation. The archetypical Japanese villains were Philip Ahn and Richard Loo.

* Furhammar and Isaksson, *Politics and Film*, Studio Vista, London, 1968.

4   Michael Caine as Harry Palmer in *The Billion Dollar Brain*.
David McCallum as Illya Kuryakin in *The Spy With My Face*.
Terence Stamp as Willie Garvin in *Modesty Blaise*.
Dirk Bogarde as Nicholas Whistler in *Hot Enough for June*.
James Coburn as Derek Flint in *In Like Flint*.
Dean Martin as Matt Helm in *The Wrecking Crew*.
Rod Taylor as Boysie Oakes in *The Liquidator*.
Ursula Andress as James Bond in *Casino Royale*.
David Niven as Dr Jason Love in *Where the Spies Are*.

5   1.   *The Ipcress File* (1965)
   2.   *A Dandy in Aspic* (1966)
   3.   *Torn Curtain* (1966) – Hitchcock again
   4.   *The Spy Who Came In from the Cold* (1965)
   5.   *The Prize* (1964)

5 Romance

The romantic drama is another of Hollywood's contributions to popular culture. The glamour of the stars and the magic of the great screen partnerships probably provoke the greatest old-movie nostalgia. No matter how contrived the situation, how banal the dialogue or anachronistic the costumes, the appeal of the great romantic films, especially those of the thirties and forties, remains.*

1   The supreme romantic lady of the thirties (and for some, for all time) was Greta Garbo. Pushed ruthlessly by MGM, she averaged more than one film a year in the thirties and then retired at the height of her career.

1.   Her leading men were all big names (although she once refused Laurence Olivier as her partner). Who were they in:
   Susan Lenox: Her Fall and Rise (1931)?
   Grand Hotel (1932)?
   Queen Christina (1933)?
   Anna Karenina (1935)?
   Camille (1936)?
   Marie Walewska [*Conquest*] (1937)?

2.   For which film did Garbo win an Academy Award?

3.   What was the title of her last film?

4.   Which film was advertised as 'Garbo Talks!', and what were the first lines she spoke on the screen?

5.   One of her best films was re-made twice: which one was it, and what can you remember about the re-makes?

2   Many of the great romantic couples have been characters in novels. Can you remember who played:

* Answers on page 77.

66

1. Darcy and Elizabeth in Jane Austen's *Pride and Prejudice* (1940)?

2. Catherine and Heathcliffe in Emily Brontë's *Wuthering Heights* (1939)?

3. Natasha and Andrei in Tolstoy's *War and Peace* (1956)?

4. Elizabeth Barrett and Robert Browning in Beiser's *The Barretts of Wimpole Street* (1934)?

5. Alice Aisgill and Joe Lampton in John Braine's *Room at the Top* (1959)?

6. Pip and Estella (as adults) in Dickens's *Great Expectations* (1946)?

7. Lara and Zhivago in Boris Pasternak's *Dr Zhivago* (1965)?

8. Jake Barnes and Lady Brett Ashley in Hemingway's *The Sun Also Rises* (1957)?

9. Rochester and Jane in Charlotte Brontë's *Jane Eyre* (1944)?

10. Gerald Crich and Gudrun Brangwen in D. H. Lawrence's *Women in Love* (1969)?

3 Vivien Leigh was another all-time great romantic lead. Who were her leading men in the following films?
Fire over England (1936)
Gone with the Wind (1939)
Waterloo Bridge (1940)
Lady Hamilton [*That Hamilton Woman*] (1941)
Anna Karenina (1948)
A Streetcar Named Desire (1951)
The Roman Spring of Mrs Stone (1961)

4 The greatest he-man romantic lead in the movies was surely Clark Gable. During his career of nearly thirty years, he appeared with almost every leading lady in the business. Who are the leading ladies with him in the pictures overleaf from some of his films, and can you name the films as well?

5 In most romantic films, the man and the woman meet in extraordinary and often inauspicious circumstances. What can you remember about these encounters?

1. Marilyn Monroe and Tom Ewell in *The Seven Year Itch* (1955)
2. Audrey Hepburn and Cary Grant in *Charade* (1963)
3. Sean Connery and Ursula Andress in *Dr No* (1962)
4. Dirk Bogarde and Yoko Tani in *The Wind Cannot Read* (1957)
5. Melina Mercouri and Tony Perkins in *Phaedra* (1961)
6. Julie Andrews and Christopher Plummer in *The Sound of Music* (1965)
7. Ryan O'Neal and Ali McGraw in *Love Story* (1971)
8. Rex Harrison and Elizabeth Taylor in *Cleopatra* (1963)
9. Jane Fonda and Michael Sarrazin in *They Shoot Horses, Don't They?* (1969)
10. Anouk Aimée and Jean-Louis Trintignant in *A Man and a Woman* (1966)
11. Trevor Howard and Celia Johnson in *Brief Encounter* (1946)
12. Bette Davis and Paul Henried in *Now, Voyager* (1942)

6 Tarzan and Jane may not be everyone's idea of the perfect romantic couple, but one has to admire their durability. Who played them in:

1. *Tarzan of the Apes* (1918)?
2. *The Return of Tarzan* (1920)?
3. *The Adventures of Tarzan* (1921)?
4. *Tarzan and the Golden Lion* (1927)?
5. *Tarzan the Ape Man* (1932)?
6. *Tarzan the Fearless* (1933)?
7. *Tarzan's Revenge* (1938)?
8. *Tarzan and the Amazons* (1945)?
9. *Tarzan and the She-Devil* (1952)?

7 The only big romantic pair of recent years has been Elizabeth Taylor and Richard Burton. How many of the films that they made together can you remember?

8 Romantic couples, however, are almost a thing of the past, when certain pairs of names always seemed to go together. How many films did each of the following pairs make together, and how many titles can you remember?
1. Judy Garland and Mickey Rooney
2. Katharine Hepburn and Spencer Tracy
3. Joan Crawford and Clark Gable
4. Olivia de Havilland and Errol Flynn
5. Ginger Rogers and Fred Astaire
6. Lauren Bacall and Humphrey Bogart

9 True or False?
1. Grace Kelly and Ava Gardner chased the same man in Africa in 1953.
2. Omar Sharif and Charles Boyer have played the same romantic lead at different times.
3. James Stewart played a musician married to June Allyson.
4. Rita Tushingham fell in love with Peter Finch in Ireland.
5. Oliver Reed and Heather Sears were trapped together in Canada.
6. Michael Caine was involved with Jane Fonda in Mexico.
7. Dirk Bogarde played a Spanish priest who fell in love with Capucine during the Spanish Civil War.
8. Leslie Caron slept with Tom Courtenay in a bedsitter in London.
9. Julie Christie went to a Parisian orgy with Terence Stamp.

10 Who are 'he', 'she', and 'they' in the following statements, and in which films would you expect to find them?

1.   She wore a scarlet dress to attract her man in Warner Brothers' challenge to *Gone with the Wind* (1939).

2.   They embraced in the raging Hawaiian surf following a moonlight swim in December 1941.

3.   She seduced him while they danced to 'Moonglow'.

4.   She rose out of the bushes, drank his 'gentleman's wine', and led him back into the undergrowth.

5.   While they lay in bed, he played his Stradivarius to calm her nerves.

6.   She ran away from royal protocol and fell in love with an American reporter.

7.   He interviewed her in a man-on-the-street television programme on the King's Road; he lost her to others, and wouldn't have her when she tried to come back.

8.   He tried to drive her out of his flat the morning after by playing brass band records.

9.   He arrived encased in black leather, and just before her wedding to another, she ran off with him into the Mexican hills.

10.   They had arranged an assignation in a Los Angeles hotel, but his courage failed, and he telephoned her from the lobby as she sat in the bar.

11.   He was an off-duty police officer looking for a missing friend, and she was being terrorized by a sex maniac.

12.   They stood in the shower, he fully dressed, she stark naked, paralysed because the villain was on the other side of the curtain. She dropped the soap; he picked it up.

11   Can you identify these leading ladies?

1.   Hollywood's greatest sex goddess of the thirties was portrayed in the film *The Carpetbaggers* (1963). Who was she, and who played her?

This actress was also portrayed in two inaccurate biographies in 1965. Who were the two actresses who impersonated her in these films?

Her first film helped to fix her public image. What was it?

2. Who was 'The Sweater Girl'?

3. Whose career was launched in 1943 with publicity which described her as '. . . mean, moody and magnificent'?

4. Who was the movie queen who began as a dancer named Margarita Cansino and moved from musicals to more sultry roles?

5. Who, described as '. . . a sizzling, husky, sultry wolverine', married her most famous co-star?

12 The triangle is one of the principal ingredients of romantic drama, although in recent films, situations are frequently more polygonal than triangular. Who was involved with whom in:

1. *Dr Zhivago* (1965)?
2. *The Servant* (1963)?
3. *Life at the Top* (1965)?
4. *X, Y and Zee* [*Zee and Co*] (1972)?
5. *Accident* (1967)?
6. *The Flesh and the Devil* (1927)?
7. *Sweet Bird of Youth* (1962)?
8. *Red Dust* (1932)?
9. *The Killing of Sister George* (1968)?
10. *Dreaming Lips* (1937)?
11. *The Night of the Iguana* (1964)?
12. *Design for Living* (1934)?
13. *L'Amant de Cinq Jours* (1961)?
14. *Carnal Knowledge* (1971)?
15. *A Stolen Life* (1946)?

13 Peter Finch has probably been involved in more, and more varied, triangles than any other actor. Who were the others in his life in:

1. *The Trials of Oscar Wilde* (1960)?
2. *I Thank a Fool* (1962)?
3. *The Pumpkin Eater* (1964)?
4. *Sunday, Bloody Sunday* (1971)?

4

14 Although she had made several films in the twenties, it wasn't until 1930 and *The Blue Angel* that Marlene Dietrich became an international success.
Who are the leading men with whom she is pictured here, and what are the titles of the films?

15 In which films did these triangles occur?
1. Michael Caine, Shirley Anne Field, Jane Asher, Vivien Merchant, etc.
2. George C. Scott, Shirley MacLaine, Alain Delon
3. George C. Scott, Julie Christie, Richard Chamberlain
4. Ava Gardner, Robert Taylor, Mel Ferrer

5.   Rod Steiger, Claire Bloom, Judy Geeson
6.   Elizabeth Taylor, Richard Burton, Peter Ustinov
7.   Elizabeth Taylor, Richard Burton, Eva Marie Saint
8.   Tyrone Power, Linda Darnell, Rita Hayworth
9.   Gary Cooper, Tallulah Bankhead, Charles Laughton
10. Fredric March, Greta Garbo, Basil Rathbone

16   It's difficult to say who are today's great romantic stars. There are a few likely candidates, although their appeal is more sexual than romantic.
Can you identify the actor or actress being described in the following 'scenarios'?

1.   She ran a brothel for her rather hopeless man; she was seduced by a famous Irish playwright; she ruined a man's life because she used him to deliver letters to her lover.

2.   An extremely wealthy woman, she fell in love with a poor and humble doctor who kept rejecting her; as an aristocrat, she had a little shipboard romance; more recently she was seen in Russia, searching for her husband who was lost during the Second World War.

3.   He was a deranged German general; he was harassed by his royal wife and three disappointing children; he had a more peaceful time as a gentle schoolmaster, but has recently become a deranged nobleman.

4.   She had a fruitless liaison with a photographer in swinging London; then she fell for a king; after a brief career as a dancer, she fell in love with a gallant young Victorian officer, but he was killed in action.

Romance — Answers

1   1.   *Susan Lenox: Her Fall and Rise:* Clark Gable ('What a pair of screen lovers they make!')
    Grand Hotel: John Barrymore
    Queen Christina: John Gilbert (rather than Olivier)
    Anna Karenina: Fredric March
    Camille: Robert Taylor
    Marie Walewska: Charles Boyer
2.   Not for any film, but she was awarded one in 1954 for '. . . her unforgettable screen performances . . .'
3.   *Two-Faced Woman* (1941), not a great success.
4.   *Anna Christie* (1931). Her first words were 'Giff me a whisky, ginger ale on the side — and don't be stingy, baby.'
5.   It was *Ninotchka* (1939) — 'Garbo Laughs!' The original was directed by Lubitsch; both re-makes were in 1955. One was the musical *Silk Stockings*, with Cyd Charisse taking over the Garbo role. The other was *The Iron Petticoat*, with Katharine Hepburn.

2   1.   Laurence Olivier and Greer Garson
2.   Merle Oberon and Laurence Olivier
3.   Audrey Hepburn and Mel Ferrer
4.   Norma Shearer and Fredric March
5.   Simone Signoret and Laurence Harvey
6.   John Mills and Valerie Hobson (as children, they were played by Anthony Wager and Jean Simmons)
7.   Julie Christie and Omar Sharif
8.   Tyrone Power and Ava Gardner
9.   Orson Welles and Joan Fontaine
10. Oliver Reed and Glenda Jackson

3   *Fire over England:* Laurence Olivier
Gone with the Wind: Clark Gable and Leslie Howard (it really couldn't be left out)
Waterloo Bridge: Robert Taylor
Lady Hamilton: Laurence Olivier (as Lord Nelson)
Anna Karenina: Kieron Moore
A Streetcar Named Desire: Marlon Brando
The Roman Spring of Mrs Stone: Warren Beatty

4   1.   *It Happened One Night* (1934), with Claudette Colbert
2.   *Love on the Run* (1937), with Joan Crawford
3.   *Gone with the Wind* (1939), with Vivien Leigh
4.   *Honky Tonk* (1941), with Lana Turner
5.   *It Started in Naples* (1959), with Sophia Loren

5   1.   She accidentally pushed a tomato plant off her balcony on to his patio, and almost got him with it.
2.   They met at a ski resort in the Alps; he returned her friend's little boy, who let him have it in the face with a water pistol.
3.   He was on the beach, and she rose out of the sea, wearing an almost non-existent bikini and a knife at her waist.
4.   She came to give him Japanese lessons when he was stationed in India during the Second World War.
5.   They met at the Elgin Marbles in the British Museum.
6.   She was sent from her convent, where she was a novice, to be governess to his motherless children.
7.   She gave him a hard time when he, a Harvard student, came to borrow a book from the Radcliffe library, where she worked and studied.
8.   She was concealed in a carpet, a gift for Caesar, and was tumbled out across the floor as it was unrolled.
9.   He got unwillingly roped into being her partner in a thirties dance marathon when her partner walked out on her.
10. Each of them widowed, they met when they went to visit their children, who were at the same boarding school in Deauville.

11. She got a cinder in her eye while waiting on a station platform, and he said 'May I help? I'm a doctor.'

12. They met on a ship. She was there under psychiatrist's orders, and he was trying to escape from his unhappy marriage.

6   1.   Elmo Lincoln and Enid Markey
2.   Gene Polar and Karla Schramm
3.   Elmo Lincoln and Louise Lorraine
4.   James Pierce and Dorothy Dunbar
5.   Johnny Weissmuller and Maureen O'Sullivan
6.   Buster Crabbe and Jacqueline Wells
7.   Glenn Morris and Eleanor Holm
8.   Johnny Weissmuller and Brenda Joyce
9.   Lex Barker and Joyce MacKenzie

Of these, the most famous pair was Johnny Weissmuller and Maureen O'Sullivan, who made sixteen films in this seemingly endless series. There appear to have been more than sixty films made, with at least fourteen different Tarzans. In addition to the seven noted above, there have been P. Dempsey Tabler (*Son of Tarzan*, 1920, with Kamuela C. Searle in the title role), Frank Merrill (*Tarzan the Mighty*, 1928), Bruce Bennett (*Tarzan and the Green Goddess*, 1935, made under his real name, Herman Brix), Gordon Scott (*Tarzan's Hidden Jungle*, 1955), Denny Miller (*Tarzan the Ape Man*, 1960), Jock Mahoney (*Tarzan Goes to India*, 1962) and Mike Henry (*Tarzan and the Jungle Boy*, 1968).

7   At the time of writing, they had made ten: *Cleopatra* (1962); *The VIPs* (1963); *The Sandpiper* (1965); *Who's Afraid of Virginia Woolf?* (1966); *The Comedians* (1967); *The Taming of the Shrew* (1967); *Doctor Faustus* (1967); *Boom* (1968); *Under Milk Wood* (1971); *Hammersmith Is Out* (1972).

8   1.   There were eight: *Thoroughbreds Don't Cry* (1937); *Love Finds Andy Hardy* (1938); *Babes in Arms* (1939);

Andy Hardy Meets Debutante (1940); *Babes on Broadway* (1941); *Girl Crazy* (1943); *Thousands Cheer* (1943); *Words and Music* (1948).

2. There were nine: *Woman of the Year* (1941); *Keeper of the Flame* (1943); *Without Love* (1945); *Sea of Grass* (1947); *State of the Union* (1948); *Adam's Rib* (1949); *Pat and Mike* (1952); *The Desk Set* (1957); *Guess Who's Coming to Dinner* (1967).

3. There were eight: *Dance Fools Dance* (1931); *Laughing Sinners* (1931); *Possessed* (1932); *Dancing Lady* (1933); *Forsaking All Others* (1934); *Chained* (1934); *Love on the Run* (1936); *Strange Cargo* (1940).

4. There were eight: *Captain Blood* (1935); *The Charge of the Light Brigade* (1936); *The Adventures of Robin Hood* (1937); *Four's a Crowd* (1938); *Dodge City* (1939); *Elizabeth and Essex* (1939); *Santa Fe Trail* (1940); *They Died with Their Boots On* (1941).

5. There were ten: *Flying Down to Rio* (1933); *The Gay Divorce[e]* (1934); *Roberta* (1934); *Top Hat* (1935); *Follow the Fleet* (1935); *Swing Time* (1936); *Shall We Dance?* (1937); *Carefree* (1938); *The Story of Vernon and Irene Castle* (1939); *The Barkleys of Broadway* (1949).

6. Surprisingly, Humphrey Bogart and Lauren Bacall only made four films together: *To Have and Have Not* (1945); *The Big Sleep* (1946); *Dark Passage* (1947); *Key Largo* (1948).

Other notable pairs: Janet Gaynor and Charles Farrell (11); Myrna Loy and William Powell (12); Jeannette MacDonald and Nelson Eddy (8); Greer Garson and Walter Pidgeon (8); Bette Davis and George Brent (7).

9 1. True. Clark Gable in *Mogambo*.
2. True. Both have played Austrian Archduke Rudolph, who was found dead in the hunting lodge at *Mayerling*. The

respective Marie Vetseras were Danielle Darrieux (1936) and Catherine Deneuve (1968). The director of the original, Anatole Litvak, made a TV version with Audrey Hepburn and Mel Ferrer in 1956.

3. True. In *The Glenn Miller Story* (1954).

4. True. In *The Girl with Green Eyes* (1964).

5. False. He was with Rita Tushingham in *The Trap* (1966).

6. False. They did, however, make a film set in the deep south – *Hurry Sundown* (1967) – in which he played a plantation owner and she was his tormented wife.

7. False. It was Ava Gardner, in *The Angel Wore Red* (1960).

8. False. It was Tom Bell, in *The L-Shaped Room* (1962).

9. False. She went with Laurence Harvey in *Darling* (1965).

10
1. The lady was Bette Davis, in *Jezebel* (1938).

2. In *From Here to Eternity* (1953), Deborah Kerr made out with Burt Lancaster in a torrid (for the time) prelude to the attack on Pearl Harbor.

3. Kim Novak and William Holden in Joshua Logan's *Picnic* (1955).

4. Diane Cilento, seducing Albert Finney in *Tom Jones* (1963).

5. Peter Sellers made this unsuccessful attempt to relax Capucine in *The Pink Panther* (1963).

6. Audrey Hepburn played the princess on the loose to Gregory Peck's newspaper man in search of a story in *Roman Holiday* (1953).

7. They were Dirk Bogarde and Julie Christie in *Darling* (1965).

8. He was Dustin Hoffman, making an unsuccessful attempt to rid himself of Mia Farrow in *John and Mary* (1969).

9. Dirk Bogarde and Mylene Demongeot in *The Singer Not the Song* (1960).

10. Dustin Hoffman and Anne Bancroft in *The Graduate* (1967).

11. Donald Sutherland and Jane Fonda in *Klute* (1971).

12. Gregory Peck and Sophia Loren in *Arabesque* (1966).

11 1. She was Jean Harlow, and she was played in *The Carpetbaggers* by Carroll Baker. The two 1965 *Harlows* were Carol Lynley and Carroll Baker again. Harlow's first film, *Hell's Angels* (1930), showed her as a fairly loose lady being passed around a group of flyers. It was produced and directed by Howard Hughes, who also turned up, slightly disguised, in *The Carpetbaggers*, impersonated by George Peppard.

2. Lana Turner, who began her career in 1937 as one of MGM's girl-next-door types and quickly changed her image.

3. Jane Russell, another Hughes discovery, in *The Outlaw*. Because of censor problems, the film wasn't released until 1946.

4. She changed her name to Rita Hayworth, and her subsequent films (*Gilda*, 1946; *Salome*, 1953) were a far cry from *Cover Girl* (1944).

5. Lauren Bacall, who married Humphrey Bogart.

12 1. Geraldine Chaplin, Omar Sharif and Julie Christie

2. Dirk Bogarde, Sarah Miles, James Fox and Wendy Craig

3. Jean Simmons, Laurence Harvey and Honor Blackman

4. Elizabeth Taylor, Michael Caine and Susannah York

5. Dirk Bogarde, Stanley Baker, Jacqueline Sassard, Vivien Merchant and Michael York

6. Lars Hanson, Greta Garbo and John Gilbert

7. Geraldine Page, Paul Newman and Shirley Knight

8. Jean Harlow, Clark Gable and Mary Astor (re-made as *Mogambo* (1953) with Ava Gardner, Clark Gable and Grace Kelly)

9. Beryl Reid, Susannah York and Coral Browne

10. Raymond Massey, Elisabeth Bergner and Romney Brent

11. Richard Burton, Deborah Kerr, Ava Gardner and Sue Lyon

12. Gary Cooper, Miriam Hopkins, Fredric March and Edward Everett Horton

13. Jean-Pierre Cassel, Micheline Presle, Jean Seberg and François Dérier

14. Jack Nicholson, Candice Bergen, Ann-Margaret and Arthur Garfunkel (also numerous other ladies, mostly involved with Mr Nicholson, but two with Mr Garfunkel)

15. Bette Davis, Glenn Ford and Bette Davis (in a double role)

13
1. John Fraser and Yvonne Mitchell
2. Susan Hayward and Diane Cilento
3. Anne Bancroft and Maggie Smith
4. Glenda Jackson and Murray Head

14
1. Robert Donat in *Knight Without Armour* (1937)
2. Charles Boyer in *The Garden of Allah* (1936)
3. Ray Milland in *Golden Earrings* (1947)
4. Gary Cooper in *Morocco* (1930), her first American picture

15
1. *Alfie* (1966)
2. The middle episode of *The Yellow Rolls Royce* (1964)
3. *Petulia* (1968)
4. *The Knights of the Round Table* (1954), as Guinevere, Lancelot and Arthur, respectively.
5. *Three into Two Won't Go* (1969)
6. *The Comedians* (1967)
7. *The Sandpiper* (1965)
8. *Blood and Sand* (1941)
9. *The Devil and the Deep* (1932)
10. *Anna Karenina* (1935)

16 1. Julie Christie. She was a madam for Warren Beatty in *McCabe and Mrs Miller* (1972), seduced by Rod Taylor as a thinly disguised Sean O'Casey in *The Young Cassidy* (1964), and made a neurotic mess of Dominic Guard/Michael Redgrave in *The Go-Between* (1971).

2. Sophia Loren. As *The Millionairess* (1961) she fell in love with Indian doctor Peter Sellers, and got him in the end; she had an affair at sea with Marlon Brando in *A Countess From Hong Kong* (1966), and searched for lost husband Marcello Mastroianni in *Sunflower* (1970).

3. Peter O'Toole. In one of the title roles in *Night of the Generals* (1966); he was nagged by Katharine Hepburn in *The Lion in Winter* (1968) and married to Petula Clark in *Goodbye Mr Chips* (1969), which was obviously too much for him, as *The Ruling Class* (1972) showed.

4. Vanessa Redgrave. She seduced David Hemmings in *Blow-Up* (1967), married Richard Harris in *Camelot* (1967) but played around with Franco Nero; danced as *Isadora* (1968), and had another encounter with David Hemmings in *The Charge of the Light Brigade* (1968).

6 Horror

Hollywood imported the horror movie from Germany in the twenties. The thirties were the genre's golden age, when its traditions were established by its greatest exponents. Decline began in the forties and continued into the fifties. Horror films have more recently been enjoying a renaissance, although pure horror has been bypassed for light entertainment.*

1.   1.   In 1931, Boris Karloff, who had already some sixty films to his credit, achieved stardom with his basically sympathetic portrayal of the monster in James Whale's production of *Frankenstein*. The phenomenal success of this film led to a fantastic number of Frankenstein successors, a few of which are listed below. In which ones did Karloff appear as the monster?

> *Bride of Frankenstein* (1935)
> *Son of Frankenstein* (1939)
> *Frankenstein Meets the Wolf Man* (1943)
> *House of Frankenstein* (1945)
> *The Curse of Frankenstein* (1956)
> *Frankenstein 1970* (1958)

2.   Who played the title roles in these Frankenstein films?
   a. *The Bride of Frankenstein* (1935)
   b. *Son of Frankenstein* (1939)
   c. *The Ghost of Frankenstein* (1942)

3.   Who was the novelist who wrote the original *Frankenstein*, in what film was this author portrayed, and by whom?

* Answers on page 93.

2   1.   The first three-act stage version of Bram Stoker's novel *Dracula* was written and produced by (and starred) Hamilton Deane, who toured Britain with it in the twenties. 1931 was the year of the film version, in which Hungarian actor Bela Lugosi transferred his own stage performance to the screen. He subsequently appeared in three Dracula sequels, and became one of the stock horror movie stars. In the films listed below, he did not play a vampire: can you remember the role he did play, and the name and the role of the famous actor who played opposite him?

    a.   *The Raven* (1935)
    b.   *Frankenstein Meets the Wolf Man* (1943)
    c.   *Island of Lost Souls* (1932)

2.   The first screen vampire of any note appeared some years before Lugosi's *Dracula*, in 1922. What was his name, and who played him?

3   1.   There have been at least nine versions of Robert Louis Stevenson's *Dr Jekyll and Mr Hyde*, not to mention several sequels of the *Son of . . .* and *Daughter of . . .* variety. There is even a cartoon version starring Sylvester. Four famous actors have played the dual role in straight versions of the story, in 1920, 1921, 1932 and 1941. Who were they?

2.   In the 1941 version, two famous actresses were flogged by the star (in a dream sequence). Can you remember them?

4   Quickies:

1.   In *Dead of Night* (1945), who was the famous British actor who played the actor possessed by his dummy?

2.   Which horror superstar played the role of Ygor in *Son of Frankenstein* (1939), and what was Ygor's principal claim to fame?

3.   Who played Frankenstein's supposed second son in *The Ghost of Frankenstein* (1942)?

4.   Who were the two leads in the 1939 version of John Willard's horror-comedy *The Cat and the Canary*?

5. Tom Ewell took Marilyn Monroe to a horror movie in *The Seven Year Itch* (1955). Which one was it, and what was her reaction to it?

5   Can you identify these four characters and their films?

6 Who played
  1. *The Phantom of the Rue Morgue* (1954)?
  2. *The Phantom of the Opera* (1943)?
  3. *The Invisible Man* (1933)?
  4. *Svengali* (1931)?
  5. *The Mummy* (1932)?
  6. *The Ghoul* (1933)?
  7. *Dracula's Daughter* (1936)?
  8. *The Werewolf of London* (1935)?
  9. *Son of Dracula* (1943)?
  10. *M* (1930)?

7 In the forties and fifties, two American comedians made a series of films in which they met a variety of monsters, films which typified the level to which horror films had sunk. Who were the comedians, and how many titles can you remember?

8 *King Kong* (1933) was the first, and possibly the best, of all the monster horror films, and although it has given rise to a host of imitators (*Rodan*, *Gorgo*, *Godzilla* and several Japanese *Kongs*), it remains technically and dramatically more exciting than any of its successors. Can you remember the stars of this classic (other than Kong himself), and the name of the second-rate sequel, made in 1934?

9 Horror-realism, along the lines of Hitchcock's *Psycho* (1960) and Aldrich's *Whatever Happened to Baby Jane?* (1962) was the new type of horror film made by the major studios in the fifties and sixties. Its roots, though, were in the thirties and forties – or perhaps even earlier (*The Cabinet of Dr Caligari*, 1919).

  1. Who were the psychotics, and who were they after, in
    a. *Gaslight* (1939 and 1944)?
    b. *Night Must Fall* (1937 and 1963)?
    c. *The Collector* (1965)?

2. Who played the title-role villains in
   a. *The Lodger* (1944)?
   b. *Bluebeard* (1944)?
   c. *Monsieur Verdoux* (1947)?

3. Who murdered whom in
   a. *Hush, Hush, Sweet Charlotte* (1964)?
   b. *Psycho* (1960)?
   c. *Night of the Hunter* (1955)?
   d. *Strangers on a Train* (1951)?

10 Can you identify these frightened ladies, and the films in which they are being terrorized?

11   One of the last refuges of the B-movie is the horror film of the sixties and seventies; in other genres the Bs have been replaced by bad television films.

    1.   In 1954, American-International Pictures was founded. One of its earliest recruits, a young writer-producer-director, turned out more than fifty films in ten years, and became known as King of the Bs. Some of his most successful productions were loose adaptations of the macabre works of a nineteenth-century American writer. Who is the film-maker, on whose works did he base these films, and who was the star of most of them?

    2.   Along with the star mentioned above, many of these films featured well-known horror actors as co-stars. Who were the principal players in:

       a. *Tales of Terror* (1962)?
       b. *Comedy of Terrors* (1964)?
       c. *The Raven* (1963)?

    3.   At least two of American-International's horror adaptations have featured being buried alive and its associated problems. Can you name two male stars who have been involved in this practice, the titles of the films, and the ladies with whom they were associated?

12   American-International's British counterpart has been Hammer Films* who, with *The Curse of Frankenstein* (1956), embarked on a long and successful series of re-makes and sequels.

    1.   If sequels and re-makes are any indication of longevity, then vampires surely hold the record. Who is Hammer's most famous vampire?

    2.   Another male star has been closely associated with this studio since its first film; he is usually a goodie. Who is he?

    3.   The seemingly endless list of Hammer vampire flicks, such as *Dracula, Prince of Darkness* (1965); *Dracula Has Risen from the Grave* (1968 — you can't keep a

---

* It's perhaps worth noting that, apparently, A-I and Hammer (and Disney) are the only studios to make money consistently over the past fifteen years or so.

good vampire down); *Taste the Blood of Dracula* (1970) and *Scars of Dracula* (1970), have not only perpetuated but also extended our knowledge of vampirology. The possibilities seem endless, what with lesbian vampires (*The Vampire Lovers*, 1970) and black vampires (*Blacula*, 1972). What happens to a vampire if you:

a. Expose him to sunlight?

b. Brandish a crucifix in his direction? or place it on his forehead?

c. Put garlic at your bedroom doors and windows?

d. Throw water on him?

How do you permanently dispatch a vampire?

13 What have the names in each of the following groups in common?

1. *Topper* (1939)
   The Uninvited (1943)
   Portrait of Jennie (1943)
   Blithe Spirit (1945)

2. Walter Huston
   Ray Milland
   Stanley Holloway
   Benjamin Christensen

3. *Rosemary's Baby* (1968)
   The Dunwich Horror (1969)
   The Black Cat (1934)
   The Seventh Victim (1943)

4. Margaret Hamilton
   Lisbeth Martin
   Veronica Lake
   Kim Novak

5. Catherine Deneuve
   Francesca Annis
   Ruth Gordon
   Françoise Dorléac

14   In another recent trend, established movie queens have taken to horror films: *Whatever Happened to Baby Jane?* (1962) was the first and most famous of the lot, followed by *Lady in a Cage* (1963) and *Hush, Hush, Sweet Charlotte* (1964). Even Hayley Mills has tried it (*Twisted Nerve*, 1968).

Who are the well-known lady stars of these recent films?

1.   *Whatever Happened to Aunt Alice?* (1970)
2.   *What's the Matter with Helen?* (1971)
3.   *Whoever Slew Auntie Roo?* (1971)

Horror — Answers

1. Boris Karloff was the monster in both *Bride of Frankenstein* and *Son of Frankenstein*. He was in *House of Frankenstein*, but Glenn Strange (!) played the monster. His last Frankenstein film was *Frankenstein 1970*, in which he played Baron Victor von Frankenstein, the great grandson of the original. The role was played by Bela Lugosi in *Frankenstein Meets the Wolf Man*, and in *The Curse of Frankenstein* it was Christopher Lee.

2. a. The title role was taken by Elsa Lanchester. This was the first film to begin the confusion between Frankenstein (the German baron-scientist) and the monster he created. Miss Lanchester was supposed to be the bride of the *monster*, not the baron. But even she, who was not particularly lovely as the she-monster, couldn't stand poor Boris.

b. The *Son of Frankenstein* was Basil Rathbone, a fairly major figure in horror films, although this was his only 'monster' movie.

c. The title role was played by Lon Chaney Jr. Maybe. There is some doubt as to who the 'ghost' was meant to be, but if you assume that the ghost was the monster, then the answer is Chaney.

3. The original novel *Frankenstein* was the creation of Mary Shelley, wife of poet Percy Bysshe, who wrote it during a long, wet English summer. She was featured in the film *Bride of Frankenstein*, for reasons which are not clear, as she certainly didn't write this or any other sequel. She was played by the same actress who played the *Bride*: Elsa Lanchester.

1. a. He played a mad scientist-surgeon, opposite mad

killer-on-the-loose Boris Karloff, who had dropped in for a spot of plastic surgery.

b. He played the monster to Lon Chaney Jr's *Wolf Man*.

c. He played one of the ape men created by mad scientist Charles Laughton.

2. His name was the same as that of the film: *Nosferatu*, directed by F. W. Murnau. Although no credit was given, the film was again a direct adaptation of the Bram Stoker original. The title role in this classic German film was played by an actor named Max Schreck; 'Schreck' translates as 'terror'.

Nosferatu is often credited as being the first vampire film, but there were at least two earlier ones: *Vampyr* (1912; Denmark) and *The Vampire* (1914; USA).

3 1. In 1920: Conrad Veidt
In 1921: John Barrymore
In 1932: Fredric March
In 1941: Spencer Tracy
2. In the dream, Tracy was driving a coach and whipping the team of Ingrid Bergman and Lana Turner.

4 1. Michael Redgrave, in an Ealing film, a collection of five ghost stories, one of the few films to treat the subject seriously.
2. Bela Lugosi. Ygor had been hanged but had survived, somewhat deformed by his broken neck. He had a bad habit of knocking his knuckles against the (anatomically ludicrous) protruding bone.
3. Cedric Hardwicke, who at about that time appeared in several horror films including *On Borrowed Time* (1939), in which he played Death, and *The Hunchback of Notre Dame* (1940).
4. Paulette Goddard and Bob Hope. This was the third version of the stage hit: the first, silent, starred Laura la Plante and Creighton Hale, and was made in 1927. A sound

re-make in 1930 was called *The Cat Creeps*, and starred Helen Twelvetrees and Raymond Hackett. The Goddard/ Hope version was the best.

5. He took her to see *The Creature from the Black Lagoon* (1954). She felt sorry for the Creature.

5 All four are pictures of Lon Chaney, *The Man of a Thousand Faces* (the title of a biographical film made in 1957). His characters were not so much horrible or terrifying as they were grotesque. These are good examples:

1. *The Phantom of the Opera* (1925), in which he played the embittered, disfigured composer who haunts the sewers under the Paris Opera, and eventually sacrifices himself for his protégée with whom he has fallen in love. Certainly the best of the three versions of this story.

2. *West of Zanzibar* (1928), with Chaney as the bitter, vicious magician who gives his unfaithful wife's daughter to cannibals, only to find that she is (you guessed it) his own child. He perishes in the attempt to rescue her.

3. *Laugh, Clown, Laugh* (1928), with Chaney in the title role of the clown who can't laugh. He is matched with the count who can't stop laughing. The count falls in love with Chaney's girl-friend and after much suspicion and acrimony, the tragic clown kills himself.

4. *The Unknown* (1927), in which Chaney played a murderer with two thumbs on one hand. To escape detection he masquerades as an armless man in a sideshow. After he falls in love he has to maintain the disguise by amputating his arms, but the girl he loves loves another. His bitterness leads to plots of revenge, but he is trampled to death in the attempt.

6 1. Karl Malden
2. Claude Rains
3. Rains again

4. John Barrymore
5. Boris Karloff
6. Karloff again
7. Gloria Holden
8. Henry Hull
9. Lon Chaney Jr
10. Peter Lorre

7   The comedians were Bud Abbott and Lou Costello, and the films were:

Abbott and Costello Meet: Frankenstein (1949)
                          The Killer (1950)
                          The Invisible Man (1951)
                          Dr Jekyll and Mr Hyde (1953)
                          The Mummy (1954)

There was also a film in 1941, *Hold That Ghost*, which was along the same lines, even though the title doesn't really fit with the others.

8   The stars of this Merian C. Cooper/Ernest B. Schoedsack film were Fay Wray, Robert Armstrong and Bruce Cabot. Edgar Wallace received a credit for the screenplay, as he was in on the first discussions about the film, but he died before shooting actually started.

The sequel was *Son of Kong*, naturally.

9   1. a. Charles Boyer tried to drive Ingrid Bergman out of her mind, in order to lay claim to her fortune. The earlier version, with the same name, was made by Thorold Dickinson, with Anton Walbrook and Diana Wynyard. Its negative was bought (and destroyed!) by MGM to make way for the re-make. In Britain the later version was called *The Murder in Thornton Square*. A few prints of the 1939 version apparently still exist in the United States, where it is called *Angel Street*.

b. In the original version of Emlyn Williams's play about a homicidal Welshman, Robert Montgomery was after Rosalind Russell. The later version had Albert Finney pursuing Susan Hampshire.

c. Terence Stamp, unsuccessfully uglified, was trying to add Samantha Eggar to his collection of butterflies.

2. a. Laird Cregar, as a slightly disguised Jack the Ripper.

b. John Carradine, another horror standby (*House of Frankenstein*, 1945, as Dracula; *House of Dracula*, 1945; *The Mummy's Ghost*, 1946).

c. Charles Chaplin, in this *Bluebeard* variation.

3. a. Mary Astor murdered her husband, as he was Charlotte's lover and she was understandably upset. Subsequently, Olivia de Havilland murdered the faithful family retainer/eccentric Agnes Moorehead, but Bette Davis finally got Olivia and her conspirator Joseph Cotten in the end.

b. Anthony Perkins murdered Janet Leigh and later Martin Balsam when he came looking for her.

c. Robert Mitchum murdered Shelley Winters (and several other murders of his were mentioned). Lillian Gish almost got Mitchum when he attempted to get at his two stepchildren.

d. Robert Walker, as the (probably homosexual) psychopath, murdered Farley Granger's wife. He was eventually killed, but not murdered, by a runaway roundabout in the fairground where he had committed the murder.

10 1. Vera Miles, in Alfred Hitchcock's *Psycho* (1960), who has just seen something nasty in the cellar.

2. Mia Farrow, seeing *Rosemary's Baby* (1968) for the first time.

3. Deborah Kerr in Jack Clayton's *The Innocents* (1961), the film version of Henry James's *The Turn of the Screw*, which has recently been followed by a sort of forerunner,

The Nightcomers (1972), which attempts to tell what happened before James's original.

4.   Claire Bloom and Julie Harris in Robert Wise's *The Haunting* (1963), the film version of Shirley Jackson's *We Have Always Lived in the Castle*. Some unknown force is trying to break down the bedroom door.

11 1.   Roger Corman. His source was Edgar Allen Poe. Most of the films (*The Fall of the House of Usher*, 1961; *The Pit and the Pendulum*, 1961; *The Tomb of Ligeia*, 1964; *The Masque of the Red Death*, 1964) starred Vincent Price.

2.   Along with Vincent Price were:
   a. Boris Karloff, Peter Lorre and Basil Rathbone.
   b. The same again, in another send-up of the genre.
   c. Peter Lorre was in the title role, with magician Boris Karloff. Rathbone missed this one.

3.   In *The Fall of the House of Usher* (1960) he was (surprise) Vincent Price. His family was cursed with incurable hereditary catalepsy, and eventually he buried alive his sister (Myrna Fahey).

In *The Premature Burial* (1961), Ray Milland was buried alive by his scheming wife (Hazel Court, another Corman favourite). She was able to do this because the family was cursed with incurable hereditary catalepsy.

Notice the similarity? Not only were both very loose Poe adaptations, directed by Roger Corman, but A-I's slim budgets were reflected in the use of the same sets for both pictures. See also *The Pit and the Pendulum* (1961), in which similar situations plague Vincent Price and Barbara Steele.

12 1.   Who else but Christopher Lee?

2.   Peter Cushing, who has played not only vampire-destroyers (*Brides of Dracula*, 1960), but also more down-to-earth characters like Sherlock Holmes (*The Hound of the Baskervilles*, 1959). Christopher Lee has also played Holmes, but only in German films.

3. a. He (or she) turns to dust.

b. He is instantly repelled. A crucifix to the forehead will brand him (but for this, you have to catch him in his grave, during the day).

c. He can't get in. Purists maintain that it has to be a *ring* of garlic, but it seems sufficient, judging by recent films, if only the entrances to the room are so protected.

d. He dies, but by what means is not too clear.

Permanent dispatch is more difficult. You must catch him during the daylight hours (when he is confined to his coffin, because of the sunlight, you see) and drive a wooden stake through his heart. In the good old days, it was also necessary to cut off his head, but this doesn't seem called for any more: he generally distintegrates before decapitation. With the speed with which Christopher Lee keeps coming back, one wonders why they bother at all.

13 1. In all four, at least one of the principal characters was a ghost.

In *Topper*, the ghosts were Constance Bennett and Cary Grant.

In *The Uninvited*, the ghost was disembodied, didn't respond to Ray Milland's challenges, and drove Cornelia Otis Skinner mad.

In *Portrait of Jennie*, the ghost was Jennifer Jones.

In *Blithe Spirit*, it was Kay Hammond, who was latterly joined by Constance Cummings.

2. All these gentlemen have played the devil:
Huston in *All That Money Can Buy* (1941).
Milland in *Alias Nick Beal* [*The Contact Man*] (1949).
Holloway in *Meet Mr Lucifer* (1953).
Christensen in *Witchcraft Through the Ages* (1921), still one of the best films of its type, which Christensen also directed. It has recently been re-released with sound effects and music.

3. All were films which involved the principal characters

in devil worship, in one form or another. All were made by noted directors of horror-type films: Roman Polanski, Daniel Haller (with Roger Corman producing), Edgar G. Ulmer and Mark Robson respectively.

4.   All have played witches:
Margaret Hamilton in *The Wizard of Oz* (1939)
Lisbeth Martin in Carl Dreyer's *Day of Wrath* (1943)
Veronica Lake in *I Married a Witch* (1942)
Kim Novak in *Bell, Book and Candle* (1957)

5.   All were leading ladies in horror films by one of the few directors in this genre to be taken 'seriously' (although afficionados of the genre take *all* the directors seriously): Roman Polanski.
Catherine Deneuve in *Repulsion* (1965)
Francesca Annis in *Macbeth* (1972)
Ruth Gordon in *Rosemary's Baby* (1968)
Françoise Dorléac in *Cul de Sac* (1966)

14   1.   Geraldine Page and Ruth Gordon, in another film by Robert Aldrich.
2.   Shelley Winters, Debbie Reynolds and Agnes Moorehead in a film written by Henry Farrell, author of the screenplay of *Baby Jane* (1962).
3.   Shelley Winters again, in another film directed by Curtis Harrington, director of *What's the Matter with Helen?* (1971).

7 Comedies

No definition of comedy could adequately embrace the Keystone Cops, Bob Hope, Chaplin, Hepburn and Tracy, *M*A*S*H*, Norman Wisdom, Alec Guinness, Keaton and Billy Wilder. All that can be said is that comedies make us laugh, that comedy is one of the cinema's most enduring accomplishments, and that more comedies have been produced than any other type of film.*

1 The Marx Brothers provoke more argument about what is funny than any other comedians. They came to the screen from vaudeville but never really changed their tactics for the new medium. Their thirteen star vehicles provide some of the funniest set-pieces and non-sequiturs on film.
1. What were the names of the *five* Marx Brothers?
2. Who was Groucho's long-suffering straight lady?
3. Who played these characters, and in what films?
   a. Rufus T. Firefly
   b. Professor Quincy Adams Wagstaff
   c. Wolf J. Flywheel
   d. Hugo Z. Hackenbush
   e. Otis B. Driftwood

2 Who was (or were)
1. *Ninotchka* (1939)?
2. *The Beautiful Blonde from Bashful Bend* (1949)?
3. *The Reluctant Debutante* (1958)?
4. *The Major and the Minor* (1942)?
5. *The Man Who Came to Dinner* (1941)?
6. *The Bank Dick* [*The Bank Detective*] (1941)?

* Answers on page 110.

7. *Auntie Mame* (1957)?
8. *The Inspector General* (1949)?
9. *Born Yesterday* (1951)?
10. *The Constant Husband* (1955)?
11. *The Odd Couple* (1968)?
12. *The Father of the Bride* (1950)?
13. *Harold and Maude* (1971)?
14. *The Madwoman of Chaillot* (1969)?
15. *Barefoot in the Park* (1967)?

3 One of the best-known comedies of the forties was Frank Capra's adaptation of Joseph Kesselring's *Arsenic and Old Lace* (1944). Who were the principal characters and who played them?

4 Successful comedies have often depended on the talents of a large stock of familiar faces, usually in small roles. Here are eight: how many can you identify?

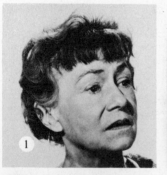

5 For decades, Charles Chaplin has been the acknowledged king of comedy.

1. Listed here are some of his best films. Who were his leading ladies?

    a. *Tillie's Punctured Romance* (1914)
    b. *Shoulder Arms* (1918)
    c. *City Lights* (1931)
    d. *Modern Times* (1936)
    e. *The Great Dictator* (1940)
    f. *Limelight* (1952)

2. Who is the best-remembered heavy from the early Chaplin two-reelers?

3. What was Chaplin's most recent film, and who were its stars?

6 Many people think that Buster Keaton was an even greater talent than Chaplin. He was a major star in the twenties, but

it wasn't until forty years later that critical opinion acknowledged his particular genius.

1.   Keaton began his film career in 1917, playing in a series of short comedies with the well-established comedian —— ——.

2.   His leading ladies in *The Navigator* (1924), *The General* (1926) and *Go West* (1925) were —— ——, —— ——, and —— ——.

3.   Along with several other well-known faces, he played himself in the 1950 film —— ——.

4.   He appeared with Chaplin once, in ——.

5.   His only 'serious' film was his penultimate one, in 1965. It was called ——, and was written by —— ——.

7   The so-called 'Ealing comedies' were the hallmark of British film humour from the late forties to the early sixties.

1.   Who were the members of *The Lavender Hill Mob* (1951)?

2.   Who were *The Ladykillers* (1955), and who was the lady they couldn't kill?

3.   Who was Siggy Schmaltz, and in what film did he appear?

4.   Who was 'Nosey' Parker in *Two-Way Stretch* (1960)?

5.   Dennis Price's best performance was in *Kind Hearts and Coronets* (1949) where he murdered eight people on the way to the family title. Whom did he murder, and who were the two women in his life?

6.   In a later film, five people tried to murder Dennis Price. Who were they, what was the film, and did they succeed?

7.   Who was *The Rebel* (1961), what form did his rebellion take, and who (eventually) became his muse?

8.   Who was *Genevieve* (1953), and who were her co-stars?

9.   Why was it necessary to have a *Passport to Pimlico* (1948)?

8   Can you identify these stars (right) of some of the great silent comedies?

9   Quickies:
1.   Who were the stars of *My Little Chickadee* (1940)?
2.   Who were *Scared Stiff* (1953)?
3.   Who were the stars of *Once More with Feeling* (1959)?
4.   Who was the comedian who was Britain's top box office star in 1939?
5.   Who played the flute and who conducted the orchestra in *Hot Millions* (1968)?
6.   Who taught whom *How To Steal a Million* (1966)?
7.   Who was the movies' most professional virgin, who starred in a series of 'sophisticated' comedies in the fifties and sixties?

10   True or False?
1.   *The Comedians* (1967) was a comedy starring Alec Guinness and Peter Ustinov.
2.   James Stewart played *Harvey* (1950).
3.   In *The Knack ... and How to Get It* (1965), Ray Brooks, who had it, lost Rita Tushingham to Michael Crawford, who didn't.
4.   The 1951 comedy-adventure *The African Queen* starred Katharine Hepburn, Humphrey Bogart and Robert Morley.
5.   Judy Holliday divorced Paul Douglas in *Phffft* (1954).

11   Great directors of comedy are rare, but up to the early forties a number of them flourished. Each of the following groups of films has a common director: who?
1.   *The Lady Eve* (1941)
The Great McGinty (1940)
The Palm Beach Story (1942)

2.   *It Happened One Night* (1934)
The Strong Man (1926)
You Can't Take It With You (1938)

3.   *The Shop Around the Corner* (1940)
Trouble in Paradise (1932)
Design for Living (1933)

4. *Mickey* (1918)
    The Shriek of Araby (1923)
    Comrades (1911)

12 Fill in the blanks:

1. —— —— and —— —— were the stars of *Pat and Mike* (1952).

2. —— —— played Titania to —— ——'s Bottom in *A Midsummer Night's Dream* (1935).

3. —— ——, —— —— and —— —— were the stars of *The Philadelphia Story*. The musical re-make was called —— —— and starred —— ——, —— —— and —— —— in the leading roles.

4. —— —— starred with stand-up comedian —— —— in *Fancy Pants* (1949).

5. —— —— played Lady Bracknell and —— —— played Miss Prism in the film version of —— ——'s comedy —— —— —— —— —— (1952).

6. In *The Wrong Box* (1966), —— —— and —— —— played the feuding brothers, while —— —— and —— —— supplied the love interest.

7. In *One Way Pendulum* (1964), —— —— taught speak-your-weight machines to sing the Hallelujah Chorus. —— —— played his mother.

8. In *The Magic Christian* (1969), —— —— adopted —— ——.

13 In the sixties, the movies began to take a more cynical look at the battle of the sexes. The ending was still usually a happy one, but it was also a compromise, acceptable because it was the least of the evils encountered on the way. Who were the protagonists in these films?
1. *Divorce American Style* (1967)
2. *The Apartment* (1960)

3. *A New Leaf* (1971)
4. *Love with the Proper Stranger* (1964)
5. *Morgan, A Suitable Case for Treatment* (1966)

14 1. In *The Smallest Show on Earth* (1957), Virginia McKenna and Bill Travers inherited a run-down cinema. Who were the equally decrepit employees they inherited with it?
2. Jane Fonda, Jim Hutton, Anthony Franciosa and Lois Nettleton starred in an early Tennessee Williams comedy. Can you name it?
3. Who was the lady in all the Hope−Crosby *Road* shows, and how many of the titles can you name?
4. *Bedazzled* (1967) was the eleventh re-make (at least) of a classic story. What is the original on which it was based, and who were its stars?

15 In the past decade, black comedy has become a respectable screen subject: *Arsenic and Old Lace* (1944), *Kind Hearts and Coronets* (1949) and *The Trouble With Harry* (1956) were the predecessors of the recent films. What 'serious' subjects were treated comically in:
1. *The Loved One* (1965)?
2. *The Best of Friends* (1971)?
3. *A Day in the Death of Joe Egg* (1972)?
4. *M*A*S*H* (1970)?
5. *No Way to Treat a Lady* (1968)?
6. *The Anniversary* (1967)?
7. *Black Flowers for the Bride* [*Something for Everyone*] (1971)?
8. *The Hospital* (1972)?
9. *Loot* (1971)?

16 Can you identify the people in these photographs? What are the films from which the pictures are taken?

Comedies – Answers

1   1.   Yes, there were five: Chico, Harpo, Groucho, Zeppo and Gummo. Zeppo soon dropped out of their films, after a few attempts at playing romantic leads. Gummo was with them in their vaudeville days, but left the others long before they reached films.

2.   Margaret Dumont (who should have been decorated). Her last film, which she made at the age of seventy-four, was *What a Way to Go* (1964); she died the following year.

3.   All of them are outrageous characters played by Groucho:
   a.   Firefly was the president of Freedonia in *Duck Soup* (1933).
   b.   Wagstaff was the college president in *Horse Feathers* (1932).
   c.   Flywheel was the detective in *The Big Store* (1941).
   d.   Hackenbush was the masquerading vet in *A Day at the Races* (1937).
   e.   Driftwood was the would-be impresario in *A Night at the Opera* (1935).

2   1.   Greta Garbo
2.   Betty Grable
3.   Sandra Dee
4.   Ray Milland and Ginger Rogers
5.   Monty Wooley
6.   W. C. Fields
7.   Rosalind Russell
8.   Danny Kaye
9.   Judy Holliday
10.   Rex Harrison

11. Jack Lemmon and Walter Matthau
12. Spencer Tracy
13. Bud Cort and Ruth Gordon
14. Katharine Hepburn
15. Robert Redford

3

The hero, Mortimer Brewster, was overplayed by Cary Grant, but the rest of the cast was superb:
The murderous Aunts Abby and Martha were Josephine Hull and Jean Adair.
Mad brother Jonathan ('just like Karloff') was Raymond Massey.
His cringing companion, plastic surgeon Dr Einstein, was Peter Lorre.
Elaine, Grant's fiancée, was played by Priscilla Lane.
Mad brother Teddy (who thought he was Theodore Roosevelt) was John Alexander.
The stage-struck Officer O'Hara ('I was born during the third act, and Mother made the finale') was played by Jack Carson.

4

1. Thelma Ritter, acid-voiced and razor-tongued character actress, always ready with a bit of homely advice which will go unheeded. She played this role in both comedies and non-comedies (*All About Eve*, 1950; *Titanic*, 1953; *Rear Window*, 1954), and also enlivened several otherwise dull comedies (*Pillow Talk*, 1959; *Move Over, Darling*, 1963).

2. Richard Wattis, who always plays harassed, servile, sceptical characters. His spectacles and facial expression are his most important and memorable characteristics; both show well here in *The Captain's Table* (1958). Similar roles include the Ministry of Education official in the *St Trinian's* films and the airport official in *The VIPs* (1963).

3. Phil Silvers, ex-vaudeville comedian who played second lead and smart-aleck friend-of-the-hero in a number of musicals and comedies: *Cover Girl* (1944); *Summer Stock*

(1950); *Lucky Me* (1954); *A Funny Thing Happened on the Way to the Forum* (1966); *Follow That Camel* (1967).

4.   Irene Handl, the typical Cockney mum/maid/char, in such films as *Two-Way Stretch* (1960), *Heavens Above* (1963) and *Morgan* (1966). One of her best roles: Peter Sellers's rebellious wife in *I'm All Right, Jack* (1959).

5.   Fred Clark, the explosive loser of many American comedies such as *The Solid Gold Cadillac* (1956), *Don't Go Near the Water* (1956) and *The Mating Game* (1959), as well as small appearances in non-comedies like *Sunset Boulevard* (1950) and *The Court Martial of Billy Mitchell* (1955).

6.   Eve Arden, an ex-Ziegfeld girl, who became the typical wisecracker and friend-of-the-heroine in a number of forties films (*Comrade X*, 1940; *Mildred Pierce*, 1945), and continued the role in a variety of comedies (*We're Not Married*, 1952; *Our Miss Brooks*, 1955) and non-comedies (*Song of Scheherazade*, 1948; *Anatomy of a Murder*, 1959).

7.   Terry-Thomas, typically the public school villain/underdog (here in *School for Scoundrels*, 1960), whose best roles were in films like *Private's Progress* (1956), *Carleton Browne of the FO* (1958) and *I'm All Right, Jack* (1959). Recently, he has been playing, less successfully, Hollywood Englishmen in films like *How to Murder Your Wife* (1965) and *Monte Carlo or Bust* (1969).

8.   Joyce Grenfell, archetypal spinster, often in pursuit of the man no one else wants. Splendid performances in *Genevieve* (1953), *The Happiest Days of Your Life* (1949) and the *St Trinian's* films, and as Emily's scatty mother in *The Americanization of Emily* (1964).

5   1.   a. Mabel Normand, a leading silent comedienne and frequent partner of Chaplin's. The film also marked the movie début of Marie Dressler.
b. Edna Purviance, another of Chaplin's favourite leading ladies, of the girl-next-door type.

  c. Virginia Cherrill, in the first role of her brief career, which ended in 1936.

  d. Paulette Goddard, in her first feature role.

  e. Paulette Goddard again (by this time Mrs Chaplin).

  f. Claire Bloom, in her second screen appearance.

2. Eric Campbell, whose partnership with Chaplin might have continued, but he died in 1917.

3. He directed (and made a brief appearance, as a waiter, in) *A Countess from Hong Kong* (1966) starring Sophia Loren and Marlon Brando.

6

1. Fatty Arbuckle.

2. Kathryn McGuire, Marion Mack and Kathleen Myers. Like Chaplin, Keaton preferred unknowns opposite him. His one criterion (other than beauty) was that his ladies didn't break up during his clowning. None of his leading ladies became established stars (except for Phyllis Haver, in *Baloonatic*, 1923).

3. *Sunset Boulevard.* Others included Erich von Stroheim and Anna Q. Nilsson.

4. *Limelight* (1952).

5. *Film*, an almost-silent movie, written by Samuel Beckett.

7

1. They were Alec Guinness, in one of his finest roles, Stanley Holloway, Sid James and Alfie Bass.

2. Led by a somewhat mad professor, played by Alec Guinness (virtually unrecognizable), they were Herbert Lom, Cecil Parker, Peter Sellers and Danny Green. The lady was Katie Johnson who, after a long screen career, became a star in this, her penultimate film, made when she was seventy-seven.

3. He was an important explosives expert of Teutonic origins, played by Tutte Lemkow (more recently seen in the title role of *Fiddler on the Roof*, 1971), in *The Wrong Arm of the Law* (1963).

4.   Lionel Jeffries, who seemed in those days to be constantly on the receiving end of Peter Sellers's antics.

5.   He murdered Alec Guinness, in what must be the only octuple role in films. He jilted Joan Greenwood to marry Valerie Hobson, but was then manoeuvred into a more convenient position by Miss Greenwood by a touch of blackmail.

6.   They were Terry-Thomas, Peter Sellers, Shirley Eaton, Peggy Mount and Joan Sims, in *The Naked Truth* (1958). They were being blackmailed by Price, and finally, with considerable assistance from numerous other victims, kidnapped him. He met his end accidentally by walking out of the dirigible in which they were transporting him.

7.   He was Tony Hancock. He discarded his businessman's suit for an artist's smock, went to Paris, and founded the Infantile school of painting, but eventually ended up where he started, in suburban London, with landlady Irene Handl.

8.   She was a 1904 Darracq, and her co-stars, in this story of the veteran car run from London to Brighton, were Kenneth More, John Gregson, Dinah Sheridan and Kay Kendall.

9.   Because an ancient writ, dug up in a bomb site, showed that this part of London really belonged to France.

8 1.   Harold Lloyd (1893–1971), one of Keaton's and Chaplin's few rivals who, with spectacles and shy, college-boy image, was best known for his acrobatic tricks, usually involving hanging from high buildings. His best-known films include *Safety Last* (1923), *Girl Shy* (1924) and *The Freshman* (1925). His sound films were not particularly successful.

2.   Harry Langdon (1884–1944), another silent clown and, in the mid-twenties, a serious Keaton–Chaplin rival. He made many shorts and some twenty-four features, the

best of which were *Tramp Tramp Tramp* (1926), in which his co-star was Joan Crawford, *The Strong Man* (1926) and *Long Pants* (1927). His sound films were never more than routine.

3.   Fatty Arbuckle (1887–1933), the star of several funny two-reelers, whose career ended abruptly with Virginia Rappé's death and the subsequent investigation. Later, he directed a few comedies under the pseudonym Will B. Good.

4.   Ben Turpin (1874–1940), one of the most popular slapstick clowns of the two-reelers, most notable for his burlesques of successful 'serious' films: *The Shriek of Araby* (1923), in which he parodied Valentino, and *Three and a Half Weeks* (1924), his take-off of Elinor Glyn's Ruritanian nonsense *Three Weeks* (1924), and which included his impersonation of Erich von Stroheim.

5.   Stan Laurel (1890–1965) and Oliver Hardy (1892–1957), the greatest comedy partnership in the movies. Both had several years' film experience before teaming up to make *Putting Pants on Philip* (1926), a merger which continued with varying success until 1950. Many of their best films were directed by Laurel, although he did not always receive credit for it. Their best work includes *Big Business* (1929), *Way Out West* (1937) and *A Chump at Oxford* (1940).

9   1.   Mae West and W. C. Fields, performing their own script.
2.   Dean Martin and Jerry Lewis, in a re-make of *The Ghost Breakers* (1915; 1922; 1940).
3.   Kay Kendall and Yul Brynner.
4.   George Formby, who made twenty repetitive comedies between 1933 and 1946.
5.   A very pregnant Maggie Smith played Mozart; husband Peter Ustinov conducted.

6.   Peter O'Toole, insurance investigator, taught Audrey Hepburn, daughter of art forger Hugh Griffith.

7.   Doris Day. Who else?

10   1.   False. It was not a comedy, but an adaptation of Graham Greene's novel about political corruption in Haiti, and the impossibility of doing anything about it.

2.   False. He played Elwood P. Dowd. Harvey, the invisible six-foot rabbit, was his constant companion.

3.   True. Donal Donnelly looked on.

4.   True. Hepburn and Morley were a brother and sister missionary team, and Bogart was the drunken skipper with whom she had to cope.

5.   False. She divorced Jack Lemmon. She *married* Paul Douglas in *The Solid Gold Cadillac* (1956).

11   1.   Preston Sturges. A writer-turned-director who made eleven films between 1940 and 1949, including *Sullivan's Travels* (1941), *The Miracle of Morgan's Creek* (1943), *Unfaithfully Yours* (1948) and *The Beautiful Blonde from Bashful Bend* (1949). He made only one more film (*The Diary of Major Thompson*, 1956) before his death in 1959.

2.   Frank Capra directed Harry Langdon's most successful comedies, made several successful talkies in the thirties and war documentaries in the forties. His most recent films are *A Hole in the Head* (1959) and *A Pocketful of Miracles* (1961, a re-make of his own 1933 *Lady for a Day*).

3.   Ernst Lubitsch, a German actor-turned-director who went to Hollywood in 1922 and was involved in more than thirty features, mostly as director; he eventually became Paramount's leading producer. His last film, *That Lady in Ermine* (1948), was unfinished when he died, and was completed by Otto Preminger.

4.   Mack Sennett, the most outstanding producer-director of silent films, inventor of the Keystone Cops and the first to

utilize the talents of Chaplin, Keaton, Mack Swain, Louise Fazenda and countless others. Sound, for some reason, never appealed to him, and he dropped out of the movies. He died in 1960.

12 1. Katharine Hepburn and Spencer Tracy. Aldo Ray was in it too.

2. Anita Louise and James Cagney.

3. Katharine Hepburn, Cary Grant and James Stewart. The re-make, *High Society* (1956), mangled the original story to make a part for Frank Sinatra. The other two leads were Grace Kelly and Bing Crosby.

4. Lucille Ball and Bob Hope.

5. Edith Evans and Margaret Rutherford in Oscar Wilde's *The Importance of Being Earnest*.

6. John Mills and Ralph Richardson were the brothers, Nanette Newman and Michael Caine the young lovers.

7. Jonathan Miller and Mona Washbourne.

8. Peter Sellers adopted Ringo Starr.

13 1. The re-united couple was Debbie Reynolds and Dick van Dyke. They came together again because she couldn't stand any of the available men and he couldn't afford to go on supporting her and the kids, in a very underrated film directed by Bud Yorkin.

2. Shirley MacLaine and Jack Lemmon ended up together because her boss (Fred MacMurray) finally dumped her in favour of his wife and family.

3. Walter Matthau decided that he couldn't bring himself to murder Elaine May, because she was so dependent on him, even though he couldn't stand her and was only interested in her money.

4. Natalie Wood and Steve McQueen, having failed to go through with an abortion and having botched up their other relationships (with Tom Bosley and Edie Adams respectively) ended up together, but still unmarried.

5. Vanessa Redgrave divorced David Warner, but she ended up pregnant by him rather than by her new husband (Robert Stephens). Warner ended up a complete wreck, tending the flowers in a mental hospital, but happier than ever before.

14
1. Margaret Rutherford, Peter Sellers and Bernard Miles.
2. *A Period of Adjustment* (1962).
3. She was Dorothy Lamour. Altogether, there were seven: *The Road to Singapore* (1940), *Zanzibar* (1941), *Morocco* (1942), *Utopia* (1946), *Rio* (1947), *Bali* (1952) and *Hong Kong* (1962). In the last, the leading lady was Joan Collins, but Miss Lamour made a guest appearance.
4. The story is *Faust*. The stars of this comedy version were Peter Cook as Mephistopheles, Dudley Moore as Faust, Eleanor Bron as Marguerite and Ursula Andress as Helen of Troy (presumably).

15
1. The American way of death: funeral parlours, mortuaries, the undertaking business, Los Angeles.
2. The medical profession and friendship.
3. A spastic child, daughter of stars Alan Bates and Janet Suzman.
4. Medicine, the army, war.
5. Murder, and the Oedipus complex.
6. The family and mother love (very black, with Bette Davis as Mother).
7. Family life, German aristocratic traditions; multiple sexual relationships allow anti-hero Michael York to achieve his goals by any means, including murder.
8. Medicine (again), murder, death, impotence and religion too, peripherally.
9. It's difficult to be specific when Joe Orton is the writer: death, certainly, but just about everything else as well: bodies, the police, human relationships, money, etc.

16　1.　Alastair Sim as the headmistress in *The Belles of St Trinian's* (1954).

2.　Stan Laurel in *Bohemian Girl* (1936).

3.　Edna May Oliver as the Nurse in *Romeo and Juliet* (1936).

4.　Alec Guinness as the suffragette-balloonist knocked off by Dennis Price in *Kind Hearts and Coronets* (1949).

5.　Jack Benny, as one of the many who have played *Charley's [American] Aunt* (1941).

6.　Lon Chaney in *The Unholy Three* (1930), a re-make of his 1925 silent version.

7.　Danny Kaye in *On the Double* (1962), doing something of a Dietrich imitation.

Musicals

In effect, the screen musical means the Hollywood musical. Good stories, scores, performances and production skills combined to create a unique art form. Most of the best musicals were made by MGM in the period bounded by *Meet Me in St Louis* (1944) and *Singin' in the Rain* (1952), although the foundations were laid elsewhere, in the thirties, by people like Al Jolson, Busby Berkeley and Ginger Rogers and Fred Astaire.*

1   1.   Probably the best-remembered double act in musicals was Fred Astaire and Ginger Rogers. Many of the songs which they sang and danced to have become all-time classics: some of them are listed below. In which films did they occur?
     a. 'The Carioca'
     b. 'The Continental'
     c. 'Let's Face the Music and Dance'
     d. 'Cheek to Cheek'
     e. 'I Won't Dance'
     f. 'Let's Call the Whole Thing Off'

2.   As well as making films together, they both played opposite other stars. Fred Astaire made his film début in 1933, in a musical in which the leads were not people whom one usually associates with musicals. Can you name the film, and the two leading players in it?

3.   Who were Astaire's leading ladies in:
     a. *You Were Never Lovelier* (1942)?
     b. *Easter Parade* (1948)?

* Answers on page 132.

    c. *Royal Wedding* (1951)?

    d. *The Belle of New York* (1952)?

4.   Ginger Rogers made a few musicals with other leading men before turning to straight parts, usually in comedies. Who were her leading men in:

    a. *Twenty Million Sweethearts* (1934)?

    b. *Lady in the Dark* (1943)?

2   True or False?

1.   In *The Wizard of Oz* (1939), Billie Burke played the Wicked Witch of the West.

2.   In *Love Me or Leave Me* (1955), Doris Day played Marilyn Miller, star of twenties and thirties stage musicals.

3.   In *There's No Business Like Show Business* (1954), Johnnie Ray gave up show business for the priesthood.

4.   In 1940, Judy Garland starred in the musical *Little Nellie Kelly*.

5.   Julie Andrews married James Fox in *Thoroughly Modern Millie* (1967).

6.   *Oklahoma!* (1955) was Rod Steiger's first film and only musical.

7.   The role of Gypsy Rose Lee in *Gypsy* (1962) was played by Rosalind Russell.

8.   Shirley Jones won an Academy Award (Best Supporting Actress) for her role as Julie Jordan in the musical *Elmer!* (1960).

9.   Gene Kelly played D'Artagnan to June Allyson's Constance Bonacieux in the musical version of *The Three Musketeers* (1948).

10.   Frank Sinatra played opposite Kathryn Grayson in the 1948 musical *The Kissing Bandit*.

3   1.   One of the easiest ways to make a musical is to adapt the biography of a well-known and popular composer. Can you name the composers portrayed in these films?

    a. *Rhapsody in Blue* (1945)

    b. *Night and Day* (1945)

  c. *Yankee Doodle Dandy* (1942)
  d. *A Song to Remember* (1945)
  e. *Till the Clouds Roll By* (1946)
  f. *Words and Music* (1948)

2. In 1936, MGM made *The Great Ziegfeld*, the biography of the man who created and produced the famous Ziegfeld Follies. Two of the characters in this film were well-known Ziegfeld discoveries: Fannie Brice and Ray Bolger. Who played them in this film?

4 What do these three stills have in common, and what films are they taken from?

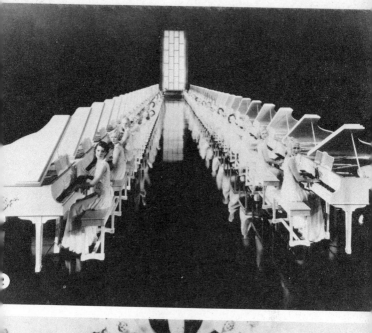

5 1. *Showboat*, based on Edna Ferber's novel, has been transferred to the screen three times – in 1929, 1936 and 1951. The last two adaptations have been the most memorable. In them, who played:

Magnolia Hawks?
Gaylord Ravenal?
Joe?
Julie?

2. The music for *Showboat* was written by Jerome Kern; the lyrics and adaptation of the novel by Oscar Hammerstein II. But there was one song in which Hammerstein had no part; it was a relic of Kern's period in England in the early twenties, and the lyrics were written by a well-known English humorist. What was the song, and who wrote the lyrics for it?

6 1. Many people regard *Singin' in the Rain* (1952) as the best screen musical ever made. With its parody of Hollywood in the twenties and the advent of the talkies, it was almost sure to be a success. From the following list of songs, two were *not* in *Singin' in the Rain*. Which ones?

'All I Do Is Dream of You'
'Wedding of the Painted Doll'
'Yes Sir, That's My Baby'
'Good Morning'
'You Are My Lucky Star'
'Five Foot Two'
'You Were Meant For Me'

2. 1927 is often regarded as a landmark in the evolution of the screen musical. Why?

3. If you don't agree that *Singin' in the Rain* is the all-time great musical, you probably think that *On the Town* (1949) is better. There were six stars in this film, four of them well known, the other two not so well known. How many can you name?

4. In the forties and early fifties, MGM produced more good musicals than any other studio. One man, a producer, was responsible for nearly all of these. He is credited with fostering the careers of people like Gene Kelly, Stanley Donen, Michael Kidd, Vincente Minnelli and André Previn. He was also half of the song-writing team which was responsible for dozens of songs, including most of the ones in *Singin' in the Rain*. Like all good producers, he could recognize talent, but he had the good sense to allow it to develop with as little interference from the studio as possible. Who is he?

7

1. Judy Garland was one of the outstanding talents in musicals, and the films she made for MGM remain some of the best of the late thirties and of the forties. Can you name the films in which she sang these songs?
   a. 'The Man That Got Away'
   b. 'Oh You Beautiful Doll'
   c. 'On the Acheson, Topeka and the Santa Fe'
   d. 'If You Feel Like Singing, Sing'
   e. 'Dear Mr Gable (You Made Me Love You)'

2. Who were her leading men in:
   a. *I Could Go On Singing* (1963)?
   b. *Babes in Arms* (1939)?
   c. *In the Good Old Summertime* (1949)?
   d. *Meet Me in St Louis* (1944)?
   e. *The Pirate* (1947)?

3. What was Judy Garland's first stage name?

8

Pictured overleaf are several ladies who appeared in many musicals in the thirties, forties and fifties. They either never became great musical stars, or retired and faded from the scene before musicals got really great. Nevertheless, some of them had considerable impact on the scene in their day. Can you identify them?

9 The only actor-singer-dancer-choreographer-producer-director in musicals has been Gene Kelly. He has probably been associated with more great musicals than any other individual (except possibly Arthur Freed). Can you match the following lists of his movies, leading ladies and songs?

'When You Wore a Tulip'	Lucille Ball	*Cover Girl* (1944)
'Do I Love You?'	Rita Hayworth	*It's Always Fair Weather* (1955)
'I Got Rhythm'	Cyd Charisse	*For Me and My Gal* (1942)
'Long Ago and Far Away'	Judy Garland	*An American in Paris* (1951)
'I Like Myself'	Leslie Caron	*Dubarry Was a Lady* (1943)

10 Quickies:
1. Who was the Brazilian Bombshell?
2. What film is generally regarded as the first talkie?
3. Who was the Boop-a-Doop Girl?
4. In what film featuring his own songs did Irving Berlin appear?
5. Who were *Les Girls* (1957)?

11 Pairs of names – of writers, composers or actors – have often been associated with musicals. Each of the following groups of films has a particular pair associated with it. Who are they?
1. *The Barkleys of Broadway* (1949)
   The Band Wagon (1953)
   It's Always Fair Weather (1955)

2. *Maytime* (1937)
    Girl of the Golden West (1938)
    Naughty Marietta (1935)

3. *Footlight Parade* (1933)
    Forty-Second Street (1933)
    Dames (1934)

4. *My Friend Irma* (1949)
    At War with the Army (1950)
    Hollywood or Bust (1956)

5. *Camelot* (1967)
    Gigi (1958)
    Brigadoon (1955)

6. *West Point Story* (1950)
    On Moonlight Bay (1952)
    By the Light of the Silvery Moon (1952)

12 Good songs tend to be used again and again – 'St Louis Blues' has been used in nine different musicals, and 'Pretty Baby' in eight. But the following songs have been used only once in a movie musical. Can you name the film, and the performer(s)?

1. 'Two Little Girls from Little Rock'
2. 'The Hostess with the Mostest'
3. 'Sisters'
4. 'How Long Has This Been Going On?'
5. 'It's Spring, Spring, Spring'
6. 'Hey There'
7. 'I Believe in You'
8. 'A Room in Bloomsbury'
9. 'Piccadilly'
10. 'The Rhythm of Life'
11. 'Over and Over Again'
12. 'I Love Louisa'

13 Who played:
1. The female leads in *Singin' in the Rain* (1952)?
2. Riff in *West Side Story* (1961)?
3. *The Great Caruso* (1951)?
4. Adelaide in *Guys and Dolls* (1955)?
5. *The Kid from Brooklyn* (1946)?
6. Glenn Miller in *Orchestra Wives* (1942)?
7. The title song in *High Society* (1956)?
8. *Gilbert and Sullivan* (1953)?
9. *Scrooge* (1971)?

14 Many of Walt Disney's films have been musicals. Can you name the cartoon characters who sang the following songs, and the films in which they sang them?
1. 'Some Day My Prince Will Come'
2. 'Who's Afraid of the Big Bad Wolf?'
3. 'Bibbidi-Bobbidi-Boo'
4. 'When You Wish Upon a Star'
5. 'The Bare Necessities'

15 By the end of the fifties, the *original* screen musical was dead. Stage musicals were being transferred to the screen virtually intact (*Oklahoma*, 1955; *Carousel*, 1956; *The King and I*, 1956; *South Pacific*, 1958; *West Side Story*, 1961), and the musical professionals like Minnelli and Donen were passed over for directors with no experience in musicals. The stars were non-singers and non-dancers, and the films were constructed to hide these shortcomings, giving the films a plastic, processed look. Who were the unlikely stars of these musicals from this period?
1. *West Side Story* (1961)
2. *The King and I* (1956)
3. *Bye Bye Birdie* (1963)
4. *My Fair Lady* (1964)
5. *Camelot* (1967)
6. *Oliver!* (1968)

16   The fifties and sixties produced a spate of films to cash in on the Rock and Roll phenomenon. The Elvis pictures were the most notable. The Rock pictures used tenuous plots to introduce Rock and Roll guest stars, most of whom couldn't be called upon to act. The pictures opposite are of rock stars from such movies: can you name the stars and the movies?

17   By the mid-sixties, a few new talents began to appear, and some hopeful signs of a revival of exciting movie musicals could be found. Some of the songs from some such films are listed below: which films are they taken from, and who sang them?

1.   'I Talk to the Trees'
2.   'Just Leave Everything to Me'
3.   'Look to the Rainbow'
4.   'My Favourite Things'
5.   'Don't Rain on My Parade'
6.   'Matchmaker, Matchmaker'
7.   'Money Money Money'

Musicals – Answers

1
    1. a. *Flying Down to Rio* (1933)
       b. *The Gay Divorce[e]* (1934)
       c. *Follow the Fleet* (1935)
       d. *Top Hat* (1935)
       e. *Roberta* (1934)
       f. *Shall We Dance?* (1937)

2. The film was *Dancing Lady*, and the stars were Joan Crawford, whose early career included several musicals, and Clark Gable, then almost unknown.

3. a. Rita Hayworth
    b. Judy Garland
    c. Jane Powell
    d. Vera-Ellen

4. a. Dick Powell
    b. Ray Milland

2
    1. False. She played Glenda, the Good Witch of the North. Margaret Hamilton was the Wicked Witch of the West.

2. False. She played Ruth Etting. In *Till the Clouds Roll By* (1946) Judy Garland was one of the 'guest stars', and played Marilyn Miller.

3. True. Probably just as well, as he wasn't much of an actor.

4. True.

5. True.

6. False. It is his only musical to date, but his first film was *Teresa* in 1951.

7. False. Rosalind Russell played her mother. Natalie Wood was Gypsy Rose Lee.

8.   False. She won her award for her portrayal of the good-girl-turned-whore in *Elmer Gantry* (1960), which was not a musical. Julie Jordan was the heroine of *Carousel* (1956), and was played by Shirley Jones.

9.   False. *The Three Musketeers* was not a musical, although Gene Kelly did make a rather balletic D'Artagnan.

10.   True.

3   1.   a. George Gershwin, many of whose scores have been used in a variety of musicals. His original film scores, with lyrics by brother Ira, include *Shall We Dance?* (1937) and *The Goldwyn Follies* (1938).

b. Cole Porter, who wrote scores for some twenty screen musicals, either originals or adaptations of his own stage musicals: *Anything Goes* (1936, 1956); *Kiss Me Kate* (1953); *Can Can* (1960), etc.

c. George M. Cohan, the first really big multiple talent on Broadway in the first two decades of this century. He wrote, composed, acted, sang, directed and produced, but never really liked Hollywood, and was associated only with this one film.

d. Frédéric Chopin, played by Cornel Wilde! Merle Oberon was Georges Sand.

e. Jerome Kern, with more than twenty musicals to his credit: *Swing Time* (1936), *High, Wide and Handsome* (1937), *Centennial Summer* (1946), etc.

f. Richard Rodgers and Lorenz Hart. Hart was Rodgers's first lyricist, and their scores included *Love Me Tonight* (1932), *On Your Toes* (1939), *The Boys from Syracuse* (1940), *Pal Joey* (1957) and many others.

2.   Not surprisingly, they were played by Fannie Brice and Ray Bolger.

4   All come from films choreographed by Busby Berkeley. He did more than anyone else in the thirties to influence the development of the musical, especially in the way he photographed his dance numbers and created such spectacular set-pieces. He has been associated with more than forty musicals, either as director or choreographer.

These stills are from
1. *Fashions of 1934*
2. *Gold Diggers of 1935*
3. *Dames* (1934)

5   1. In 1936, they were played by Irene Dunne, Allan Jones, Paul Robeson and Helen Morgan. The film was directed by James Whale.

George Sidney's 1951 production had Kathryn Grayson, Howard Keel, William Warfield and Ava Gardner.

(In the 1929 version, directed by Harry Pollard, the two romantic leads were Laura la Plante and Joseph Schildkraut.)

2. The song was 'Bill', and the lyrics were by P. G. Wodehouse.

6   1. 'Yes Sir, That's My Baby' was in *Broadway* (1942), *Yes Sir, That's My Baby* (1949), *I'll See You In My Dreams* (1951) and *The Eddie Cantor Story* (1953).

'Five Foot Two' was in *Has Anybody Seen My Gal* (1950) and *Love Me or Leave Me* (1955).

(Neither of them was in *Singin' in the Rain*.)

2. 1927 was the Year of the Talkies. Before that, musicals were impossible.

3. They were Gene Kelly, Frank Sinatra, Ann Miller, Vera-Ellen, Jules Munshin and Betty Garrett.

4. Arthur Freed, one of whose minor contributions to musicals was his dubbing of the singing voice of Leon Ames in *Meet Me In St Louis* (1944).

7 1. a. *A Star is Born* (1954)
  b. *Girl Crazy* (1943)
  c. *The Harvey Girls* (1945)
  d. *Summer Stock* [*If You Feel Like Singing*] (1950)
  e. *Broadway Melody of 1938*

  2. a. Dirk Bogarde
  b. Mickey Rooney
  c. Van Johnson
  d. Tom Drake
  e. Gene Kelly

  3. In her early career on stage, she was known as Baby Frances Gumm.

8 1. Lucille Ball, the screen's best female clown, who began her career as a Goldwyn Girl, appearing in twenty-five musicals, some (*Roman Scandals*, 1933; *Roberta*, 1934; *Follow the Fleet*, 1935; *The Ziegfeld Follies*, 1944) more memorable than others (*Bottoms Up*, 1934; *That's Right, You're Wrong*, 1939; *Too Many Girls*, 1940) before giving up musicals in 1950 for comedy (mostly on TV). She ended up buying the studio (RKO) which first employed her.

  2. Alice Faye (in *Music is Magic*, 1935), one of the best musical stars of the thirties and forties, who made twenty-eight films between 1934 and 1944, and then retired while still at the top. Her best films include *Alexander's Ragtime Band* (1938), *Rose of Washington Square* (1939) and *Hello Frisco, Hello* (1943). She has made one appearance since her retirement, in the 1962 re-make of *State Fair*.

  3. Jane Powell, first a teenage actress, who became the star of some unmemorable musicals (*Nancy Goes to Rio*, 1949; *Rich, Young and Pretty*, 1951, and several others) and a few better ones, including *Royal Wedding* (1951), from which this still is taken, and *Seven Brides for Seven Brothers* (1954).

4.   June Allyson (in *Good News*, 1947), who made several MGM musicals in the forties (*Girl Crazy*, 1943; *Till the Clouds Roll By*, 1946; *Words and Music*, 1948). She then turned to non-musical roles with less success, except for *The Glenn Miller Story* (1954), a semi-musical in which she had no musical numbers.

5.   Sonja Henie, the Norwegian girl who became an Olympic skating champion and subsequent star of several custom-made Fox B-musicals, including *Thin Ice* (1937), *Sun Valley Serenade* (1941) and *The Countess of Monte Cristo* (1946), following which she retired.

6.   Esther Williams, another MGM B-musicals star, whose principal films (*Bathing Beauty*, 1944; *Neptune's Daughter*, 1949; *Pagan Love Song*, 1950; *Dangerous When Wet*, 1953) were designed to exploit her championship swimming.

9   He sang (and usually danced):
'When You Wore a Tulip' with Judy Garland in *For Me and My Gal*.
'Do I Love You?' in *Dubarry Was a Lady*, with Lucille Ball.
'I Got Rhythm' in *An American in Paris*, with Leslie Caron.
'Long Ago and Far Away' with Rita Hayworth in *Cover Girl*.
'I Like Myself' in *It's Always Fair Weather*, with Cyd Charisse.

10   1.   Carmen Miranda (*Down Argentine Way*, 1940; *That Night in Rio*, 1941; *A Weekend in Havana*, 1941; *Copacabana*, 1947; *Nancy Goes to Rio*, 1949, etc).
2.   *The Jazz Singer* (1927), in fact only part-talkie, starring Al Jolson.
3.   Helen Kane, who was first on the stage (with the Marx Brothers), then made a few musicals (*Paramount on Parade*, *Heads Up*, *Dangerous Nan McGrew*) in 1930. She was played by Debbie Reynolds in *Three Little Words* (1950), for which she dubbed the singing voice.

4.   *This Is the Army* (1943).

5.   Mitzi Gaynor, Kay Kendall and Taina Elg, starring with Gene Kelly; songs by Cole Porter.

11   1.   Betty Comden and Adolph Green wrote the screenplays.

2.   Nelson Eddy and Jeanette MacDonald were the stars.

3.   The romantic leads were Dick Powell and Ruby Keeler.

4.   All were Dean Martin-Jerry Lewis films – not true musicals, really.

5.   Lyrics and music were by Allan Jay Lerner and Frederick Loewe.

6.   All three starred Doris Day and Gordon Macrae.

12   1.   Jane Russell and Marilyn Monroe in *Gentlemen Prefer Blondes* (1953).

2.   Ethel Merman in *Call Me Madam* (1953).

3.   Rosemary Clooney and Vera-Ellen in *White Christmas* (1954). You'll also remember that there was a reprise, sung by Bing Crosby and Danny Kaye in semi-drag.

4.   Audrey Hepburn (undubbed) in *Funny Face* (1956).

5.   The six brides and six brothers left when you take away Jane Powell and Howard Keel from the *Seven Brides for Seven Brothers* (1954).

6.   John Raitt in *The Pajama Game* (1957).

7.   Robert Morse and Michele Lee in *How to Succeed in Business Without Really Trying* (1966).

8.   Twiggy and Christopher Gable in *The Boyfriend* (1971).

9.   Julie Andrews, Bruce Forsyth and Beryl Reid in *Star!* (1968).

10.   Sammy Davis Jr in *Sweet Charity* (1968).

11.   Doris Day in [*Billy Rose's*] *Jumbo* (1962).

12.   Fred Astaire and Oscar Levant in *The Band Wagon* (1953).

13   1.   Debbie Reynolds was the Sweet Young Thing and Jean Hagen was the Bitch-Star.

2.   Russ Tamblyn

3. Mario Lanza
4. Vivian Blaine
5. Danny Kaye
6. Glenn Miller (under a slightly fictionalized name)
7. Louis Armstrong and his band
8. Robert Morley and Maurice Evans
9. Albert Finney

14
1. Snow White, in *Snow White and the Seven Dwarfs* (1937)
2. *The Three Little Pigs*, in one of the *Silly Symphony* series
3. The Fairy Godmother in *Cinderella* (1950)
4. Jiminy Cricket in *Pinocchio* (1940)
5. Balou in *The Jungle Book* (1967)

15
1. Natalie Wood and Richard Beymer, with Russ Tamblyn, Rita Moreno and George Chakiris.
2. Deborah Kerr and Yul Brynner (he played the part on Broadway as well).
3. Dick van Dyke and Janet Leigh, with Ann-Margret, Bobby Rydell, Paul Lynde and Maureen Stapleton.
4. Rex Harrison and Audrey Hepburn, with Stanley Holloway, Wilfred Hyde-White, Jeremy Brett, Gladys Cooper, Theodore Bikel and Mona Washbourne.
5. Vanessa Redgrave, Richard Harris and Franco Nero, with David Hemmings and Lionel Jeffries.
6. Ron Moody, Shani Wallis, Harry Secombe, Oliver Reed, Mark Lester, Jack Wild and Peggy Mount.

16
1. Gene Vincent in *The Girl Can't Help It* (1957)
2. The Platters in *Rock Around the Clock* (1956)
3. Bill Haley in *Don't Knock the Rock* (1957)
4. Jerry Lee Lewis in *High School Confidential* (1960)

17
1. *Paint Your Wagon* (1969): Clint Eastwood (!)
2. *Hello, Dolly* (1969): Barbra Streisand

3.   *Finian's Rainbow* (1968): Fred Astaire, Petula Clark and Don Franks

4.   *The Sound of Music* (1965): Julie Andrews

5.   *Funny Girl* (1968): Barbra Streisand

6.   *Fiddler on the Roof* (1971): Rosalind Harris, Michele Marsh and Neva Small

7.   *Cabaret* (1972): Liza Minnelli and Joel Grey

ꝯ Crime

Like the western, the crime movie owes much of its popularity to its formalized conventions. Although the first gangster film, *The Musketeers of Pig Alley*, was made in 1912, the traditions and archetypes of screen crime were not really established until the thirties. Succeeding decades have all produced their crime classics, although today's equivocal characters have undermined the certainties of the past, when good always triumphed over evil and motives were never suspect.*

1   In 1930, Darryl F. Zanuck decreed that as much of Warner's production as possible should be based on 'real-life stories'. The four actors pictured here are all shown as characters from four such films. Who are they, who are they portraying, and in what films?

* Answers on page 152.

1

2

2

1. Three names are outstanding in the annals of movie gangsterism: James Cagney, Edward G. Robinson and Humphrey Bogart, synonymous with the vigorous, direct style of screen crime.

Which of them appeared in these films?

 a. *The Widow from Chicago* (1930)
 b. *The Hatchet Man* (1931)
 c. *Taxi* (1932)
 d. *The Mayor of Hell* (1933)
 e. *Lady Killer* (1934)
 f. *Dead End* (1937)
 g. *Racket Busters* (1938)
 h. *King of the Underworld* (1938)
 i. *A Slight Case of Murder* (1938)
 j. *You Can't Get Away with Murder* (1939)
 k. *Larceny Inc* (1942)
 l. *13 Rue Madeleine* (1946)
 m. *Dead Reckoning* (1947)
 n. *Hell on Frisco Bay* (1955)
 o. *We're No Angels* (1955)
 p. *Tribute to a Bad Man* (1956)

4

    q. *Never Steal Anything Small* (1959)

    r. *The Cincinatti Kid* (1965)

2.   True or False?

a. Bogart appeared in more films with Edward G. than with Cagney.

b. Bogart survived most of his encounters with each of them.

c. Cagney, Robinson and Bogart never appeared together in the same film.

d. Robinson made more films than either Cagney or Bogart.

e. Bogart never made a film with Spencer Tracy.

f. Bogart made only one film with George Raft.

3   Sidney Greenstreet became famous for his 'Mr Gutman' in *The Maltese Falcon* (1941). Others, like George Sanders and Walter Slezak, developed the style of the suave villain, but Greenstreet remains *the* Mr Big. How many other films of the forties featured him?

4   James Cagney began his career as a song-and-dance man, but moved into crime in *Public Enemy* (1931). In this still from that film, who is the lady with the faceful of grapefruit? Who was the 'other woman' who drove Cagney to such Gothic behaviour? Zasu Pitts, Susan Hayward, Fay Spain, Jean Harlow or Ida Lupino?

5 Jules Dassin's *The Naked City* (1948) was a serious police thriller, one of the first to use a semi-documentary approach to crime. It had a famous closing line, which was used in all ninety-nine episodes of the subsequent TV series.
What is that line?

6 Quickies:
1. Who was Maisie?
2. Who were *The Killers* (1946)?
3. Who was the fat boss of *Underworld USA* (1960)?
4. *Kiss Me Deadly* (1955) was based on which mythological story?
5. Who got *A Hole in the Head* (1959)?
6. Who first blew the gaff on *Murder Inc* [*The Enforcer*] (1951), and who made him do it?
7. Who were Bullweed, Feathers McCoy and Rolls Royce?
8. Who was the T-man in *Undercover Man* (1949)?

7 What is the common factor in each of the following groups?
1. *On Friday at 11* (1960)
   The Asphalt Jungle (1950)
   Rififi (1954)

2. *The Glass Key* (1942)
   Detective Story (1951)
   The Dark Corner (1946)

3. Mr Moto
   The Thin Man
   Charlie Chan

4. *Double Indemnity* (1944)
   Strangers on a Train (1951)
   Farewell My Lovely (1944)

5. *The League of Gentlemen* (1960)
   The Strange Affair (1968)
   Robbery (1967)

6.   *Spin of a Coin* [*The George Raft Story*] (1961)
     The Rise and Fall of Legs Diamond (1960)
     The Big Operator (1951)

8   Few stars have made a living by always playing bad guys.
Here are several stars who are best known as good guys but
who were not nearly so nice in some of their earlier days,
shown here. Who are they? Which films do these scenes
come from?

9

1. In *The Third Man* (1949), Orson Welles played Harry Lime, the arch-racketeer who was eventually hunted down in the sewers of Vienna. But two years earlier, in one of his own films, Welles fell innocent victim to a group of swindlers. What was the film, and who was his principal antagonist?

2. In 1959, Marilyn Monroe was peripherally involved with George Raft and several other mobsters in *Some Like It Hot*. In an earlier film, she was something of a moll, playing the crooked lawyer's girlfriend. What was the film?

10 Crime films usually feature a particular racket. Here are some examples. Can you match the films with the rackets?

The Big Sleep (1946)	Liquor
All the King's Men (1950)	Boxing
The Wet Parade (1932)	Drugs
The Harder They Fall (1956)	Labour
The French Connection (1971)	Gambling
On the Waterfront (1954)	Politics

11 Overleaf are some characters in bad shape through their involvement with crime. Who are the actors, and from which films are the pictures taken?

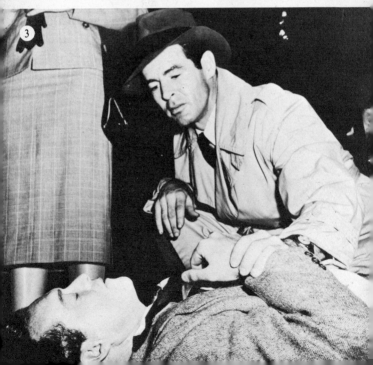

4

5

6

12 Underworld slang has become common language through its use in the movies. What do these words mean?
1. roscoe
2. snow
3. soldier
4. mug
5. heeled
6. stool pigeon
7. hit
8. heist
9. G-man
10. shamus
11. the big house

13 Crime movies are full of quotable lines, but it's not so easy to remember who said them, and in what film, especially when they are often used more than once. What films do these lines come from?
1. Edward G. Robinson: 'You can dish it out, but you can't take it any more.'
2. Gloria Grahame: 'I've had it rich, and I've had it poor. Believe me, rich is better.'
3. Peter Lorre: 'We may be rats, crooks and murderers . . . but we're *Americans*!'
4. Humphrey Bogart: 'Play it, Sam.'
5. Lauren Bacall: 'If you want anything, just whistle. You know how to whistle . . . you just put your lips together and blow.'
6. James Cagney: 'I'm from the collection agency . . . I've come to collect my wife.'
7. Maxine Cooper: 'Don't stand too near the window, honey. Someone might blow you a kiss.'
8. Emile Meyer: 'Come here, Sidney – I want to chastise you.'

14 1. In *Bonnie and Clyde* (1967), Faye Dunaway and Warren Beatty gave us a new, glamorized picture of the gangster's life and death. Who played Clyde's brother and sister-in-law? Which one received an Academy Award for the performance?

2.   Another glossy gangster film set in the thirties was *Borsalino* (1970), which showed the Gallic fascination with American-style gangsterism. Who were its two male stars?

3.   In contrast to these two was Roger Corman's *Bloody Mama* (1971), set in the same period. Although derived from *Bonnie and Clyde*, with all the decorative period settings and music, the characters were ugly and repellent. Who was the real-life Mama, who played her, and who played her dumb daughter-in-law?

4.   In 1971, MGM released a film based on the exploits of Crazy Joe Gallo and his gang, responsible, among other misdeeds, for the shooting of Joe Colombo at an Italian-American civil rights meeting. What was the title of the film, and who played Crazy Joe?

5.   Who was *The Canary That Sang* and what recent film was based on his testimony?

15   Many of the big-time tough guys found themselves behind bars in one or more of their films, often facing the dreadful prospect of the walk through the little green door leading to *The Last Mile* (1937). Who were the notable stars behind bars in:

1.   *The Last Mile* (1959)?
2.   *20,000 Years in Sing Sing* (1932)?
3.   *San Quentin* (1937)?
4.   *The Last Gangster* (1938)?
5.   *Each Dawn I Die* (1939)?
6.   *Riot in Cell Block 11* (1954)?
7.   *Cell 2455 Death Row* (1955)?
8.   *The Birdman of Alcatraz* (1962)?
9.   *I Want to Live* (1958)?

16 The world of gangsters and the detectives is primarily male. Ladies are usually involved at their peril, though a few have shown themselves capable of holding their own. Who are the molls pictured here, and what films are these stills taken from?

17 The hero of the detective/crime film of the sixties and seventies is a more ambivalent character. In the thirties and forties, there was little doubt about good and bad; today's hero is not so clear-cut, and frequently achieves his ends by dubious means. Here is a list of some of these characters: who played them?

1. Lew Harper
2. Frank Bullitt
3. Tony Rome
4. Walker
5. Daniel Madigan
6. Popeye Doyle
7. Virgil Tibbs
8. Inspector Clouseau
9. John Shaft
10. Harry Callahan

Crime – Answers

1 The character in each case is Al Capone. Pictured here are:

1. Rod Steiger as *Al Capone* (1950). The publicity for the film made much of the resemblance between Steiger and the King of the Underworld, and the movie started a vogue for reprises of gangland themes.

2. Jason Robards Jr in Roger Corman's story of *The St Valentine's Day Massacre* (1967), one of the key events of Capone's career. The massacre was also featured, slightly fictionalized, in *Some Like It Hot* (1959).

3. Paul Muni in *Scarface* (1932). Capone (then in prison) insisted on seeing the script, but declined an invitation to appear in the film.

4. Neville Brand as the leader of *The Scarface Mob* (1960). Brand also played Capone in a guest appearance in *Spin of a Coin* [*The George Raft Story*] (1961).

2 1. a. *The Widow from Chicago* – Robinson
   b. *The Hatchet Man* – Robinson
   c. *Taxi* – Cagney
   d. *The Mayor of Hell* – Cagney
   e. *Lady Killer* – Cagney
   f. *Dead End* – Bogart
   g. *Racket Busters* – Bogart
   h. *King of the Underworld* – Bogart
   i. *A Slight Case of Murder* – Robinson
   j. *You Can't Get Away with Murder* – Bogart
   k. *Larceny Inc* – Robinson
   l. *13 Rue Madeleine* – Cagney
   m. *Dead Reckoning* – Bogart
   n. *Hell on Frisco Bay* – Robinson
   o. *We're No Angels* – Bogart

p. *Tribute to a Bad Man* – Cagney
q. *Never Steal Anything Small* – Cagney
r. *The Cincinatti Kid* – Robinson

2. a. True. Bogart appeared with Robinson in *Bullets or Ballots* (1936), *Kid Galahad* (1937), *The Amazing Dr Clitterhouse* (1938), *Brother Orchid* (1940) and *Key Largo* (1948).

He appeared with Cagney only in *Angels with Dirty Faces* (1938) and *The Roaring Twenties* (1939).

b. False. He was shot in nearly all of them. Edward G. poisoned him in *The Amazing Dr Clitterhouse*, but he managed to shoot Robinson, without getting shot himself, in *Key Largo*.

c. True. But Cagney and Robinson did appear together once: in *Smart Money* (1931).

d. True. Cagney has made sixty, Bogart made seventy-five and Robinson made eighty.

e. False. They made *Up the River* together in 1930; it was Bogart's third film.

f. False. They appeared together in two films: *Invisible Stripes* (1939) and *They Drive by Night* (1940).

3 After *The Maltese Falcon*, he made:
1942: *They Died with Their Boots On*, *Across the Pacific* and *Casablanca*.
1943: *Background to Danger*.
1944: *Hollywood Canteen*, *Passage to Marseilles*, *Between Two Worlds*, *Devotion*, *The Conspirators* and *The Mask of Dimitrios*.
1945: *Conflict*, *Pillar to Post* and *Christmas in Connecticut*.
1946: *Three Strangers* and *The Verdict*.
1947: *That Way with Women* and *The Hucksters*.
1948: *The Woman in White*, *The Velvet Touch* and *Ruthless*.
1949: *Flamingo Road*, *It's a Great Feeling* and *Malaya*.
He made no more films, and died in 1954.

4   The unfortunate lady is Mae Clarke. 1931 was her busiest year, and she appeared in *Waterloo Bridge* and *Frankenstein* as well.

The 'other woman' was Jean Harlow; Zasu Pitts was hardly the moll type, Fay Spain wasn't born in 1931, and even Susan Hayward was only thirteen at the time. Ida Lupino was also in the film, however.

5   'There are 8 million* stories in *The Naked City*. This has been one of them . . .'

6   1.   Maisie was a girl detective played by Ann Sothern, and a very resourceful one, judging by the number of films she made: *Maisie* (1939), *Congo Maisie* (1940), *Gold Rush Maisie* (1940), *Maisie Was a Lady* (1941), *Ringside Maisie* (1941), *Maisie Gets her Man* (1942), *Swing Shift Maisie* (1943), *Maisie Goes to Reno* (1944), *Up Goes Maisie* (1946) and *Undercover Maisie* [*Undercover Girl*] (1947).

2.   Harry Hayden and Charles McGraw were *The Killers*, although some people may better remember Burt Lancaster, in his film début, as the victim. A silent 1929 feature called *Walking Back* featured two similar characters who indulged in some crackling dialogue (on title cards), and it was rumoured that this was the source of Hemingway's original story. Clu Gulager and Lee Marvin played the title roles in Don Siegel's 1964 re-make.

3.   He was played by Robert Emhardt (former understudy for Sidney Greenstreet). He was the chief of National Projects and responsible for most of the nastiness in this film by Samuel Fuller. He ends up dead in his own penthouse swimming pool.

4.   The film was based on the theme of Pandora's Box. Everyone was after a lead box containing an unspecified but

---

* New York was smaller then.

dreadful radioactive substance. The villainess opened the box in the end and burned herself to a cinder.

5.   Nobody. The title refers to the mentality of the central character, played by Frank Sinatra ('. . . soft-hearted, hard-boiled, white-souled black sheep . . .' as one critic put it), who conspires to raise money to keep his swish Miami hotel running and his young son by his side.

6.   Zero Mostel played Abe 'Kid Twist' Reles, the squealer who told all to D.A. William O'Dwyer (Humphrey Bogart).*

7.   The characters in an early influential crime movie, *Underworld* (1927). They were played by George Bancroft, Evelyn Brent and Clive Brook respectively. The film was written by Ben Hecht and directed by Joseph von Sternberg. Its European title was *Paying the Penalty*.

8.   Glenn Ford was the Federal tax agent who finally nailed Al Capone. Capone received an eleven-year sentence for tax evasion.

7   1.   Each was about a major robbery: in *On Friday at 11* they robbed the Monte Carlo Casino; a big jewel raid was the central set piece in *The Asphalt Jungle*, as it was in *Rififi* (see Foreign Movies, 12.5).

2.   William Bendix, classic exponent of the Dumb Ox character, appeared in all three.

3.   All were detectives who made series of films. Peter Lorre was Mr Moto, William Powell was The Thin Man and Warner Oland, Sidney Toler and Roland Winters all had a go at being Charlie Chan.

---

* Murder Inc was the real-life nation-wide execution cooperative, organized at a pan-American meeting of criminal chiefs in New York. Capone, who had called the meeting, failed in his attempt to set up a national crime syndicate.

4. Raymond Chandler. He wrote the screenplay for *Double Indemnity* (with Billy Wilder), collaborated with Czenzi Ormonde on the script for *Strangers on a Train*, and wrote the novel *Farewell My Lovely*.

5. Three British crime films; *Robbery* featured the Great Train Robbery, *The League of Gentlemen* explored the benefits of army discipline when applied to bank robbery and *The Strange Affair* was concerned with bent policemen.

6. Ray Danton. He played the lead in the first two, and supported Mickey Rooney in the third. They were the high points in his Hollywood career.

8   1. Clark Gable played several smooth gangsters early in his career: here, in *A Free Soul* (1931), which was followed by *The Finger Points* in the same year.

2. Robert Mitchum, in *His Kind of Woman* (1951), playing the gambler given a free holiday by his racketeer employer. In *Build My Gallows High* [*Out of the Past*] (1947), he played the ex-hoodlum whose violent and complicated past eventually catches up with him.

3. Alan Ladd, in *Lucky Jordan* (1942), the follow-up to the previous year's *This Gun for Hire*, his first big film, in which he played a ruthless killer.

4. Gary Cooper, being very tough in *City Streets* (1932). He was already a star, having made his first impact in *The Winning of Barbara Worth* in 1926.

5. Frank Sinatra as the psychopathic killer in *Suddenly* (1954), invading a typical American home to get a good shot at the President. In the end his nerves give out, and he gets shot.

6. Kirk Douglas, the smooth corporation crook, having

trouble with erstwhile companion Burt Lancaster, the old-fashioned gangster, in *I Walk Alone* (1947).

9   1.   In *The Lady from Shanghai* (1947), Welles, with a bizarre Irish accent, was the shambling fall-guy framed by Everett Sloane. The shoot-out in the Hall of Mirrors of the deserted fun-fair was memorable.

2.   In *The Asphalt Jungle* (1950), directed by John Huston, Marilyn had a small role, considered her first important appearance.

10   *The Big Sleep:* Gambling. Much of the action was concerned with a casino.
All the King's Men: Politics. Broderick Crawford used gangland tactics to further his career; a slightly fictionalized life of Louisiana's Huey Long.
The Wet Parade: Liquor. Jimmy Durante and Robert Young were the crusaders against the bootleggers.
The Harder They Fall: Boxing. This film was Bogart's swansong. A courageous sportswriter, he ends up trying to outlaw boxing, having been involved in too much fight-fixing. Earlier in his career (*Kid Galahad*, 1937), Bogart had also been mixed up in boxing rackets.
The French Connection: Drugs. The story, based on fact, tells how heroin was smuggled into the United States, and how most of the hoods involved got away with it. Since the film, someone got away with the heroin.
On the Waterfront: Labour. Marlon Brando took on single-handed the labour-based protection rackets of the New York docks.

11   1.   Mickey Rooney as *Baby Face Nelson* (1957), ambushed by the G-men, dies in the arms of Carolyn Jones.
2.   Lionel Stander, long-time influential hoodlum involved in a caper gone wrong, ends up at Donald Pleasence's manse in *Cul de Sac* (1966).

3.   Fate, in the person of assassin Robert Ryan, catches up with Van Heflin, who can't live down his past, in *Act of Violence* (1948).

4.   Lee Marvin in a scene from *The Big Heat* (1953), paying for scalding Gloria Grahame with boiling coffee.

5.   Cliff Robertson, having been worked over during his inquiries into *Underworld USA* (1960). David Kent may also be recognized under the plaster.

6.   Down and out and mortally wounded, James Cagney finally pegs out on the church steps in *The Roaring Twenties* (1939), after his final and mutually fatal interview with Bogart.

12   1.   A gun. As in: 'Somewhere a roscoe coughed. She went limp in my arms. She was as dead as vaudeville.' (Paraphrase of S. J. Perelman)

2.   Heroin. This is the term used by the pushers, not the junkies.

3.   The hitman (professional assassin).

4.   Three possibilities here: the face.

> a nice guy/obvious victim – e.g. Elisha Cook Jr.
>
> to strike on the head with a blackjack.

5.   Armed, either with money or a gun.

6.   Squealer.

7.   What soldiers (see above) are contracted to do *or* to raid an institution, usually a bank.

8.   A robbery, or the proceeds therefrom.

9.   Government (FBI) agent. The term is said to have been coined by George 'Machine Gun' Kelly on his arrest in 1934.

10.   A private eye. Usually used by jealous/frustrated policemen.

11.   San Quentin prison, as in *The Big House* (1930) and *Mutiny in the Big House* (1939).

13 1. *Little Caesar* (1930)
2. *The Big Heat* (1953)
3. *Seven Miles from Alcatraz* (1943)
4. *Casablanca* (1942)
5. *To Have and Have Not* (1945)
6. *Man of a Thousand Faces* (1957). The biography of Lon Chaney, and thus hardly a crime movie, but the line was just too good to leave out.
7. *Kiss Me Deadly* (1955)
8. *The Sweet Smell of Success* (1957)

14 1. Gene Hackman as Buck Barrow and Estelle Parsons as his wife Blanche. Miss Parsons was voted Best Supporting Actress.

2. Alain Delon and Jean-Paul Belmondo. The two had previously appeared together in *Is Paris Burning?* (1966).

3. Ma Barker was played by Shelley Winters in a really fantastic performance. Ma and her boys were shot down at Lake Weir, Florida, in 1935, after a series of bank raids and hold-ups in the Bonnie-and-Clyde style. Diane Varsi played the woolly-headed daughter-in-law.

4. Jerry Orbach played Gallo in *The Gang That Couldn't Shoot Straight*. The novel on which the film was based was written by Jimmy Breslin, whose wife wrote a screenplay called *A-Block* (never produced) in association with Crazy Joe himself before he was rubbed out at Umberto's Clam House in Manhattan in retaliation for the Colombo shooting. Parts of Gallo's life feature in *The Godfather* (1972), apparently made with the aid of Colombo's organization.

5. Joseph Valachi broke the vow of silence and told all about the Cosa Nostra on his arrest in 1960. He died in prison (of natural causes) in 1971; *The Valachi Papers* was released in 1972.

15 1. Mickey Rooney was the thoroughly bad prisoner who started a riot on Death Row in this re-make of the 1937 original.

2. Spencer Tracy, in one of his several early hard-guy roles, before he settled on the right side of the law.

3. Humphrey Bogart, who also went through a very mean phase before becoming an acceptable hero in 1941.

4. Edward G. Robinson became very bitter during his long stretch, mostly because nice James Stewart had stolen his wife during his incarceration.

5. Crusading reporter James Cagney, wrongly imprisoned, found himself behind bars with big-time gangster George Raft. Raft helped Cagney to nail the guys responsible for his frame-up.

6. Neville Brand was the leader of the prison revolt. Another tough film by Don Siegel, its views were based on the experiences of writer-producer Walter Wanger, who had actually been inside for a while.

7. William Campbell, in the biography of convicted murderer Caryl Chessman, reviewed his life in flashback while in San Quentin on stay of execution. The book caused a sensation, but not the film.

8. Burt Lancaster was the life-sentence murderer who was brutal with people but a lover of bird life.

9. Susan Hayward won an Academy Award for her portrayal of a woman sent to the gas chamber maintaining her quite possible innocence, in this film biography directed by Walter Wanger.

16 1. Doris Day as singer Ruth Etting in *Love Me or Leave Me* (1955). She is married to gangster James Cagney, but really loves Cameron Mitchell. Cagney machine-guns him.

2. Judy Holliday, wiping the floor with mobster Broderick Crawford as they play gin rummy, in *Born Yesterday* (1951). Her dumb blonde had first been seen two years earlier in *Adam's Rib* where she gunned down straying husband Tom Ewell.

3.   Lana Turner in a characteristically melodramatic pose in *Johnny Eager* (1941). She has played a long series of broads-cum-hard-ladies in her thirty-five-year career, in films like *Slightly Dangerous* (1943), *The Postman Always Rings Twice* (1945) and *The Three Musketeers* (1948).

4.   A very young and effective Shelley Winters as the sad floozie in *Cry of the City* (1949). In almost thirty years, she has played most of the hard ladies: junkie (*Let No Man Write My Epitaph*, 1961); moll (*Johnny Stool Pigeon*, 1950); alcoholic (*Harper*, 1966); shopgirl (*The Gangster*, 1948); and whore (*A House is Not a Home*, 1964).

5.   Gloria Grahame gets her own back in *The Big Heat* (1953). She never really got the parts she deserved, although she gave fine performances as the fallen woman in *It's a Wonderful Life* (1947) and the sensible girl who sorts out Bogart in *In a Lonely Place* (1952).

6.   Peggy Castle doing heroic things for Anthony Quinn in Mickey Spillane's *The Long Wait* (1953), before finally copping it herself. Definitely a minority interest, she featured in fifties Bs such as *The Counterfeit Plan* (1956) and *Hell's Crossroads* (1957).

17   1.   Paul Newman in *Harper* [*The Moving Target*] (1966). The film had a contemporary setting, although novelist John Ross McDonald wrote the original some twenty years earlier.

2.   Steve McQueen. The original book, *Mute Witness*, by Robert L. Pike, had a central character called Lt Clancy. 'Bullitt' was something of an inspired change.

3.   Frank Sinatra played him in 1967, in the film of the same name. He went on to play similar roles in *The Detective* (1968) and *Lady in Cement* (1968).

4.   Lee Marvin was the revenge-bent crook in *Point Blank*

(1967), who tracked down the organization that shopped him.

5.   Richard Widmark was *Madigan* (1968), a long way from his catarrhal hood of *Street With No Name* of twenty years earlier.

6.   Gene Hackman hit the big time with his portrayal of the zealous, brutal, trigger-happy cop who established *The French Connection* (1971).

7.   Sidney Poitier, the black cop from Philadelphia who successfully confronted southern sheriff Rod Steiger in Norman Jewison's *In the Heat of the Night* (1967). Tibbs was also the hero of some indifferent sequels (*They Call Me Mister Tibbs*, 1971, and such).

8.   Hardly a tough cop, but a bumbling fool of a French inspector. Created by Peter Sellers in *The Pink Panther* (1963), followed by *A Shot in the Dark* (1964), and taken over by Alan Arkin in *Inspector Clouseau* (1968). The sequels were both markedly inferior to the original.

9.   Richard Rountree is now the Number 1 tough black cop as a result of *Shaft* (1971), notable for its music track and as the first film to capitalize on the audience potential of the urban black population. Rountree played a similar type in *Embassy* (1972).

10. Clint Eastwood was *Dirty Harry* (1972), in a slick, realistic and unsentimental film by Don Siegel.

10 Epics and Costume Dramas

Spectacles of epic proportions, with lavish settings and casts of thousands, were early cinematic triumphs. All the highlights of history were re-created on film, convincingly if somewhat inaccurately. But now a lack of new material has created problems. Recent history (*Nicholas and Alexandra*, 1971, *Lawrence of Arabia*, 1962) lacks the epic scale of the biblical and Roman sagas, and costume dramas seem to have exhausted the possibilities of pirates, musketeers and Robin Hood.*

1   D. W. Griffith made *Intolerance* ('Love's Struggle through the Ages') in 1915, the year after *Birth of a Nation*. It told four separate stories: a modern story of the slums, the story of Christ, the massacre of the Huguenots, and the sacking of Babylon. Who were the leading players in each of the four stories?

2   Epic films are commonly associated with Cecil B. de Mille. His films were notable for their spectacle, their tame debauchery, their star names, and their strong moral tone.

    1.   What was his first talkie pseudo-biblical spectacular, and who were its stars?

    2.   Several of his earlier epics were re-made. Which ones, and who were the directors of the re-makes?

    3.   *The Ten Commandments* (1956) was a typical de Mille epic: huge sets and set-pieces and lots of stars. Who played Moses?
        Pharaoh?

* Answers on page 174.

Pharaoh's son? and the son's wife?
the evil slave master Yochabel?
Joshua? and his mother?
the traitorous Jew Dathan?

4.   Another great all-star de Mille production was *The Greatest Show on Earth* (1952), set in and around the Ringling Brothers-Barnum and Bailey Circus. Who were the stars of this film?

5.   De Mille's last film, made in 1958, starred two of his leads from *The Ten Commandments* (1956). Who were they, and what is the interesting historical note about the making of his final epic?

3   The most famous Cleopatra is Elizabeth Taylor, but no one knows how many other Cleopatras there have been, or how many films. Name the ladies and the films built around Cleopatra in 1911, 1917, 1934, 1945, 1963 and 1972.

4   The classic Ruritanian costume adventure is *The Prisoner of Zenda*. There have been three notable versions, in 1923, 1937 and 1952. Who were the two male leads in each?

5   Robin Hood has featured in countless British and American films. There were early versions of this story, in 1909, 1912 and 1913, but the first really great version was made by Alan Dwan in 1922.

1.   Who played *Robin Hood* (1922)?

2.   How many Robin Hoods can you identify in this list?
The Adventures of Robin Hood (1938)
The Bandit of Sherwood Forest (1946)
Prince of Thieves (1948)
Rogues of Sherwood Forest (1950)
Tales of Robin Hood (1952)
The Story of Robin Hood [and His Merrie Men] (1952)
Men of Sherwood Forest (1956)

Son of Robin Hood (1959)
The Sword of Sherwood Forest (1961)
A Challenge for Robin Hood (1967)

3. There was a comedy-musical loosely based on the Robin Hood legend, made in 1956. What was it called, and who was its star?

4. What 1952 film with the Taylors (Robert and Elizabeth, that is) had in it a brief appearance by Robin Hood?

Fill in the blanks:
1. —— —— starred in both *Ben Hur* (1959) and *Tom Jones* (1963).
2. —— —— played Paul in *The Robe* (1953).
3. —— —— played John the Baptist in *Salome* (1953).
4. —— —— was Nero in *Quo Vadis* (1951) to —— ——'s Poppea.
5. —— —— was Marcus Aurelius in *The Fall of the Roman Empire* (1964).
6. Beau Geste has been played by —— —— in 1926, —— —— in 1939 and —— —— in 1966.
7. —— —— twisted a lion's head in *Demetrius and the Gladiators* (1954), sequel to the previous year's *The Robe*.
8. —— —— was Crassus in *Spartacus* (1960), while —— —— played his slave.
9. In *Helen of Troy* (1956), —— —— played the title role, —— —— was Achilles and —— —— was King Priam.
10. —— —— was Atahualpa in *The Royal Hunt of the Sun* (1969).
11. —— —— played the title role in *Alfred the Great* (1969).
12. —— —— played *Lord Jim* (1965).
13. —— —— was Prince Feisal in *Lawrence of Arabia* (1962).
14. —— —— was *Alexander the Great* (1956).

15. ——— ——— and ——— ——— played *Samson and Delilah* (1950).

7 Can you identify these ladies, and the epics from which these pictures are taken?

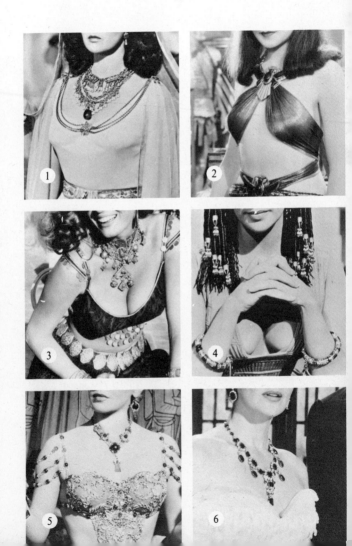

8   Much of Shakespeare has been transferred to the screen. In
1908, Griffith made a version of *The Taming of the Shrew*;
in 1913, there was a *Hamlet* (with Forbes Robertson), and
in 1916 another, this time with Beerbohm Tree.

Who played the following Shakespearean characters?

1.   Petruchio and Katharine in *The Taming of the Shrew*
(1929 and 1966). What was the musical version called, and
who were its leads?

2.   *Romeo and Juliet* in 1909, 1916, 1936, 1954 and
1968. There was also a musical version of this play. What
was its title, and who were the ill-fated lovers?

3.   *Henry V* (1944)

4.   *Macbeth* in 1948, 1957, 1960 and 1972

5.   *King Lear* (1970)

6.   Mark Antony and Brutus in 1953 and 1970

7.   *Hamlet* in 1948 and 1964

8.   Orlando and Rosalind in *As You Like It* (1936)

9.   *Othello* in 1922, 1951, 1955 and 1966

9   What do the films and actors in each of these groups have in common?

1. *The Bible* (1966)
   55 Days at Peking (1962)
   The Naked Maja (1958)

2. *The Sign of the Pagan* (1954)
   The Mongols (1960)
   The Horsemen (1971)

3. Max von Sydow
   Jeffrey Hunter
   H. B. Warner

4. Elisabeth Bergner
   Marlene Dietrich
   Bette Davis

5. *Androcles and the Lion* (1953)
   Veils of Baghdad (1954)
   The Egyptian (1955)

6. Rex Harrison
   Claude Rains
   Louis Calhern

10   The vast bulk of epic and costume drama has concentrated on either the ancient Mediterranean or on Tudorbethan England. Notable and honourable exceptions to this have been the Scandinavian epics.

1. Who was the leading man, and who was the villainous prison master, in *The Long Ships* (1964)? What were they all after?

2. Name the three male stars of *The Vikings* (1958). One of them had lost an eye: how? Who played father to whom, and who was the girl they fought over?

11   True or False?

1. Charlton Heston once played a Spanish explorer in search of Inca gold.

2.   Ward Bond had a small part in *Gone With the Wind* (1939).

3.   George C. Scott has played Moses.

4.   Vincent Price has played Sir Walter Raleigh.

5.   Kirk Douglas once played Hector.

6.   Jack Hawkins played a mad priest in Africa.

7.   Errol Flynn once played Soames in *The Forsyte Saga*.

8.   Clark Gable and Marlon Brando have played the same role (in different films).

9.   Richard Chamberlain has played in Shakespeare opposite John Gielgud.

10. Richard Boone was once Charlton Heston's faithful servant.

12   Kings and queens of Britain, traditional Hollywood favourites, have normally been played by distinguished British actors.

1.   What actor has played the same king in two films, once as a young man, and later as a middle-aged one?

2.   What king do Cedric Hardwicke and George Sanders have in common?

3.   How many English kings has Laurence Olivier played?

4.   What four British actors have played Henry VIII in a major role?

5.   Henry's daughter Elizabeth I has been another film favourite. Which actresses have played her, and in which films?

6.   Which ladies have played Elizabeth's rival Mary, in 1936 and 1972?

7.   Who played Richard III in *The Tower of London* (1940 and 1962)?

8.   Who played Prince Hal in *Chimes at Midnight* (1966)?

9.   In 1966 Anne Boleyn appeared as a supporting character; in 1970 and 1972 she was a more central figure. Who played her on each occasion?

10. Charles I has appeared only once on the screen. What was the film, and who played him?

13 One of the essentials of costume drama is, of course, the costume, however inaccurate. Who are the actors in these stills, and from which film is each one taken?

6

14 Other major names from history are perennial movie favourites:

1. Napoleon made his first major appearance in Abel Gance's *Napoleon* in 1925, in which he was played by Albert Dieudonné. Who played the part in:
   a. *Marie Walewska [Conquest]* (1937)?
   b. *Désirée* (1954)?
   c. *The Black Book* (1949)?
   d. *Austerlitz* (1960)?
   e. *The Young Mr Pitt* (1941)?
   f. *War and Peace* (1956)?
   g. *Waterloo* (1970)?

2. Abraham Lincoln's first important appearance was in Griffith's *Birth of a Nation* (1914), played by Joseph Henaberry. Who played the part in:
   a. *Abraham Lincoln* (1925)?
   b. *Abraham Lincoln* (1930)?
   c. *Young Mr Lincoln* (1939)?
   d. *Abe Lincoln in Illinois* (1939)?

3. Religion, revolution, royalty, sex and hypnotic powers are all combined in any film featuring Rasputin. Who played the part in:
   a. *Rasputin* (1930)?
   b. *Rasputin and the Empress* (1932)?
   c. *Nights of Rasputin* (1960)?
   d. *Rasputin the Mad Monk* (1966)?
   e. *I Killed Rasputin* (1968)?
   f. *Nicholas and Alexandra* (1971)?

15 No one seems to swashbuckle any more.
1. Who played:
   a. *The Black Pirate* (1926)?
   b. *The Sea Hawk* (1940)?
   c. *The Crimson Pirate* (1952)?
   d. *Captain Blood* (1924 and 1935)?
   e. *Son of Captain Blood* (1962)?

2. There were two other Captain Blood films, both in the fifties. Who was the actor who played him, and what were the titles of the films?

3. Who played Long John Silver in 1935, 1950 and 1954?

4. What is the only pirate musical, and who were the pirates in it?

Epics and Costume Dramas – Answers

1 Most of Griffith's leads were not well known at the time, but many of them became famous.

1. The Modern Story: Mae Marsh, Robert Harron, Fred Turner, Sam de Grasse and Vera Lewis.

2. The Judean Story: Howard Gaye, Lillian Langdon, Olga Grey and Bessie Love.

3. The French Story: Margery Wilson, Eugene Pallette, Spottiswoode Aitken, Ruth Handford and Frank Bennett.

4. The Babylonian Story: Constance Talmadge, Elmer Clifton, Alfred Paget, Seena Owen, Carl Stockdale, with Ruth St Denis, Natalie Talmadge, Colleen Moore, Ethel Terry and, as extras, Douglas Fairbanks, Beerbohm Tree, Donald Crisp and thousands of others.

The stories were linked by the figure of The Woman Who Rocks the Cradle, played by Lillian Gish.

Griffith used six assistant directors: George Siegmann, W. S. van Dyke, Joseph Henaberry, Erich von Stroheim, Edward Dillon and Tod Browning. All of them played small parts in the film as well.

2 1. In *The Sign of the Cross* (1932) the stars were Fredric March and Claudette Colbert.

2. *King of Kings* (1927) was re-made by Nicholas Ray in 1961.

Cleopatra (1934) was re-made by Joseph L. Mankiewicz (and uncredited others) in 1962.

The Ten Commandments (1923) was re-made by de Mille himself, in 1956. In the latter version, he omitted the second half of the original, a modern story pointing out the evils and misfortunes which befall when one strays from the Mosaic tenets.

3.   Charlton Heston was Moses.
Cedric Hardwicke was Pharaoh, Yul Brynner the son who succeeded him, and Anne Baxter was Brynner's wife.
Vincent Price was the villain.
Joshua was played by John Derek. He provided the only love interest (assisted by Debra Paget). His mother was Yvonne de Carlo.
The double-dealing Dathan was Edward G. Robinson.

4.   Charlton Heston (in one of his few modern-dress roles), Betty Hutton, James Stewart, Gloria Grahame, Dorothy Lamour, Cornel Wilde, Frank Wilcox, Emmett Kelly and Lyle Bettger.

5.   *The Buccaneer*, with Yul Brynner in the title role as the French pirate Jean Lafitte; he produced a head of hair for this picture, but not much of a performance. His adversary, Andrew Jackson, was played by Charlton Heston. De Mille died before the film was finished, and it was completed by Anthony Quinn, the only film that he has directed.

3   The early *Cleopatra*s, in 1908 and 1909, were unidentified. Helen Gardner played the role in 1911; Theda Bara in 1917. Cleopatra talked for the first time in de Mille's *Cleopatra* (1934), with Claudette Colbert. In 1945, she was played by Vivien Leigh, in *Caesar and Cleopatra*. Another British actress, Amanda Barrie, took over the role in *Carry On, Cleo* (1963). The most recent one is Hildegarde Neil, in *Antony and Cleopatra* (1972).

4   Lewis Stone and Ramon Novarro in 1923.
Ronald Colman and Douglas Fairbanks Jr in 1937.
Stewart Granger and James Mason in 1952.
The first in each pair played the King and his double, the valiant Englishman who stands in for him to foil the enemies

of the throne. The second in each case played the villainous
Rupert of Hentzau.

The 1937 film is held to be the classic version.

5
1. Douglas Fairbanks Sr.
2. Errol Flynn (1938)
   Cornel Wilde (1946; Robin's son)
   Jon Hall (1948)
   John Derek (1950; the son again)
   Robert Clarke (1952)
   Richard Todd (1952; notable for being made on
   location in Sherwood Forest)
   Don Taylor (1956)
   June Laverick (1959; the son turns out to be a girl)
   Richard Greene (1961; he went on to make 165
   television episodes)
   Barrie Ingham (1967).
3. *The Court Jester*, with Danny Kaye. He played the title
   role, a member of a band of outlaw patriots living in the
   forest, whose leader was The Fox, who wished to restore the
   rightful king to the throne, etc, etc. His love was Glynis
   Johns, the villains Cecil Parker and Basil Rathbone, and the
   femme fatale Angela Lansbury.
4. *Ivanhoe*. Robin was played by Harold Warrender.

6
1. Hugh Griffith
2. Michael Rennie
3. Alan Badel
4. Peter Ustinov and Patricia Laffan
5. Alec Guinness
6. Ronald Colman, Gary Cooper and Guy Stockwell
7. Victor Mature*
8. Laurence Olivier and Tony Curtis
9. Rosana Podesta, Stanley Baker and Cedric Hardwicke
10. Christopher Plummer

* Who, when told that the lion was toothless, is said to have remarked, 'Yeah, but
who wants to be gummed to death?'

11. David Hemmings
12. Peter O'Toole
13. Alec Guinness
14. Richard Burton
15. Victor Mature and Hedy Lamarr

7

1. Susan Hayward in *David and Bathsheba* (1952)
2. Claudette Colbert as *Cleopatra* (1934)
3. Anita Ekberg in *Zarak* (1957)
4. Elizabeth Taylor as *Cleopatra* (1963)
5. Lana Turner in *The Prodigal* (1955)
6. Ava Gardner in *55 Days at Peking* (1962)
7. Rita Hayworth as *Salome* (1953)

8　1.　In 1929, Douglas Fairbanks and Mary Pickford.

In 1966, Richard Burton and Elizabeth Taylor.

The musical was *Kiss Me Kate* (1953), in which the parts were played by Howard Keel and Kathryn Grayson.

2.　In 1909, Paul Panzer (looking remarkably like Charles Chaplin) and Florence Lawrence.

In 1916, Francis X. Bushman and Beverly Bayne.

In 1936, Leslie Howard and Norma Shearer.

In 1954, Laurence Harvey and Susan Shentall.

In 1968, Leonard Whiting and Olivia Hussey.

The musical was *West Side Story* (1961), and the parts were played by Richard Beymer and Natalie Wood.

3.　Laurence Olivier.

4.　In 1948, Orson Welles.

In 1957, Toshiro Mifune in Kurosawa's Japanese version, *Throne of Blood*.

In 1960, Maurice Evans.

In 1972, Jon Finch.

5.　Paul Scofield.

6.　In 1953, Marlon Brando and James Mason.

In 1970, Charlton Heston and Jason Robards Jr.

7.　In 1948, Laurence Olivier.

In 1964, Innokenti Smoktunovsky.*

8.　Laurence Olivier and Elisabeth Bergner.

9.　In 1922, Emil Jannings.

In 1951, Orson Welles.

In 1955, Sergei Bondartchuk.

In 1966, Laurence Olivier.

9　1.　Ava Gardner was in all of them.

2.　Jack Palance.

3.　All have played Christ: von Sydow in *The Greatest Story Ever Told* (1965); Hunter in *King of Kings* (1961); Warner in *King of Kings* (1927).

4.　All played Catherine the Great: Bergner in *Catherine*

---

* A 1964 Electronovision version of John Gielgud's stage production has been released on film (1972), starring Richard Burton.

the Great (1934); Dietrich in *The Scarlet Empress* (1934); Davis in *John Paul Jones* (1959).

5. Victor Mature.

6. All played Julius Caesar: Harrison in *Cleopatra* (1962); Rains in *Caesar and Cleopatra* (1945); Calhern in *Julius Caesar* (1953).

10 1. The lead was Richard Widmark, the villain Sidney Poitier. They were all after an enormous legendary golden bell.

2. Ernest Borgnine played father to one-eyed Kirk Douglas, whose other eye had been plucked out by an eagle. The other leading man was Tony Curtis, and the lady in the middle was Janet Leigh.

11 1. False. He was an American, looking for gold plate from the Temple of the Sun in *The Secret of the Incas* (1954).

2. True. He was one of the young Yankee officers.

3. False. He played Abraham in *The Bible* (1966).

4. True. In *Elizabeth and Essex* (1939).

5. False. He played *Ulysses* (1954).

6. True. In *Zulu* (1963).

7. True. Greer Garson was his Irene in *The Forsyte Saga* [*That Forsyte Woman*] (1948).

8. True. Fletcher Christian in *Mutiny on the Bounty* in 1935 and 1962 respectively. Their Captain Blighs were Charles Laughton and Trevor Howard.

9. True. In *Julius Caesar* (1970).

10. True. In *The Warlord* (1965).

12 1. Peter O'Toole as Henry II in *Becket* (1964) and *The Lion in Winter* (1968).

2. Charles II: Cedric Hardwicke in *Nell Gwynn* (1934) and George Sanders in *Forever Amber* (1947).

3. Two. *Henry V* (1944) and *Richard III* (1956).

4. Charles Laughton in *The Private Life of Henry VIII*

(1932); Robert Shaw in *A Man For All Seasons* (1966); Richard Burton in *Anne of the Thousand Days* (1970); Keith Michell in *Henry VIII and his Six Wives* (1972).

5.   Flora Robson in *Fire Over England* (1936) and *The Sea Hawk* (1940); Bette Davis in *Elizabeth and Essex* (1939) and *The Virgin Queen* (1955); Jean Simmons in *Young Bess* (1954); Irene Worth in *Seven Seas to Calais* (1963); Amanda Jane Smythe (as a child) in *Anne of the Thousand Days* (1970); Glenda Jackson in *Mary, Queen of Scots* (1971).

6.   Katharine Hepburn in *Mary of Scotland* (1936) and Vanessa Redgrave in *Mary, Queen of Scots* (1971).

7.   Basil Rathbone (1940) and Vincent Price (1962).

8.   Keith Baxter.

9.   Vanessa Redgrave in *A Man for All Seasons* (1966), in a brief appearance in the wedding breakfast scene, Genevieve Bujold in *Anne of the Thousand Days* (1970); Charlotte Rampling in *Henry VIII and his Six Wives* (1972).

10. Alec Guinness in *Cromwell* (1969).

13   1.   Tyrone Power in *Blood and Sand* (1941)

2.   Robert Taylor in *The Adventures of Quentin Durward* (1956)

3.   Tyrone Power in *The Prince of Foxes* (1949)

4.   Robert Taylor as Lancelot in *Knights of the Round Table* (1954)

5.   Tyrone Power as the *Captain from Castille* (1947)

6.   Robert Taylor as *Ivanhoe* (1952)

14   1.   a. Charles Boyer

           b. Marlon Brando

           c. Arnold Moss

           d. Pierre Mondy

           e. Herbert Lom

           f. Herbert Lom again

           g. Rod Steiger

2.   a. George A. Billings

           b. Walter Huston, in one of Griffith's rare talkies.

    c. Henry Fonda
    d. Raymond Massey

3.   a. Conrad Veidt
    b. Lionel Barrymore
    c. Edmund Purdom
    d. Christopher Lee
    e. Gert Frobe
    f. Tom Baker

15 1.   a. Douglas Fairbanks Sr
      b. Errol Flynn
      c. Burt Lancaster
      d. J. Warren Kerrigan (1924) and Errol Flynn (1935)
      e. Sean Flynn, son of Errol Flynn

2.   Played by Louis Hayward, they were *The Fortunes of Captain Blood* (1950) and *Captain Blood, Fugitive* (1952).

3.   In 1935, Wallace Beery in *Treasure Island*.
In 1950, Robert Newton, in Disney's re-make. He later made a starring film, *Long John Silver* (1954), and a television series.

4.   *The Pirate* (1947), with Gene Kelly as the would-be pirate, and Walter Slezak as the retired (and undiscovered) pirate.

11 Novels and Plays into Movies

Plays

1 The temptation to adapt well-known or popular plays for the screen has usually been too great to resist. In 1908, Vitagraph made one-reelers of *Romeo and Juliet*, *The Merchant of Venice*, *Antony and Cleopatra* and *Richard III*, and the trend has continued. The success of adaptations has been variable. Frequently, the original cannot be recognized, or it has been treated with such reverence that the film, as a film, has been a disaster. The successful transition from stage to film is a rare event. Who played these well-known parts in the film versions of these stage successes?*

1. Big Momma and Big Daddy in Tennessee Williams's *Cat on a Hot Tin Roof* (1958)
2. Willie Loman in Arthur Miller's *Death of a Salesman* (1952)
3. Nick and Honey in Edward Albee's *Who's Afraid of Virginia Woolf?* (1966)
4. The Tyrones in Eugene O'Neill's *Long Day's Journey into Night* (1962)
5. Eliza Doolittle and Henry Higgins in Bernard Shaw's *Pygmalion* (1938)
6. Archie Rice in John Osborne's *The Entertainer* (1960)
7. Mick, Aston and Davies in Harold Pinter's *The Caretaker* [*The Guest*] (1963)
8. Mr Sloane in Joe Orton's *Entertaining Mr Sloane* (1970)
9. Doc and Lola Delaney in William Inge's *Come Back, Little Sheba* (1952)

* Answers on page 185.

10. Amanda Wingfield in Tennessee Williams's *The Glass Menagerie* (1950)

11. Gwendolyn Fairfax and Cicely Cardew in Oscar Wilde's *The Importance of Being Earnest* (1953)

12. The Countess Aurelia in Jean Giraudoux's *The Madwoman of Chaillot* (1969)

13. Pizarro in Peter Shaffer's *The Royal Hunt of the Sun* (1969)

14. Arkadina and Nina in Chekhov's *The Seagull* (1969)

15. Frank and Ethel Gibbons in Noel Coward's *This Happy Breed* (1944)

Novels

2 Novels are natural sources for film stories. Like plays, though, their adaptations have often been unsuccessful, because of the need to avoid censor problems and keep the film to a manageable length. Can you name the actors who have played these well-known characters from novels adapted for the screen?

1. Fagin in Dickens's *Oliver Twist* (1948)

2. Ma and Tom Joad in Steinbeck's *The Grapes of Wrath* (1940)

3. Squire Western and his sister Miss Western in Fielding's *Tom Jones* (1963)

4. Wolf Larsen in Jack London's *The Sea Wolf* (1941)

5. George and Lenny in Steinbeck's *Of Mice and Men* (1939)

6. Holly Golightly in Truman Capote's *Breakfast at Tiffany's* (1961)

7. The de Winters in Daphne du Maurier's *Rebecca* (1940)

8. Gabriel Oak and Bathsheba Everdene in Hardy's *Far From the Madding Crowd* (1967)

9. Aschenbach in Thomas Mann's *Death in Venice* (1971)

10. Catherine Sloper in Henry James's *The Heiress* (1949)

11. Sidney Carton in Dickens's *A Tale of Two Cities* (1935 and 1958)

12. Phineas Fogg in Jules Verne's *Around the World in 80 Days* (1956)

13. Claggart in Herman Melville's *Billy Budd* (1962)

14. Pinkie in Graham Greene's *Brighton Rock* (1947)

15. Pilar in Hemingway's *For Whom the Bell Tolls* (1943)

16. Mildred Rogers and Philip Carey in Maugham's *Of Human Bondage* (1934)

17. Joseph K in Kafka's *The Trial* (1963)

18. Mr Micawber in Dickens's *David Copperfield* (1934)

19. Molly and Leopold Bloom in James Joyce's *Ulysses* (1967)

20. Sir Percy and Lady Blakeney in Baroness Orczy's *The Scarlet Pimpernel* (1935)

21. Captain Yossarian in Joseph Heller's *Catch 22* (1971)

22. Lakey and Polly in Mary McCarthy's *The Group* (1966)

Novels and Plays into Movies – Answers

Plays

1

1. Judith Anderson and Burl Ives were the parents; Elizabeth Taylor and Paul Newman were the couple whose marriage was on the rocks, and Jack Carson and Madeleine Sherwood the brother and sister-in-law ignored by the parents.

2. Fredric March, with Mildred Dunnock, Cameron Mitchell and Kevin McCarthy.

3. George Segal and Sandy Dennis played the young couple subjected to the weird games of Elizabeth Taylor and Richard Burton, in Mike Nichols's directorial début.

4. The elder Tyrones were played by Katharine Hepburn and Ralph Richardson, the sons by Jason Robards Jr and Dean Stockwell.

5. Wendy Hiller and Leslie Howard, in this now almost-impossible-to-see film. Warner Brothers bought the rights to it, and withdrew it from circulation when they acquired the film rights for *My Fair Lady* (1964). Many of the set-pieces in the musical are direct copies of the original. With Scott Sunderland (Pickering) and Wilfred Lawson (Doolittle), this is the best film adaptation of any of Shaw's plays.

6. Laurence Olivier, directed by Tony Richardson, and featuring a number of then unknown names – Joan Plowright, Daniel Massey, Alan Bates and Albert Finney – in addition to Brenda de Banzie and Roger Livesey.

7.   Alan Bates, Robert Shaw and Donald Pleasence, in Clive Donner's underrated film.

8.   Peter McEnery, with Beryl Reid and Harry Andrews as the sister and brother who marry Mr Sloane; a plodding and unfunny adaptation of one of Orton's best works.

9.   Burt Lancaster and Shirley Booth, the latter making her screen début in a performance which won her the Best Actress Academy Award.

10.   Gertrude Lawrence in the best screen adaptation of any Williams play.

11.   Joan Greenwood and Dorothy Tutin, excellent (as were all the other performances) in Anthony Asquith's stagey, very funny film.

12.   Katharine Hepburn, in this star-packed (Charles Boyer, Claude Dauphin, Edith Evans, John Gavin, Paul Henreid, Oscar Homolka, Margaret Leighton, Giulietta Masina, Nanette Newman, Richard Chamberlain, Yul Brynner and Danny Kaye) but ultimately unsuccessful film directed by Bryan Forbes.

13.   Robert Shaw.

14.   Simone Signoret and Vanessa Redgrave.

15.   Robert Newton and Celia Johnson in David Lean's film of one of Coward's lesser-known plays.

Novels

2   1.   Alec Guinness. His portrayal was so effective that the film was banned in the United States for some years because of its alleged anti-semitism.

2.   Jane Darwell and Henry Fonda.

3.   Hugh Griffith and Edith Evans in Tony Richardson's best film.

4.   Edward G. Robinson, in the best of all seven screen versions of this story, directed by Michael Curtiz.

5.   Burgess Meredith and Lon Chaney Jr, directed by Lewis Milestone.

6.   Audrey Hepburn, giving an excellent performance of a character who bore little resemblance to the original.

7.   Joan Fontaine and Laurence Olivier; directed by Alfred Hitchcock.

8.   Alan Bates and Julie Christie.

9.   Dirk Bogarde, directed by Luchino Visconti.

10. Really a film of the play of the same name, adapted from James's novel *Washington Square*. Olivia de Havilland was Catherine, the heiress of the title (for which she won an Academy Award) with Ralph Richardson, Miriam Hopkins and Montgomery Clift, directed by William Wyler.

11. Ronald Colman in 1935, although the most memorable performances in that version were Blanche Yurka's Madame Defarge and Edna May Oliver's Miss Pross. In 1958 Dirk Bogarde played Carton.

12. David Niven directed by Michael Anderson and produced by Mike Todd. Shirley Maclaine was miscast as the princess.

13. Robert Ryan. This quiet film had Terence Stamp in the title role and was written, directed by, and starred Peter Ustinov.

14. Richard Attenborough, in his first starring role, under John Boulting's direction.

15. Katina Paxinou, a Greek actress, who won a Best Supporting Actress Academy Award for her performance in this fine film which also starred Gary Cooper, Ingrid Bergman and Akim Tamiroff.

16. Bette Davis, in the role that made her a star, playing opposite Leslie Howard.

17. Anthony Perkins. Orson Welles directed, and also appeared in the film.

18. W. C. Fields, in an all-star cast assembled by David O. Selznick and directed by George Cukor: Lionel Barrymore, Maureen O'Sullivan, Edna May Oliver, Freddie Bartholomew, Lewis Stone, Frank Lawton and Basil Rathbone.

19. Barbara Jefford and Milo O'Shea in Joseph Strick's film adaptation.

20. Leslie Howard and Merle Oberon in the best of the three sound versions of this story. Howard later made an updated version, *Pimpernel Smith* (1941).

21. Alan Arkin was the confused and doubting hero, directed by Mike Nichols.

22. Candice Bergen and Shirley Knight. The others in the group were Joan Hackett, Elizabeth Hartman, Joanna Pettet, Mary-Robin Redd, Jessica Walter and Kathleen Widdoes.

12 Foreign Movies

Clearly, 'foreign' is a relative term. Here it is used to describe films outside the Anglo-American orbit, an artificial classification. It is important to realize that many countries, such as India, Mexico and Japan, have huge film industries, but only a fraction of their output ever reaches the international scene. Directors like Renoir, Eisenstein and Ray have had great international influence and their work, along with that of many other directors, writers and actors, is now accepted on its own terms in America and Britain.*

1   The names of directors of foreign films are usually far more closely associated with their products than are those of their British and American counterparts. Who are the directors of these films, and what are their nationalities?
1. *Kanal* (1955)
2. *A Man and a Woman* (1966)
3. *The Ballad of a Soldier* (1959)
4. *Never on Sunday* (1960)
5. *The 400 Blows* (1959)
6. *Black Orpheus* (1958)
7. *Elvira Madigan* (1967)
8. *An Italian Straw Hat* (1928)
9. *The Bicycle Thieves* (1947)
10. *The Umbrellas of Cherbourg* (1964)
11. *The Cranes are Flying* (1957)
12. *Last Year at Marienbad* (1961)

2   What do the films in each of the groups overleaf have in common?

* Answers on page 200.

1. *Electra* (1962)
   Zorba the Greek (1965)
   The Trojan Women (1971)

2. *Miss Julie* (1951)
   Barabbas (1953)
   Karin Mansdotter (1954)

3. *He, She or It* (1962)
   To Love (1964)
   The Saragossa Manuscript (1965)

4. *Peter and Pavla* (1964)
   A Blonde in Love (1965)
   The Firemen's Ball (1968)

5. *Gertrud* (1964)
   Once Upon a Time (1922)
   Leaves From Satan's Book (1920)

6. *Naked City* (1948)
   Rififi (1954)
   Phaedra (1962)

3   In Britain and America, French cinema is reckoned to have the most literate approach to film, possibly because of the frequent close collaboration between directors and well-known writers.

1. *Drôle de Drame* (1937), *Quai des Brumes* (1938) and *Les Visiteurs du Soir* (1942) were made by the same writer-director team. Who were they, and what was the famous film they made in 1944?

2. Another director who achieved a very personal style made a film depicting the fantasies of school life (1933). He was hailed by the Surrealists as a major artist. His family changed its name to Almereyda, but he continued to work under his original name. Who was he?

3. An example of the writer-poet-film-maker was Jean Cocteau.

a. What was the short Surrealist work he wrote and directed in 1930?

b. What film, made in 1950, did he develop further in 1959?

c. Which of his novels was filmed in 1950?

d. His most famous film is one that he wrote and co-directed in 1946. What was it, and who were its stars?

4. French quickies:

a. What was René Clair's real name?

b. A successful French writer-director of suspense films made *Quai des Orfèvres* in 1947. Who is he?

c. Who directed *Les Mistons* in 1958?

d. Who made *Olympia* in 1952?

e. Who wrote and directed *A Nous la Liberté* in 1931?

f. Alexis Moncourge is the real name of which star of *La Grande Illusion* (1937)?

g. Julie Christie starred in a 1966 film by a French director. What was the film, who was the director, and who was her co-star?

h. Who featured Jack Palance in a 1963 French film, and what was its title?

4   Jeanne Moreau, one of the best-known French stars, first attracted international attention in Louis Malle's *The Lovers* (1959). Since then she has made frequent appearances in American and English films.

1. Which film did she make with
   a. Gerard Philipe (1960)?
   b. Brigitte Bardot (1965)?
   c. Rex Harrison (1964)?
   d. Marcello Mastroianni (1961)?

2. In which film was she directed by
   a. Peter Brook (1960)?
   b. Orson Welles (1966)?
   c. Tony Richardson (1966)?

5   Spanish director Luis Buñuel was closely associated with the
Surrealist movement in the twenties and thirties. He left
Spain after the Civil War and worked in Mexico for many
years, returning in 1960.

1.   What are the two films he made with Salvador Dali?

2.   In which of his films does he parody the Last Supper?

3.   He has made two films based on famous English novels.
Which ones?

4.   Occasionally he has used stars as his leading ladies, to
facilitate the commercial distribution of his films. Who were
his female stars in:

Le Journal d'une Femme de Chambre (1963)?

Belle de Jour (1966)?

Tristana (1969)?

6   The rise of the Nazis resulted in the virtual death of the
German film industry, at least in international terms, as its
most creative people fled to Britain and the United States.
Before 1933, and occasionally thereafter, many musicals
and excellent costume dramas were made in Germany.

1.   Who was the actress who starred in these films?

The Tragedy of Love (1923)

Manon Lescaut (1926)

I Kiss Your Hand, Madame (1928)

What was her most famous film, and who directed it?

2.   Who made *Der Müde Tod* (1921), *Inferno* (1922) and
The Spy (1927)?

3.   A Polish actress and former Hollywood star (who
faded with the onset of sound pictures) appeared in Gerhard
Lamprecht's *Madame Bovary* (1935). Who was she?

4.   Who was the star of *SOS Iceberg* (1933)?

5.   Which German director, famous for his Hollywood
work, began as a comic in German silent farces under the
name of Meyer?

6.   Who directed *Kameradschaft* (1931), and what was its subject?

7   Swedish films are commonly associated with the name of Ingmar Bergman. But Swedish film-makers were active as early as 1912, producing pictures about Swedish mythology and adaptations of classic dramas.

1.   Who directed *Jerusalem* in 1918, an American version of *The Scarlet Letter* in 1926, and appeared in *Wild Strawberries* in 1957?

2.   Who was Greta Garbo's director before she left Sweden for Hollywood?

3.   What were the two colourful films directed by Vilgot Sjoman which have caused something of an uproar in recent years?

4.   Who was the Swedish star of *Intermezzo* (1936), and what was the title of the 1939 re-make?

5.   What do the following films, directed by Ingmar Bergman, have in common?
   The Seventh Seal (1956)
   Wild Strawberries (1957)
   The Virgin Spring (1960)

6.   Which of these Bergman films is the odd one out, and why?
   Smiles of a Summer Night (1955)
   Now About These Women (1965)
   Sawdust and Tinsel (1954)

7.   The myth of Swedish 'progressive sex' was boosted by Bergman, whose films are often serious explorations of psycho-sexual problems. What were the sexual deviations in:
   Through a Glass Darkly (1962)?
   Persona (1965)?

8   Japanese films which have been seen abroad have generally been acclaimed for their sensitivity and universality. The Samurai has become familiar to western audiences, perhaps because of his resemblance to the hero of the western.

Pictured here are scenes from four Samurai films: can you identify them?

9   The largest film industry in the world is said to be in India, though only a few films are distributed in the west.

1.   Satyajit Ray is probably India's internationally best-known director. *The Apu Trilogy*, the saga of an Indian family and the struggles of its country-reared son trying to make a living in the city, was made in 1954, 1956 and 1959. What are the titles of the three films which comprise this trilogy?

2.   What do these Indian films have in common?

    The Householder (1962)
    Shakespeare Wallah (1964)
    The Guru (1969)

10   Latin American countries also have a vast film industry, geared almost entirely to home consumption. Only occasional Brazilian, Mexican and Argentinian films reach Europe or America. Most of the films which are seen abroad are those which are consciously political, rather than the sentimental and adventure films which are so popular in South America itself.

1.   In Brazil, the 'Cinema Novo' has been headed by Glauber Rocha. What are the titles of his three most famous films, dealing with life in the backlands of the north-east, which have won awards in America and Europe?

2.   What 1950 film about a bandit, made in Brazil, became internationally known on the strength of its title song?

3.   Who is the well-known Argentinian writer-director who has made *The House of the Angel* (1957), *The Fall* (1959) and *The Eavesdropper* (1965)?

4.   What political film, made in Argentina and lasting more than four hours, won a prize in Europe in 1968?

5.   The best-known Mexican films have been made by Buñuel: *Nazarin* (1951) and *Los Olvidados* (1950) are good examples. But there is one Mexican director, reputed to have made more films than any other director, who made a star of Pedro Armendariz and who also appeared in *Return of the Seven* (1966). Who is he?

11 Serious Italian films have remained faithful to the concept of the cinema as a force for social comment and reform, most evident in the post-war neo-realist works of Rossellini and de Sica. The films below are all stories with strong underlying socio-political themes: can you remember the basic theme in each?

1. a. *Open City* (1945)
   b. *Hands Over the City* (1963)
   c. *The Organizer* (1965)
   d. *Salvatore Giuliano* (1961)
   e. *Investigation of a Citizen Above Suspicion* (1970)

2. What major figures in the Italian cinema are associated with each of the following groups of films?

   a. *Europa 51* (1951)
      Fear (1952)
      The Lonely Woman (1952)

   b. *The Priest's Wife* (1970)
      Divorce Italian Style (1962)
      Yesterday, Today and Tomorrow (1963)

   c. *Cronaca di un Amore* (1950)
      Le Amiche (1955)
      Il Grido (1957)

   d. *Indiscretion* (1952)
      Shoeshine (1946)
      Two Women (1961)

   e. *Notti di Cabiria* (1957)
      Il Bidone (1955)
      Lights of Variety (1948)

   f. *Accatone* (1961)
      Mamma Roma (1962)
      The Gospel According to St Matthew (1964)

3. Overleaf are four bizarre characters featured in some films by Federico Fellini: which of his films are they taken from?

12 Quickies:

1. What 1961 film featured Jean-Paul Belmondo and Sophia Loren?

2. What 1962 film by Jacques Demy featured a compulsive gambler?

3. Who starred in *The Atonement of Gösta Berling* (1924)?

4. What Antonioni film featured the Milan Stock Exchange?

5. What shop was broken into in *Rififi* (1954)?

6. What recent film by Polish director Jerzy Skolimowski was set in a London swimming pool?

7. Who was Don Camillo, and who played him?

8. Who directed *The Passion of Joan of Arc* (1928)?

9. Who was *La Sirène du Mississippi* [*The Mississippi Mermaid*] (1969)?

10. Which of Roger Vadim's wives was in *Les Liaisons Dangereuses* (1959)?

Foreign Movies – Answers

1
1. Andrzej Wajda – Polish
2. Claude Lelouche – French
3. Grigori Chukrai – Russian
4. Jules Dassin – American, but he is usually placed in a European context, having made all his films there after leaving America because of the witch-hunts of the late forties and early fifties.
5. François Truffaut – French
6. Marcel Camus – French, although the film is set in Brazil.
7. Bo Widerberg – Swedish
8. René Clair – French
9. Vittorio de Sica – Italian
10. Jacques Demy – French
11. Mikhail Kalatozov – Russian
12. Alain Resnais – French

2
1. Greek director Michael Cacoyannis
2. Swedish director Alf Sjoberg
3. Polish actor Zbigniew Cybulski
4. Comedies made by Czech director Milos Forman
5. Made by Denmark's most famous director, Car Dreyer
6. Films by Jules Dassin; he starred in the latter two.

3
1. The director was Marcel Carné and the writer Jacques Prévert. In 1944, they made *Les Enfants du Paradis*, part of which had to be re-shot when they discovered that one of the actors was a collaborator.

2. Jean Vigo, one of the cinéastes' principal cult figures. The film was *Zéro de Conduite*.

3. a. *Le Sang d'un Poète*, a very Buñuel-like film in many respects.

    b. *Orphée* was subsequently extended in *Le Testament d'Orphée*.

    c. *Les Enfants Terribles*, for which he wrote the screenplay and spoke the narration.

    d. *La Belle et la Bête*, starring Josette Day, Jean Marais and Michel Auclair.

4. a. René Chouette

    b. Henri Georges Clouzot – he also made *The Wages of Fear* (1953) and *Les Diaboliques* (1954).

    c. François Truffaut – his first film

    d. Chris Marker, the best-known director of French documentaries, such as *Letter From Siberia* (1958), *Cuba Si* (1961); also *La Jetée* (1963).

    e. René Clair

    f. Jean Gabin

    g. Truffaut's *Fahrenheit 451*, with Oskar Werner

    h. Jean-Luc Godard, in *Le Mépris* (1963)

4

1. a. *Les Liaisons Dangereuses*, a huge success at the time, and one of the early frank-about-sex films.

    b. *Viva Maria*, Louis Malle's comedy-adventure about the Mexican Revolution.

    c. *The Yellow Rolls Royce*, Anthony Asquith's episodic collection of stories about the various owners of the title-role star.

    d. *La Notte*, one of Antonioni's films about boredom and alienation.

2. a. *Moderato Cantabile*

    b. *Chimes at Midnight*, Welles's version of the story of Falstaff, in which she played Doll Tearsheet to Welles's Falstaff.

    c. *The Sailor from Gibraltar*

5

1. *Un Chien Andalou* (1928) and *L'Age d'Or* (1930). Both have been analysed and re-analysed hundreds of times.

Regarded as two classics of Surrealism, the former contains the horrific eye-slitting sequence, with Buñuel himself as the man with the razor.

2.   *Viridiana* (1961). Awarded a major prize at Cannes, it was banned by the Spanish government, which had allowed Buñuel to return from exile to make it.

3.   *Robinson Crusoe* (1952) and *Wuthering Heights* (1953). The former starred Dan O'Herlihy, and was the film version which was closest to the original. Not much is known about the latter, except that Buñuel had wanted to film it since the thirties.

4.   Usually, Buñuel uses unknowns in his films, but in these three he used Jeanne Moreau in the first, and Catherine Deneuve in the other two.

6   1.   All were early star vehicles for Marlene Dietrich. Her first real hit was, of course, *The Blue Angel* (1930), directed by von Sternberg. Many believe it to be her best film.

2.   Fritz Lang, who also made *Metropolis* (1926) and *M* (1931). He went to Hollywood in 1934 and became one of the most vocal anti-fascists.

3.   Pola Negri, whose career began in 1915, and who still makes an occasional film appearance.

4.   Leni Riefenstahl, notorious for her brilliantly directed propaganda films for the Nazis such as *Triumph of the Will* (1934), the story of the Nuremberg Rally.

5.   Ernst Lubitsch. The 'Lubitsch Touch' became a catch phrase in Hollywood after his arrival there, describing his deft but light control of romantic comedy (*Ninotchka*, 1939, and *That Uncertain Feeling*, 1941).

6.   G. W. Pabst, another director who moved to Hollywood, but who never repeated his early German successes. *Kameradschaft* told the story of a French mining

disaster and the nearby German miners violating the frontier regulations to assist. The film was made with two endings, the second of which, with the international barriers once again being imposed, has only recently come to light.

7

1.   Victor Sjostrom (anglicized to Seastrom), who made several films in Hollywood in the twenties.
2.   Mauritz Stiller, who also went to Hollywood with her, but died soon after.
3.   *I Am Curious: Blue* (1967) and *I Am Curious: Yellow* (1967).
4.   Ingrid Bergman. She was also in the re-make, with Leslie Howard, which was called *Escape to Happiness* in Britain but retained the original title elsewhere.
5.   One of Bergman's favourite actors, Max von Sydow, starred in all of them.
6.   *Now About These Women* was the first film he made in colour.
7.   The first dealt with incest, the second with lesbianism.

8

1.   Toshiro Mifune swoops down on a spy in his efforts to aid silly self-righteous youths trying to stop administrative corruption in *Sanjuro* (1962).
2.   The baleful father Tatsuya Nakadai tells his tale of heroic misery at the Great House in *Hara Kiri* (1962), just before his spectacular efforts to destroy it in an attempt to avenge his son's terrible death.
3.   Kambei (Takashi Shimura), the leader of *The Seven Samurai* (1954), lets fly in the third and final day of the battle to save the village and its hopeless inhabitants from the marauding bandits.
4.   The villain's champion sets out for the show-down with *Yojimbo* (1961). Although he has a gun concealed in his robes, he is unable to defeat Mifune in the title role.

9

1.   *Pather Panchali, Aparajito* and *The World of Apu*.
2.   All three were made in India, about India, but were

made by an American, James Ivory. The films deal with the cross-cultural problems of Europeans in the Indian community.

10   1.   *Black God, White Devil* (1963), which was about revolution and messianic cults, introduced near its end a character who became the central figure in the sequel, *Antonio das Mortes* (1968). *Terra em Transe* (1967) was also concerned with similar themes.

2.   *O Cangaceiro* (*The Bandit*)

3.   Leopoldo Torre-Nilsson

4.   *The Hour of the Furnaces* (1967), directed by Fernando E. Solanas, is an examination of the last forty years of Argentinian politics, which attacks the establishment, and includes historic film and interviews with Argentinian and other South American political leaders.

5.   Emilio Fernandez. Several sources cite him as the world's most prolific director, but it seems impossible to get figures to corroborate this.

11   1.   a.   Made during the German retreat, it shows the effect of the changing forces of occupation on the Italians and on the forces themselves. It set the tone for Italian films of the next five years or so.

b.   The story of a corrupt official who tries to become mayor. The film featured the rotten politics of municipal administration, and starred Rod Steiger.

c.   Marcello Mastroianni played the title role in this film about the organization of labour in a textile mill; it is principally concerned with workers' rights.

d.   Poverty and the violence of politics in Sicily drives the hero to banditry in his fight against the corrupt forces of the law.

e.   The film attacks the fear of the police to incriminate one of their own, when all the clues in a notorious sex-murder point to the Roman Chief of Police — a murder which, in fact, he has committed

Peripherally it also attacks police treatment of left-wing students.

2.   a. Films made by Roberto Rossellini, starring Ingrid Bergman.
b. Sophia Loren and Marcello Mastroianni are the stars of all of them.
c. Early films by director Michelangelo Antonioni, better known for his glossier films (*Blow-Up*, 1966; *Zabriskie Point*, 1969).
d. Films by actor-director Vittorio de Sica, best known for *Bicycle Thieves* (1946) and many competent films of the fifties, who has recently bounced back to his old form with *The Garden of the Finzi-Continis* (1971).
e. Films which have starred Giulietta Masina, directed by her husband Federico Fellini.
f. Films by Pier Paolo Pasolini (*Oedipus Rex*, 1967; *Theorem*, 1968; *Medea*, 1970).

3.   1. A musician from one of the banquet sequences in *Fellini Satyricon* (1969).
2. *8½*. The character is Fifi the Dancer, in this at least semi-autobiographical film.
3. Giulietta's mother in *Giulietta of the Spirits* (1965).
4. Anthony Quinn as Zampano, in *La Strada* (1954, with Giulietta Masina and Richard Basehart).

2   1.   De Sica's *Two Women*, the film which made an international star of Sophia Loren.
2.   *Baie des Anges*, with Jeanne Moreau (in a blonde wig) as the woman who kept a roulette wheel in her bedroom.
3.   Greta Garbo
4.   *L'Eclisse* (1962), the final episode in the Antonioni trilogy (*L'Avventura*, 1959; *La Notte*, 1960).
5.   Mappin and Webb in the Place Vendôme, Paris.
6.   *Deep End* (1971), with Diana Dors, Jane Asher and John Moulder Brown.

7. He was the priest of an Italian village, locked in permanent combat with the communist mayor. He was played by French actor Fernandel.

8. Carl Dreyer

9. Catherine Deneuve, in a film by Truffaut.

10. Annette Stroyberg

13 War

The built-in possibilities of heroism, crisis, spectacle, pathos and rampant nationalism have stimulated film-makers to produce war films by the score. The best have been cool, retrospective studies made after the event, not the overtly propagandist movies made in the heat of the moment. Films set in wartime form a clear-cut category, but there has been a variety of approach and emphasis. The result is the following mixture of adventure, comedy, epic and polemical films, mostly of the major conflicts of the twentieth century.*

The Great War 1914–18

This was the first time the film industry found itself involved in a large propaganda effort. Most Hollywood films of the time were banal and unreal, undisguised attempts to promote a pro-war spirit in the United States. *The Fall of a Nation* (1916) and *The Little American* (1918) were typical forgettable films of the period. The best films about the First World War are nearly all talkies.

Fill in the blanks:
1. The outstanding film about this war was *All Quiet on the Western Front* (1930), adapted from Erich Maria Remarque's novel. It starred —— —— and was directed by —— ——.
2. Anna Neagle starred as —— —— —— in the film of the same name in 1939, portraying an Englishwoman shot by the Germans.
3. The only musical made about this war was —— —— —— —— ——.

---

* Answers on page 216.

4. The best silent film about the First World War starred John Gilbert, Tom O'Brien and Karl Dane. It was ―― ―― ――.

5. The 1918 comedy ―― ―― ―― ―― starred Marie Dressler as a Red Cross Nurse.

6. Gary Cooper was rescued from his crashed plane by Colleen Moore in ―― ――.

7. Several other films were made about the part the Air Force played in this war, such as *Wings* (1928), one of the last silent spectaculars, and *The Dawn Patrol* (1930), but probably the best of the lot was Howard Hughes's *Hell's Angels* (1930). Jean Harlow was the loose lady and the principal men in her life were ―― ―― and ―― ――.

8. Stanley Kubrick made a film about the First World War. It was ―― ―― ――, and starred ―― ――.

9. Not all of the Great War was fought in Europe. Aspects of the African campaign were shown in John Huston's ―― ―― ―― and of the war in the Middle East in David Lean's ―― ―― ――.

10. ―― ―― played the deserter shot by a firing squad in Joseph Losey's ―― ―― ――.

11. Two recent films about the air war in Europe were John Guillermin's ―― ―― ――, starring ―― ――, and Roger Corman's ―― ―― ――, starring ―― ―― ――.

The Second World War 1939–45

Like the films of 1914–18, those actually made during the war were mostly propaganda-oriented, and it is only in recent years that any objectivity and compassion (as opposed to sentimentality) have been achieved.

2   Many familiar faces were involved in British films made during the war. Who are these actors, and what are the films from which the stills opposite are taken?

3   Where would you expect to find*

1. Bette Davis in 1943?
2. Irene Dunn in 1942?
3. Mona Maris in 1941?
4. Peter Lorre in 1945?
5. Tallulah Bankhead in 1944?
6. John Garfield in 1945?
7. Spencer Tracy in 1944?
8. Humphrey Bogart in 1943?
9. Vivien Leigh in 1940?
10. Katharine Cornell in 1943?

4   Who was (or were)

1. *The One That Got Away* (1957)?
2. *Up in Arms* (1944)?
3. *The Young Lions* (1958)?
4. *Above Suspicion* (1943)?
5. *Mr Roberts* (1955)?
6. *Patton* (1969)?

5   1.   What film did Alfred Hitchcock make in 1938 which warned of the coming troubles in Europe?
What were his three wartime films which had war settings and plots?

2.   German Field Marshal Edwin Rommel has featured as the lead in two films (1943 and 1951). What were their titles, and who played him in each?

3.   Who were the stoic womenfolk left behind in (a) *Cry Havoc* (1943) and (b) *Since You Went Away* (1944)?

4.   Who was ordered to *Sink the Bismarck* (1960), and by whom?

5.   What are the titles of Andrzej Wajda's trilogy about wartime life in Poland?

6.   A German film, made in 1959, was a story about the last days of the war in Germany, and of the last-ditch

---

* The answers to these are all film titles.

defence of the Fatherland by a group of adolescent school-boys. What was the film, and who directed it?

7. Who was Captain Langsdorff?

Who played him?

In what film?

Where and how did he lose his ship?

8. In 1942, Ernst Lubitsch made a war comedy about a theatrical couple on the run in Poland. What was the film, and who were its stars?

9. Who was Emily, and who was responsible for her Americanization?

10. Who played General Dreedle, Nurse Duckett and Chaplain Tappman, and in what film?

11. In 1949, Henry King directed a film about American bomber pilots stationed in Britain. What was the film?

Who played the commanding officer who finally cracked up?

12. What was the 1969 film about the rise of Nazism and its effect on German society, and who made it?

13. Another recent film has dealt with the fascists in Italy and their effects on the Jewish population during the years 1938–43. What was the film, who directed it, and who was its leading lady?

14. Where was *Slaughterhouse Five* (1972), and who was in it?

6 Are these statements about prisoner-of-war films true or false?

1. James Robertson Justice played the title role, and Stanley Baker a double role, in *A Very Important Person* (1961).

2. *A Town Like Alice* (1956) was a film about civilian prisoners-of-war, and starred Virginia McKenna and Peter Finch.

3. William Holden escaped from three prisoner-of-war camps: in *Stalag 17* (1953), *The Bridge on the River Kwai* (1957) and *The Counterfeit Traitor* (1962).

4.   Of all those who took part in *The Great Escape* (1963), James Coburn and Steve McQueen were the only ones who were not recaptured.

5.   George Segal was the *King Rat* who corrupted James Fox and outwitted Tom Courtenay.

7   Smooth, suave and cultured, with a predilection for classical music and paintings, knowing the best wines and the histories of their occupied chateaux, and having sinister designs on barely-clad but brave resistance girls, the movies' conception of the Nazi villain was one of the most stereotyped. Who were the villainous Nazis in these films?
1.   *Foreign Correspondent* (1940)
2.   *The Invisible Agent* (1942)
3.   *Man Hunt* (1941)
4.   *North Star* (1943)
5.   *Desperate Journey* (1942)
6.   *Lifeboat* (1943)
7.   *All Through the Night* (1941)
8.   *Paris Calling* (1943)
9.   *Stalag 17* (1953)

The Cold War

8   Since 1945, the Communists have replaced the Nazis as the new international villains in commercial Hollywood movies. In these post-1945 conflicts, who opposed whom in
1.   *The Manchurian Candidate* (1962)?
2.   *Seven Days in May* (1964)?
3.   *The Bedford Incident* (1965)?

Foreign Wars

9   1.   Most Russian films which have had any international success have dealt with the Revolution or the related military events. What was the title of the film about
a.   The abortive 1905 revolution?
b.   The Russian defeat of the Teutonic knights?

c. The beginnings of the 1917 revolution?
Who directed these three films?

2. There have been two Anglo-American epics about Russian wars, one made in 1956, the other in 1966. What were they?
Who directed them?
Who were the leading players in each?

10 Several films have been made about the Spanish Civil War. Who were the stars, and who were the directors, of:
1. *Blockade* (1938)?
2. *For Whom the Bell Tolls* (1943)?
3. *Mourir à Madrid* (1962)?
4. *Behold a Pale Horse* (1964)?
5. *La Guerre est Finie* (1966)?

11 What do the following groups of films have in common?
1. *The Halls of Montezuma* (1950)
   The Frogmen (1951)
   Hell and High Water (1954)

2. *The Battle of San Pietro* (1944)
   The True Glory (1945)
   Fires Were Started (1943)

3. *To Hell and Back* (1955)
   Reach for the Sky (1956)
   The Story of G.I. Joe (1945)

4. *The Battle of Britain* (1969)
   The Longest Day (1962)
   Tora! Tora! Tora! (1971)

5. *The Enemy Below* (1957)
   Morning Departure (1950)
   Destination Tokyo (1943)

12 Who are the actors pictured overleaf? Each is playing the title role in a war film.

13 What wars were the settings for these films?

1. *Birth of a Nation* (1915)
2. *The Green Berets* (1968)
3. *M*A*S*H* (1970)
4. *Ohm Kruger* (1941)
5. *The Battle of Algiers* (1970)
6. *The Charge of the Light Brigade* (1968)
7. *The Inn of the Sixth Happiness* (1958)
8. *Something of Value* (1957)
9. *The Mercenaries [Dark of the Sun]* (1968)
10. *Che!* (1968)
11. *55 Days at Peking* (1962)

War – Answers

The Great War 1914–18

1

1. Lew Ayres and Lewis Milestone
2. *Nurse Edith Cavell*
3. *Oh! What a Lovely War* (1969)
4. *The Big Parade* (1925)
5. *The Cross Red Nurse*
6. *Lilac Time* (1928)
7. James Hall and Ben Lyon
8. *Paths of Glory* (1957), with Kirk Douglas.
9. *The African Queen* (1951); *Lawrence of Arabia* (1962).
10. Tom Courtenay in *King and Country* (1964).
11. *The Blue Max* (1966), with George Peppard; *The Red Baron* (1971), with John Philip Law.

The Second World War 1939–45

2

1. John Mills in *Waterloo Road* (1944), the story of a soldier, absent without leave, trying to avenge his wife's unfaithfulness. Shot mostly on location in south London slums, this film is considered the forerunner of the 'realist' British films of the fifties and sixties.

2. Eric Portman, as the Nazi submarine captain on the run with his crew in *49th Parallel* [*The Invaders*] (1941), trying to cross into the then-neutral United States. Assorted good guys were Raymond Massey, Anton Walbrook, Leslie Howard, Finlay Currie, Glynis Johns and Laurence Olivier.

3. Noel Coward in *In Which We Serve* (1942), one of the most important films about the war, which Coward produced and co-directed (with David Lean), as well as writing the script and the music.

4.   David Niven as one of *The First of the Few* (1942). The story of the invention of the Spitfire, written and directed by Leslie Howard, it was the last feature film in which Howard appeared.

5.   Rex Harrison (with Margaret Lockwood) in Carol Reed's *Night Train to Munich* (1940), a thriller which involved intrigue behind the enemy lines and paid tribute to the Czech war effort.

3   1.   Bette Davis was keeping *Watch on the Rhine*.
2.   Irene Dunn was on the *White Cliffs of Dover*.
3.   Mona Maris was *Underground*.
4.   Peter Lorre was at the *Hotel Berlin*, this time as a 'good' German.
5.   Tallulah Bankhead was adrift in a *Lifeboat*.
6.   John Garfield was in the *Air Force*.
7.   Spencer Tracy was spending *Thirty Seconds over Tokyo*.
8.   Humphrey Bogart really got around in 1943: he was in *Casablanca*, in the *Sahara*, and saw *Action in the North Atlantic*.
9.   Vivien Leigh was hanging about on *Waterloo Bridge*.
10.   Katharine Cornell was serving coffee to soldiers in the *Stage Door Canteen*.

4   1.   Hardy Kruger, as the one German prisoner-of-war who escaped during the Second World War.
2.   Danny Kaye, the hypochondriac draftee who eventually defeated all the Japanese army on his island single-handed.
3.   The Americans were Dean Martin and Montgomery Clift; the German was Marlon Brando.
4.   They were Fred MacMurray and Joan Crawford, who were tangling with Nazis in Paris and Salzburg.
5.   Henry Fonda, battling with lunatic Captain James Cagney and weak-kneed Lieutenant Jack Lemmon.

6. George C. Scott, in a performance for which he won (and refused) an Academy Award.

5 1. *The Lady Vanishes* was about spies, kidnapping and secret agents in an unnamed eastern European country. Its British stars (Michael Redgrave, Margaret Lockwood, Dame May Whitty, Basil Radford and Naunton Wayne) were definitely the goodies (except for adulterer and coward Cecil Parker, who got shot, but not for his political beliefs). During the war, *Foreign Correspondent* (1940), *Saboteur* (1942) and *Lifeboat* (1943) all relied on wartime settings and plots.

2. In 1943, Erich von Stroheim was a sinister stock German villain in Billy Wilder's *Five Graves to Cairo*. James Mason's 1951 performance in *The Desert Fox* was a much more sympathetic look at Rommel, and also more accurate.*

3. (a) Ann Sothern, Faye Bainter, Joan Blondell, Marsha Hunt and Margaret Sullivan.
(b) Claudette Colbert, Shirley Temple, Jennifer Jones, Alla Nazimova, Hattie McDaniel and Agnes Moorehead. (The introductory title to the film announced 'This is the story of an unconquerable fortress – the American Home.')

4. Kenneth More, by an off-screen voice of Winston Churchill.

5. *A Generation* (1954), *Kanal* (1956) and *Ashes and Diamonds* (1958).

6. *The Bridge*. The boys are killed one by one as they take on the American tanks with their outdated rifles. It was directed by former Swiss actor Bernard Wicki, who went on to direct *The Longest Day* (1962, with Ken Annakin), *The Visit* (1963) and *Morituri* [*Saboteur – Codename Morituri*] (1965).

* Rommel also made brief appearances in *The Night of the Generals* (1966), played by Christopher Plummer, and in *Patton, Lust for Glory* (1969) played by Karl Michael Volger.

7.   Langsdorff, played by Peter Finch, was Captain of the pocket battleship Graf Spee, in *The Battle of the River Plate* (1955). He scuttled his damaged ship in Montevideo harbour rather than have it sunk by the British.

8.   *To Be or Not To Be*, starring Jack Benny and Carole Lombard, in her last film.

9.   Julie Andrews, in *The Americanization of Emily* (1964), at the hands of James Garner, with amusing performances from Joyce Grenfell as Emily's mother and James Coburn as a career officer in the United States Navy.

10. Orson Welles, Paula Prentiss and Anthony Perkins in *Catch 22* (1969).

11. *Twelve O'Clock High*, with Gregory Peck.

12. *The Damned*, directed by Luchino Visconti.

13. *The Garden of the Finzi-Continis* (1971), made by Vittorio de Sica, starring Dominique Sanda.

14. In Dresden. Michael Sachs and fellow prisoners were billeted there at the time of the massive air raid.

6
1.   False. The double role was played by Stanley Baxter.
2.   True.
3.   False. In *The Counterfeit Traitor* he played a double agent, working out of Stockholm, not a prisoner-of-war.
4.   False. McQueen was recaptured. Coburn escaped, as did a few others, but most of the remainder were caught and massacred.
5.   True.

7
1.   Herbert Marshall
2.   Cedric Hardwicke and Peter Lorre
3.   George Sanders
4.   Erich von Stroheim
5.   Raymond Massey
6.   Walter Slezak

7.   Peter Lorre, Judith Anderson and Conrad Veidt

8.   Lee J. Cobb and Basil Rathbone

9.   Otto Preminger (one critic remarked that he could make a career of playing Erich von Stroheim).

The Cold War

8

1.   Frank Sinatra was after the brain-washed Laurence Harvey, to try to stop the attempt to plant a communist president in the White House.

2.   Kirk Douglas thwarted right-wing General Burt Lancaster's plans to overthrow the United States government by a military coup.

3.   Martin Balsam tried to stop virulently anti-communist Captain Richard Widmark from attacking a Russian submarine, but Lieutenant James MacArthur inadvertently launched a missile, and the Russians retaliated before it hit them. No one was left.

Foreign Wars

9

1.   a. *Battleship Potemkin* (1925)
     b. *Alexander Nevsky* (1938)
     c. *Strike* (1925)
     Sergei Eisenstein

2.   *War and Peace* (1956) was directed by King Vidor, and starred Audrey Hepburn, Mel Ferrer, Henry Fonda, Oskar Homolka, Herbert Lom, Anita Ekberg, John Mills and Vittorio Gassman.

Dr Zhivago (1966) was directed by David Lean, and starred Julie Christie, Omar Sharif, Geraldine Chaplin, Ralph Richardson, Tom Courtenay, Rod Steiger, Alec Guinness, Rita Tushingham and Siobhan McKenna.

10

1.   *Blockade*, with Madeleine Carroll and Henry Fonda, was directed by William Dieterle.

2.   Sam Wood's *For Whom the Bell Tolls* starred Gary Cooper and Ingrid Bergman.

3.   *Mourir à Madrid* was directed by Frederic Rossif. It had no stars, but was narrated by Irene Worth, John Gielgud and William Hutt.

4.   *Behold a Pale Horse*, directed by Fred Zinneman, starred Gregory Peck.

5.   *La Guerre est Finie* starred Yves Montand as the weary republican agent in Alain Resnais's film.

11   1.   All starred hero-figure Richard Widmark.

2.   All were Second World War documentaries.

3.   All were biographies of war heroes: *To Hell and Back* starred Audie Murphy as himself, the most-decorated American soldier; *Reach for the Sky* was the story of British pilot Douglas Bader (played by Kenneth More); and *The Story of G.I. Joe* was the biography of war correspondent Ernie Pyle, played by Burgess Meredith.

4.   All were huge, international, multi-star war movies.

5.   All were about submarine warfare during the Second World War.

12   1.   Greer Garson as *Mrs Miniver* (1942), Hollywood's sentimental and totally fictitious version of the English in wartime. It started a vogue for endings in burnt-out churches.

2.   Charles Chaplin as *The Great Dictator* (1940), a film which was naturally banned in Germany, Italy and the occupied countries.

3.   Gary Cooper as *Sergeant York* (1941), the First World War American hero. Cooper won an Academy Award for his performance in this film scripted by John Huston.

4.   Anna Neagle, portraying a wartime nurse, this time Florence Nightingale in *The Lady with a Lamp* (1951).

5.   Danny Kaye and Curt Jurgens as *Me and the Colonel* (1957), the story of a Jewish refugee and a Polish colonel on the run in front of the rapidly-advancing German army.

13   1.   The American Civil War

2.   The Vietnam War – an attempt to justify it, by actor-director John Wayne.

3.   The Korean War

4.   The Boer War. A German film made to whip up anti-British feelings by showing British soldiers committing all sorts of atrocities against the good and helpless Boers.

5.   The Algerian war of independence

6.   The Crimean War

7.   The Sino-Japanese War

8.   The Mau Mau uprising

9.   The Congolese war

10.   The Cuban revolution, and the subsequent attempts to export it.

11.   The Boxer Rebellion

14 Science Fiction

Ever since Georges Meliés's *Voyage to the Moon* (1902), the cinema has tried to portray the fantastic, dogged by the recurring problem of translating written science fiction into concrete cinematic terms. A few films of the thirties and forties seemed to overcome these problems, but it was not until the fifties that strong traditions were established, the result of a combination of original screenplays, sophisticated special effects and an audience newly aware of atomic power and the real possibility of space travel.*

1   Two early science fiction films, one German, the other British, were made in 1926 and 1936. Their political and social philosophies are now discounted, but the scale and imagination of their designs and sets are still impressive. What are the titles of these two films?
Who were the notable names associated with them?

2   Plots, creatures and locations are usually the most memorable aspects of science fiction movies. The names associated with the films tend to be forgotten. Here are five men who have made outstanding contributions to science fiction and fantasy films. Who are
1.   Willis O'Brien?
2.   Ray Harryhausen?
3.   George Pal?
4.   Byron Haskin?
5.   Jack Arnold?

3   The movie scientist has often been an equivocal figure, to whom retribution comes in the end because of his unswerving

* Answers on page 232.

223

devotion to the false god Science. Here is a selection of some such doctor-scientists. Who are they, and what are the titles of the films from which these stills are taken?

4 Lost worlds have been a recurrent theme: historical or fictional, on earth or deep in space, they have provided striking settings and plots even though, in some cases, these may verge on the ridiculous. Are the following statements about lost worlds true or false?

1. Four film versions of Rider Haggard's *She* were made between the date of the book's publication in 1887 and the earliest *surviving* film version (1916).

2. *L'Atlantide* (1934) was one of the best variations on the *She* theme. Directed by Fritz Lang, it featured a ghoulish eternal woman who kept a collection of her mummified ex-lovers.

3. In *Lost Horizon* (1934), Ronald Colman was so taken with the idea of eternal youth with Jane Wyman that he decided to stay in Shangri-La.

4. D. W. Griffith's special effects team pioneered the use of close-up photography of lizards, making them look like prehistoric monsters, for the original version of *One Million Years B.C.* (1940).

5   James Whale, who directed the original *Frankenstein* (1931), subsequently directed the first film version of H. G. Wells's *The Invisible Man* (1933). The film made a star of Claude Rains in the title role, although he appeared only briefly (and dead) at the end. The success of this film resulted in a spate of low-budget variations on this theme. Most of them were made by Universal, one of the science fiction specialist studios.

How many *invisible* films can you name?

6   In the forties, it became a vogue to try to adapt comic strip science fiction for the screen.

1.   There were three *Flash Gordon* serials; the last, in 1940, was called —— —— —— —— ——.

2.   —— ——, who had played Flash Gordon, also appeared in a 1939 science fiction serial, in which he played —— ——.

3.   —— and ——, created by artist Bob Kane, appeared in two fifteen-part serials, in 1943 and 1949. In them, their most notable opponent was —— —— ——, who played a wily and sinister Japanese gentleman.

4.   In 1967, John Philip Law appeared in two films based on comic strip characters. He played the title role in ——, a character originally created by Angela and Luciana Guissani. In the other, the title character (created by Jean Claude Forest), was called —— (played by —— ——, directed by —— ——); Law played —— —— ——.

7   A favourite pastime of both film-makers and science fiction writers has been to shrink people. Which films are described below?

Who directed and who starred in each?

1.   On their escape from a French prison, a framed ex-banker learns the miniaturization secret from a utopian scientist who wants to shrink everyone in the world to eradicate hunger and poverty. On the scientist's death, however, the banker perverts this purpose by selling mannikins

as novelty dolls and telepathically instructing them to maim and terrify his old enemies.

2.   Mad Dr Thorkel uses a Peruvian radioactive deposit to shrink a group of scientists to mouse size. After many terrors, they revenge themselves by smashing his thick glasses and causing him to fall down an abandoned mine-shaft.

3.   After a shower of mysterious crystals, Scott Carey suffers a lengthy and agonizing reduction in size, until his wife assumes that the family cat has killed him. He lives on in the cellar, battling with spiders and hopelessness.

4.   Intrepid captain, pneumatic cutie and sweating villain are miniaturized, (along with their submarine) and injected into an artery of a dying atomic scientist, to remove a clot from his brain.

8   Space travel, another favourite theme, has provided designers with exciting opportunities. Which films featured the scenes below and overleaf?

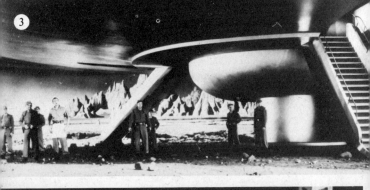

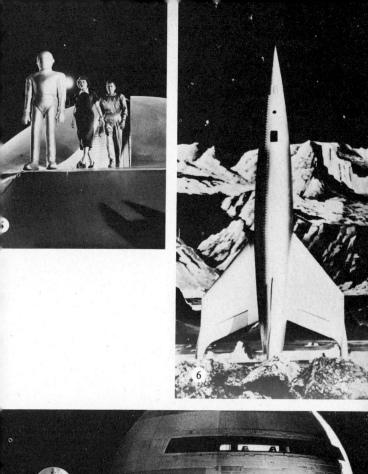

9   The effects of A-bomb testing, unwelcome aliens or secret
       drugs can lead to the awakening or uncontrolled growth of
       all sorts of creatures.
       What was the menacing creature in the following films, and
       whose inhabitants was it terrifying?
       1.   *Tarantula* (1955)
       2.   *Revenge of the Creature* (1955)
       3.   *The Beast from 20,000 Fathoms* (1953)
       4.   *Twenty Million Miles to Earth* (1957)
       5.   *Godzilla* (1955)

10 Another recurring idea is The Destruction of the World As
       We Know It: what was the world-ending threat in:
       1.   *The War of the Worlds* (1953)?
       2.   *When Worlds Collide* (1951)? – *which* worlds?
       3.   *Invaders from Mars* (1954)? – and how do they go
       about it?
       4.   *The 27th Day* (1957)?
       5.   *Quatermass and the Pit* [*Five Million Miles to Earth*]
       (1957)?
       6.   *On the Beach* (1959)?
       7.   *The Day the Earth Caught Fire* (1962)? – but how did
       it happen?
       8.   *The Invasion of the Body Snatchers* (1956)?
       9.   *Seven Days to Noon* (1950)?

11 What do the films in each of these groups have in common?
       1.   *The World, the Flesh and the Devil* (1959)
            Panic in Year Zero (1962)
            Dr Strangelove (1963)

       2.   *Moon Pilot* (1961)
            The Absent-Minded Professor (1961)
            Son of Flubber (1962)

       3.   *The Curse of the Cat People* (1944)
            The Body Snatcher (1945)
            The Andromeda Strain (1971)

4.   *Attack of the Crab Monsters* (1956)
     The Wasp Woman (1959)
     Creature from the Haunted Sea (1960)

12   1.   What was special about the apparel of *The Man in the White Suit* (1951)?
2.   What was the origin of the mysterious power of *The Man Who Could Work Miracles* (1937)?
3.   What eventually happened to the sight of *The Man with the X-Ray Eyes* (1963)?
4.   How was *The Man Who Could Cheat Death* (1959) able to do so?

13   What does each of these titles refer to?
1.   *The Power* (1967)
2.   *Them* (1954)
3.   *Donovan's Brain* (1953)
4.   *Fahrenheit 451* (1966)
5.   *The Thing* (1951)
6.   *The Blob* (1958)
7.   *The Monolith Monsters* (1957)
8.   *The Damned* (1961)

Science Fiction – Answers

1   *Metropolis*, made in Germany in 1926, directed by Fritz Lang, and based on a novel (and screenplay) by his wife, Thea von Harbou. It starred Brigitte Helm as both the altruistic nurse-heroine and the fearful robot built to impersonate her and sabotage the workers' attempts to rebel. The most memorable design work was in the models of the soaring multi-level Metropolis itself, and the nightmare subterranean powerhouse-factory.

Things to Come, made in England ten years later. H. G. Wells wrote the screenplay from his own novel; William Cameron Menzies directed. Covering the century 1936–2036, it had Raymond Massey playing two generations of technological heroes and their attempts to rescue the world from a shattering war and protect it from the forces of ignorance and chaos.

2   1.   Willis O'Brien pioneered the techniques of animating models in monster movies. He had worked on dinosaur models since the early part of the century before he made his first film contribution to the original film version of Conan Doyle's *The Lost World* (1925). This led to his work on *King Kong* (1933), his greatest achievement, and its sequels, *Son of Kong* (1934) and *Mighty Joe Young* (1949).

2.   Ray Harryhausen, O'Brien's pupil, perfected the model techniques into a system he called 'Dynamation', used in *It Came from Beneath the Sea* (1952), *Twenty Million Miles to Earth* (1957), *The Three Worlds of Gulliver* (1960), *Jason and the Argonauts* (1963), *The First Men on the Moon* (1964), *One Million Years B.C.* (1966) and *Valley of Gwangi* (1969).

3. George Pal, prolific producer of science fiction films for Paramount. He started the fifties boom with *Destination Moon* (1951), and continued with films like *When Worlds Collide* (1951), *The War of the Worlds* (1954), *The Conquest of Space* (1955), *Robinson Crusoe on Mars* (1964) and *The Power* (1968).

4. Byron Haskin, a somewhat underrated director who specialized in science fiction films, and directed most of Pal's productions, including the last four listed above. (They co-directed *The Power*.)

5. Jack Arnold, another science fiction specialist, this time for Universal. He made some powerful films of this type, including *It Came from Outer Space* (1953), *The Creature from the Black Lagoon* (1954), *Tarantula* (1955) and *The Incredible Shrinking Man* (1957).

3

1. Leo G. Carroll, intent on his misguided efforts to solve the world's food shortage (they eventually backfire, of course) in *Tarantula* (1955).

2. An ageing John Barrymore as the eccentric scientist responsible for *The Invisible Woman* (1940).

3. Boris Karloff, demonstrating his sinister machine in *The Invisible Ray* (1936), his first big film without make-up, and the one which established him in such characterizations. His power for the ray came from 'Radium X', discovered in a volcanic fissure in Africa.

4. James Mason threatening to remove one of the human obstacles on his *Journey to the Centre of the Earth* (1959). Although he wasn't particularly evil in this film, he was certainly a crack-pot.

5. Erich von Stroheim in *The Lady and the Monster* (1943), the original film version of Curt Siodmak's novel *Donovan's Brain*.

4   1.   False. At least *seven* versions were made before 1916.
2.   False. The director was G. W. Pabst.
3.   False. He left Shangri-La, then changed his mind but couldn't get back in.
4.   True. Produced by Hal Roach, it was something of a re-make of Griffith's third film, *Man's Genesis* (1912).

5   *The Invisible Man Returns* (1940), with Vincent Price; *The Invisible Woman* (1940), with Virginia Bruce; *The Invisible Ghost* (1941); *The Invisible Agent* (1942) and *The Invisible Man's Revenge* (1944), both with Jon Hall; and *The Invisible Boy* (1957). No points for *Invisible Stripes* (1939) (see Crime); *Abbott and Costello Meet the Invisible Man* (1951) (see Horror) or *The Invisible Ray* (1936) (see above).

6   1.   *Flash Gordon Conquers the Universe.*
2.   Buster Crabbe played *Buck Rogers.*
3.   Batman and Robin were up against J. Carrol Naish.
4.   *Diabolik* was the first. The second was *Barbarella*, played by Jane Fonda, directed by Roger Vadim, in which Law played Pygar the Angel.

7   1.   *The Devil Doll* (1936), directed by Tod Browning, starring Lionel Barrymore.
2.   *Doctor Cyclops* (1940), directed by Ernest B. Schoedsack (co-director of *King Kong*), starring Albert Dekker in the title role.
3.   *The Incredible Shrinking Man* (1957), directed by Jack Arnold, starring Grant Williams as the unfortunate in the title role.
4.   *Fantastic Voyage* (1966), starring Stephen Boyd, Raquel Welch and Donald Pleasence, directed by Richard Fleischer.

8   1.   A ship, loaded with samples of people and animals, takes off for safety *When Worlds Collide* (1951). Designers

Hal Pereira and Albert Nozaki had a field day with the special effects.

2.   Charlton Heston and his crew abandon ship after their crash landing on a planet they do not recognize, in the first of the *Ape* movies, *Planet of the Apes* (1967). Jack Martin Smith and Michael Crebner designed this film, but their efforts were upstaged by John Chambers's spectacular make-up.

3.   United Planets Cruiser C57D and its crew on the *Forbidden Planet* (1956), Altair IV, await the arrival of Walter Pidgeon and his naïve daughter Ann Francis. The only screen version of Shakespeare's *The Tempest*. Designer Arthur Lonergan's inventiveness made up in imagination what the film lacked in scientific authenticity.

4.   A little exterior repair work being done during *The Conquest of Space* (1955), based on the book *Mars Project* by Werner von Braun. Much of the film was taken up with extended scenes of take-offs, manoeuvrings in space and the landing on Mars. A Pal–Haskin–Pereira collaboration. Its future-ness was emphasized by showing the crew watching a 1955 musical.

5.   Robot Gort, alien Michael Rennie and earthling Patricia Neal emerge from the visitors' ship in *The Day the Earth Stood Still* (1951). The elegant flying saucer was given a dramatic setting in a park in Washington D.C., close to the Capitol.

6.   The rocketship Galileo in *Destination Moon* (1951), created by set designer Ernst Fegle, astronomical artist Chesley Bonestell and rocketeer Hermann Oberth. The film was a low-budget sleeper, but it got the science fiction boom going with some gusto.

7.   Keir Dullea pilots a pod away from the Jupiter-bound 'Discovery' in Stanley Kubrick's *2001: A Space Odyssey* (1968) in a effort to save drifting crew mate Gary

Lockwood. The scene was shot on the 54-foot model of the mother ship, with a 13-inch diameter pod. Tony Masters, Harry Lange and Ernest Archer received the Best Art Direction award from the British Film Academy for their work on this film.

9

1. An unnamed American township and the surrounding desert are ravaged by a spider which has escaped from a local laboratory. It has been injected with a secret formula developed to help alleviate the world's food shortage (see above), which causes it to grow to gigantic proportions and wreak havoc on the community.

2. The Gill Man (otherwise known as the Creature from the Black Lagoon) is put on display in Florida. He escapes and spreads terror and confusion through the streets of Miami.

3. A slumbering Rhedosaurus is awakened by an A-bomb test, and rampages through New York before being cornered and destroyed in Manhattan Beach Amusement Park.

4. A crash-landing spaceship returning from Venus turns up an egg of *Tyrannosaurus rex*. It hatches, and when it reaches maturity it ravages the villages and towns of sunny Italy.

5. An Asian dinosaur this time, with the victims being the inhabitants of Tokyo, in one of Japan's many monster movies.

10

1. Martians invade earth in flying saucers, only to be defeated by 'God's tiniest creatures', the bacteria, against which they have no defence.

2. Rogue star Bellus breaks out of its orbit and heads towards Earth. Its satellite Zyra passes close by, bringing about terrible destruction (tidal waves, earthquakes, etc.), but then goes into orbit around the sun, so that various men

and animals (see 8.1) can escape to it before the Earth is destroyed by Bellus on its collision course.

3. The Martians take over the earthlings by planting capsules in their brains which give them remote control and instant destruction when necessary.

4. Aliens from another world give five people (one on each continent) deadly capsules which contain a global poison, in order to test mankind's maturity. Despite pressure from various governments to use the capsules as weapons, the unlucky individuals refrain or are restrained.

5. A spaceship full of dead Martians is discovered on a London construction site. Investigations activate the mysterious power of the ship, which begins to sap the mental faculties of the Londoners until the hero short-circuits the ship's equipment.

6. Global atomic war has wiped out the world except for Australia. After a brief respite, the tide of radioactivity destroys that too.

7. Simultaneous atomic testing pushes the Earth off its axis, and it begins to move towards the sun. Desperate international collaboration results in another series of explosions which puts the Earth back in its correct orbit.

8. All the inhabitants of a small town are taken over by bland facsimiles of themselves, grown in pods by mysterious aliens.

9. A deranged atomic scientist threatens to destroy London unless the world agrees to his plans for world peace.

11 1. They are all about the build-up to or aftermath of atomic war. The first featured Harry Belafonte, Inger Stevens and Mel Ferrer as the three survivors of the holocaust. In the second, Ray Milland holed up in the hills after a sneak atomic attack on America, and ruthlessly defended his family. *Strangelove* detailed the irreversible tumble into total destruction brought about by psychotic Sterling Hayden's giving the secret GO code for a sneak attack on the Soviet Union.

2.   All are Disney productions.

3.   All three were directed by Robert Wise, as was *The Day the Earth Stood Still* (1951).

4.   They helped to earn director Roger Corman his 'King of the B's' title.

12   1.   It was made of material which would never wear out, thus threatening world economy.

2.   The cynical gods, looking down on the world, give one man the power to work miracles, and bet on the outcome.

3.   Unable to bear the strain of his newly-acquired power, he tears his eyes out at a prayer meeting when he hears the line 'If thine eye offend thee, pluck it out.' One of Roger Corman's better science fiction films.

4.   He regularly replaced an unspecified 'vital gland' which he obtained by murdering various donor-victims.

13   1.   It was evil Adam Hart's telepathic facility to attack the minds of those who tried to stop him. He also had powers over inanimate objects, causing carousels to speed up and doors to melt into the walls.

2.   They were monster ants, mutants from A-bomb testing, breeding in the desert.

3.   The brain of a dead, ruthless millionaire, kept alive in the laboratory. It gradually took over the scientist who was keeping it.

4.   The ignition temperature of paper, obviously important to the film's book-burning futuristic society.

5.   A vegetable humanoid (played by James Arness), found in an ice block in the Arctic wastes after the landing of an alien saucer.

6. A ferocious poisoned fungus that almost got Steve McQueen.

7. An alien element, carried to earth on a meteorite, turns people to stone. The *Monsters* were crashing crystalline monoliths which advanced on the world and threatened to destroy it.

8. A group of children treated with massive doses of radiation to enable them to survive the coming holocaust, living in a specially-built automated bunker.

15   Miscellaneous

It is impossible to categorize some films, but many which don't fit into any particular genre are too important to omit.*

Sex and Social Comment

1   The movies have generally kept clear of social problems, although a few have given serious treatment to social evils. What problem was tackled by each of these?
1. *Storm Warning* (1951)
2. *The Ox Bow Incident* (1943)
3. *Dead End* (1937)
4. *Castle on the Hudson* (1940)
5. *Tobacco Road* (1941)
6. *The Lost Weekend* (1945)
7. *Pinky* (1949)
8. *The Snake Pit* (1948)
9. *The Whistle at Eaton Falls* (1951)
10. *Gentleman's Agreement* (1947)
11. *Victim* (1961)
12. *The Whisperers* (1967)
13. *Trash* (1970)
14. *In Cold Blood* (1967)

2   Homosexuality has become an acceptable and even fashionable subject in recent years. In which films did these well-known actors play homosexual characters?
1. Laurence Olivier
2. Robert Redford
3. Rod Steiger

* Answers on page 254.

4. Rex Harrison
5. Marlon Brando
6. Richard Burton
7. Paul Newman
8. Anthony Hopkins
9. Don Murray

3 What former screen taboo was featured in each of the following groups of films?

1. *A House is Not a Home* (1964)
   Ulysses (1967)
   The Balcony (1964)

2. *Walk on the Wild Side* (1962)
   The Group (1965)
   The Haunting (1963)

3. *Peyton Place* (1957)
   Anatomy of a Murder (1959)
   Johnny Belinda (1948)

4. *The Damned* (1969)
   Dearest Love (1971)
   My Sister My Love (1965)

4 Prostitutes have been in the movies almost from the beginning, but only recently have the euphemisms been abandoned. All these leading ladies have played hookers at some time. Can you remember the films?

1. Gloria Swanson (1929)
2. Joan Crawford (1932)
3. Rita Hayworth (1956)
4. Marlene Dietrich (1931, 1932, 1939, 1957, 1958)
5. Vivien Leigh (1940)
6. Joan Bennett (1941)
7. Elizabeth Taylor (1960)
8. Bette Davis (1934, 1937)

241

9. Melina Mercouri (1960)
10. Sophia Loren (1966)

Children and Animals

From Walt Disney and Shirley Temple to Hayley Mills and
Elsa, children and animals have always been sure box-office.

5   1.   Shirley Temple, the biggest child star, was the first to
capitalize on Hollywood's shift from realism (sex and
violence) to family pictures. She quickly eclipsed stars like
Garbo and Gaynor, and between 1934 and 1940 made
eighteen pictures, six in 1935 alone.

    a. Seven of the eighteen films featured the word 'little' in
the title. How many can you remember?

    b. Two of her best-known songs were 'On the Good Ship
Lollipop' and 'Animal Crackers in my Soup'. In which
films did she sing them?

2.   Margaret O'Brien was second only to Shirley Temple.
Both began their careers at four years of age, but Miss
O'Brien made fewer pictures – fifteen between 1940 and
1950. Two of her best were *Meet Me in St Louis* (1944)
and *Little Women* (1949). Which characters did she play in
these films, and who played her sisters in each?

3.   An English child star of the forties, whose better-
known films include *How Green was my Valley* and *Man
Hunt* (both 1941) and several movies with animals, still
appears in films (*Inside Daisy Clover*, 1966; *Planet of the
Apes*, 1967; *The Poseidon Adventure*, 1972), is an outstanding photographer (stills from *Cleopatra*, 1962, in which he
also appeared), and has recently turned director. Who is he?

6   Who played
1.   *Tom Sawyer* (1929)?
2.   *The Elephant Boy* (1937)?
3.   *David Copperfield* (1934)?

4. *Oliver Twist* (1948)?
5. *Little Lord Fauntleroy* (1921)?

7   The children pictured here were all well-known child stars. Who are they?

8 *The Wizard of Oz* (1939) is one of the greatest children's pictures. In it, who played:

> Dorothy?
> The Scarecrow?
> The Tin Woodman?
> The Cowardly Lion?
> The Wizard of Oz?

9 Recently, there has been a trend to more believable children in movies, who frequently find themselves in conflict with the adult world.

1. Who played Helen Keller in *The Miracle Worker* (1962), and who played the title role?

2. Who played the three children in *To Kill a Mocking-bird* (1963)?

3. Who were the notable child stars of *Whistle Down the Wind* (1961), what were they up to, and with whom?

4. Who played the most homicidal child on film, and in what movie?

5. Who were *The Railway Children* (1971)?

10 1. The pairing of children and animals has not always produced a saccharine film. Who are these four actors, and in which films did these pairs co-star?

a   b

2.   Cartoon animals have been the most popular fauna on the screen. Disney's Mickey Mouse was the first cartoon superstar, and from him evolved a long line of fantastic creations. Here are some lesser-known cartoon animals. Who are they?

What were the feature films in which they appeared?

© Walt Disney Productions

11   Teenagers have received less attention from film-makers, perhaps because they are less good box-office material.

1.   Andy Hardy was the glamorized and sentimentalized hero of small-town America. Who played him in all fifteen *Andy Hardy* movies?
Who were the five women in his life in *Love Finds Andy Hardy* (1938)?

2.   Who was the adolescent singing star of *100 Men and a Girl* (1937) whose '... pure sweet soprano enthralled the nation and helped bring serious music much closer to public acceptance ...'?

3.   Teenage star Natalie Wood made a film about adolescents and their problems in 1955. What was the film? Who were her two male co-stars?

4.   Who were the Australian teenagers in *Walkabout* (1971)?

5.   What do actors Gary Grimes, Leonard Whiting and Timothy Bottoms have in common?

Schooldays

12 1. Who were the threatened teachers, and who their tormentors, in:
   a. *Term of Trial* (1962)?
   b. *Blackboard Jungle* (1955)?
   c. *Unman, Wittering and Zigo* (1971)?
   d. *The Prime of Miss Jean Brodie* (1969)?
   e. *The Children's Hour* [*The Loudest Whisper*] (1962)?

2. What film ended in a battle in which three English public schoolboys shot up their teachers, fellows and guests? Who played the rebels driven to violence?

3. Who were the schoolboys who ran wild in 1964? In what film?

Religion on the Screen

13 1. Priests and ministers have attracted film-makers to make much of the conflict between God and the World, the Flesh and the Devil. Who played the principal clerics in:
   a. *The Bishop's Wife* (1947)?
   b. *The Left Hand of God* (1955)?
   c. *The Christian* (1923)?
   d. *Heavens Above* (1963)?
   e. *Leon Morin, Priest* (1961)?
   f. *Fighting Father Dunne* (1947)?
   g. *The Keys of the Kingdom* (1944)?
   h. *The Night of the Hunter* (1955)?
   i. *Going My Way* (1944)?

2. Match these actor-priests with the correct film title.
   a. John Mills   *Father Brown* (1954)
   b. Frank Sinatra   *The Fugitive* (1947)
   c. Richard Burton   *The Men of Boys' Town* (1941)
   d. Karl Malden   *The Singer Not the Song* (1960)
   e. Henry Fonda   *The Miracle of the Bells* (1948)
   f. Alec Guinness   *I Confess* (1953)

g. Spencer Tracy   *The Night of the Iguana* (1964)
h. Montgomery Clift   *On the Waterfront* (1954)

3. Many Roman Catholic actor-priests have set their sights on the Head Office.

a. —— —— played the Pope in *The Agony and the Ecstasy* (1965).

b. —— —— played Cardinal Wolsey in *A Man for All Seasons* (1966).

c. —— —— played the Bishop of London in *Becket* (1964).

d. —— —— was the Pope in *The Shoes of the Fisherman* (1970).

e. —— —— played the Archbishop of Canterbury in *Becket* (1964).

f. —— —— played a cardinal in *The Shoes of the Fisherman* (1970), and was also called upon to intervene in *Becket*'s problems.

g. —— —— played the title role in *The Cardinal* (1963); —— —— played his cardinal-mentor, and —— —— was the failed parish priest.

14 Nuns have also decorated many films, although they are often ridiculed or sentimentalized out of recognition.

1. Who was the strong-willed nun that Robert Mitchum tangled with in 1956?

2. Who was *The Singing Nun* (1966)?

3. In *The Song of Bernadette*, who played the title role, and who was the principal nun?

4. In what film did Audrey Hepburn play a nun, and who were the well-known faces playing the other nuns in the same film?

5. In what film did Vanessa Redgrave play a nun?

6. Who played the two nuns who gave Hugh Marlowe a hard time in *Come to the Stable* (1949)?

7. What actress played a prostitute who disguised herself as a nun?

8.   Who played the Mother Superior, and who the novice, in *Conspiracy of Hearts* (1960)?

9.   Who is the well-known singing voice (of Deborah Kerr in *The King and I* in 1956, of Natalie Wood in *West Side Story* in 1961, of Audrey Hepburn in *My Fair Lady* in 1964, and countless others) whose only screen appearance has been as a nun?

10. Who played *Sister Kenny* (1946)?

Screen Biographies

Biopics have been numerous, entertaining, usually wildly inaccurate and, in the end, had a definite sameness about them.

15   Who are the characters portrayed here, and who is the actor playing each?

16 Painters: who were they in these films, and who played them?
1. *The Agony and the Ecstasy* (1965)
2. *Lust for Life* (1956)
3. *The Moon and Sixpence* (1942)
4. *Moulin Rouge* (1953)
5. *The Naked Maja* (1959)
6. *Montparnasse 19* (1957)

17 Composers: who played these, and in what films?
1. Handel (1942)
2. Beethoven (1960)
3. Schubert (1934)
4. Robert and Clara Schumann (1947)
5. Rimsky-Korsakov (1947)
6. Wagner (1956)
7. Liszt (1960)

18 Scientists and inventors: which ones were played by these actors?
1. Edward G. Robinson (1940; 1941)
2. Mickey Rooney (1940)
3. Spencer Tracy (1940)
4. Don Ameche (1939)
5. Paul Muni (1936)

19 Politicians. They are usually treated with a reverence bordering on the ludicrous (unless they are the villains). Who were the actors who played these political leaders?
What are the titles of the films?
1. Pitt the Younger (1942)
2. William Gladstone (1966)
3. John F. Kennedy (1963)
4. Woodrow Wilson (1944)
5. Horatio Nelson (1926; 1942; 1968)
6. The Duke of Wellington (1969)
7. Winston Churchill (1972)

8. Adolf Hitler (1961)
9. William Jennings Bryan (1960)
10. Franklin Delano Roosevelt (1960)
11. Andrew Jackson (1953)

20 Writers: which ones were portrayed by these actors?
What are the titles of the films?
1. Gregory Peck (1959)
2. Dennis Price (1948)
3. Paul Muni (1937)
4. Robert Morley (1960)
5. Peter Finch (1960)
6. Olivia de Havilland, Ida Lupino, Nancy Coleman, Arthur Kennedy and Sidney Greenstreet (1943)
7. Danny Kaye (1952)
8. Fredric March and Norma Shearer (1934)

Miscellaneous – Answers

Sex and Social Comment

1

1. The Ku Klux Klan. Other films which have attacked the Klan include *The Burning Cross* (1947), *The FBI Story* (1959) and *The Cardinal* (1963). *Birth of a Nation* (1914) is the only film to have given the Klan sympathetic treatment.

2. Lynch law. Also attacked in *Fury* (1936), *They Won't Forget* (1937) and *The Sound of Fury* (1950).

3. Juvenile delinquency. This film introduced the Dead End Kids. In sequels (*Angels with Dirty Faces*, 1938), the Kids turned to comedy, giving rise to the later Bowery Boys spin-off series.

4. Prison reform, as did films like *Each Dawn I Die* (1939) and *Riot in Cell Block 11* (1954).

5. Like *The Grapes of Wrath* (1939), another John Ford film about the plight of the destitute farmers of the Depression.

6. Alcoholism. Ray Milland won an Academy Award for his performance. Other notable film alcoholics: Frank Sinatra (*The Joker is Wild*, 1958), Lee Remick and Jack Lemmon (*Days of Wine and Roses*, 1963) and Susan Hayward (*I'll Cry Tomorrow*, 1956).

7. Race relations. Jeanne Crain played the black who could pass for white, but found herself cut off from both. Most such films are naïve (*Cry the Beloved Country*, 1952; *Guess Who's Coming to Dinner*, 1967). The best have been those treating the subject obliquely (*A Patch of Blue*, 1965; *In the Heat of the Night*, 1967).

8. Mental illness, and the horrors of mental hospitals. Olivia de Havilland won an Academy Award for this film, as did Joanne Woodward for her schizophrenic in *The Three Faces of Eve* (1957).

9. Organized labour and labour relations. Not a gripping subject for film-makers, rarely tackled (*The Organizer*, 1965; *The Molly Maguires*, 1970). The most effective of the type was a comedy, *I'm All Right, Jack* (1959).

10. Anti-semitism. Probably the most effective of many such, including *The Wandering Jew* (1933); *Jude Süss* (1934); *The Great Dictator* (1939); *The Diary of Anne Frank* (1959); *I am a Camera* (1955) and its cousin *Cabaret* (1972).

11. Homosexuality and accompanying blackmail. With Dirk Bogarde as the trapped, ambivalent barrister and Peter McEnery as the young man driven to suicide.

12. The problems of destitute old age. Edith Evans gave an outstanding performance in this film written and directed by Bryan Forbes.

13. Drug addiction. One of the controversial Warhol films, less effective than Roger Corman's *The Trip* (1967). Both are difficult to see in Britain.

14. Capital punishment. More popular, but less effective, was *I Want to Live* (1955), with an Academy Award-winning performance from Susan Hayward.

2 1. *Spartacus* (1960), in which there is an implied relationship between Olivier and his body-servant Tony Curtis. Apparently the more explicit references were written out of the script.

2. *Inside Daisy Clover* (1966), in which Redford plays the young actor who marries adolescent star Natalie Wood but runs out on her on the wedding night. Certain references

in the film indicated that some sort of relationship between Redford and Roddy McDowall had been intended.

3.   *The Sergeant* (1968), with Steiger in the title role as an officer who had a hang-up about one of his enlisted men, John Philip Law. Being queer was Steiger's less important problem in *No Way to Treat a Lady* (1968).

4.   Rex Harrison played one of the two unhappy queens in the film version of Charles Dyer's *Staircase* (1969).

5.   Marlon Brando played another army officer in pursuit of an enlisted man, who was more interested in Brando's wife, Elizabeth Taylor, in *Reflections in a Golden Eye* (1967).

6.   In 1969, he played Rex Harrison's other half in *Staircase*. This was subsequently followed by another invert role, this time in *Villain* (1971).

7.   *Cat on a Hot Tin Roof* (1958) was one of the first films to come close to admitting that homosexuality existed, although Newman's supposed relationship with his football-playing buddy who committed suicide is never made explicit.

8.   The future King Richard, he is alleged to be bisexual in *The Lion in Winter* (1968). Certainly father Henry II (Peter O'Toole) and mother Eleanor of Aquitaine (Katharine Hepburn) could be expected to have sons with problems.

9.   Don Murray played the Senator who committed suicide when a colleague tried to blackmail him by threatening to expose a homosexual relationship in his past, in *Advise and Consent* (1961).

3   1.   All three of them involved brothels of one sort or another, two of them (*A House is Not a Home* and *The Balcony*) housing Shelley Winters.

2. All of them contained implied if not explicit lesbian relationships. *Walk on the Wild Side* was also set in a brothel.

3. All of them involved rape. *Johnny Belinda* was the first to break the Hollywood taboo on the subject.

4. Incest was a topic in each of them: brother-sister in two, and mother-son (*Dearest Love*) in the other.

4 1, 2 and 3:   All three of these ladies have played Somerset Maugham's Sadie Thompson, in *Rain* (1929, the original title), *Sadie Thompson* (1932) and *Miss Sadie Thompson* (1956) respectively.

4. Dietrich has played hookers on at least five occasions: *Dishonoured* (1931), *Shanghai Express* (1932), *Destry Rides Again* (1939), *Witness for the Prosecution* (1957) and *A Touch of Evil* (1958, as a madam).

5. *Waterloo Bridge*
6. *Man Hunt*
7. *Butterfield 8*
8. *Of Human Bondage* (1934) and *Marked Woman* (1937)
9. *Never on Sunday*
10. *Lady L*

Children and Animals

5 1. a. *Little Miss Marker* (1934); *The Little Colonel* (1935); *Our Little Girl* (1935); *The Littlest Rebel* (1935); *Poor Little Rich Girl* (1936); *Little Miss Broadway* (1938); *The Little Princess* (1939). There was also *Wee Willie Winkie* (1937).

   b. *Bright Eyes* and *Curly Top* (both 1935), respectively.

2. *Meet Me in St Louis:* Tootie, loveable kid sister of Judy Garland, Louise Bremer and Joan Carroll.
Little Women: Beth (naturally), with sisters Janet Leigh, June Allyson and Elizabeth Taylor.

3. Roddy McDowall

6 1. Jackie Coogan. The part has also been played by Jack Pickford (1917) and Tommy Kelly (1938). Tom Sawyer has also been an integral part in the four (at least) versions of *Huckleberry Finn* (1919, 1931, 1939 and 1960).

2. Sabu, the Indian actor discovered by Robert Flaherty, who made several other films for the Korda brothers, in Britain and later in Hollywood: *The Drum* (1938), *The Thief of Baghdad* (1940), *The Jungle Book* (1942).

3. Freddie Bartholomew, the most successful British child actor of the thirties. Frank Lawton played the adult David. Alistair Mackenzie and Robin Phillips played the two Davids in the 1970 re-make.

4. John Howard Davies, who also made a version of *Tom Brown's Schooldays* in 1951.

5. Mary Pickford, in drag.

7 1. Bobby Driscoll, a well-known child actor of the forties and early fifties, one of the Disney stable, Academy Award winner (1949), here in one of his best roles, Jim Hawkins in Disney's *Treasure Island* (1950).

2. Jean Simmons in her best-known role as a child actress, as Estella in David Lean's *Great Expectations* (1946). She began in films in 1943, but quickly moved to older parts (*Hamlet*, 1948), and has tended to be cast in a variety of big-budget films: *The Robe* (1953); *Guys and Dolls* (1956); *The Big Country* (1957); *Spartacus* (1960), and many others.

3. Natalie Wood, here in *Father was a Fullback* (1949), who started in films at the age of five (*Happy Land*, 1943) and is still going strong.

4. Freddie Bartholomew, best known for his *David Copperfield* (1934), also appeared in many other films in the late thirties and early forties, including *Anna Karenina* (1935), *Tom Brown's Schooldays* (1939), *The Boy from Barnardo's* (1939) and *Swiss Family Robinson* (1940).

8   Judy Garland was Dorothy. The others were, respectively, Ray Bolger, Jack Haley, Bert Lahr and Frank Morgan, all in dual roles.

9   1.   Patty Duke, playing opposite Anne Bancroft as teacher Annie Sullivan. Both won Academy Awards for their performances.
2.   The leading children were Mary Badham as Scout and Philip Alford as Jem, with John Megna.
3.   The lead was Hayley Mills, then just beginning her career as the most successful child star of recent years. But in this film she was definitely outshone by Alan Barnes, who played her younger brother. They were helping to hide escaped convict Alan Bates, who they were convinced was Jesus in his second coming.
4.   Patty McCormack, in *The Bad Seed* (1956), as the child who managed to eliminate all those who opposed her. In the film, she wasn't allowed to get away with it, as she had been on stage: she was struck down by a bolt of lightning at the end.
5.   They were Jenny Agutter, Sally Thomsett and Gary Warren as the intrepid Edwardians who set out to prove their father's innocence.

10   1.   a. Kevin Corcoran, as a 'typical' Disney American boy, with *Old Yeller* (1957).
b. Dai (David) Bradley with *Kes* (1969), the most recent, and certainly one of the best, of the children-and-animals genre.
c. Elizabeth Taylor and The Pie in *National Velvet* (1944), which many consider her best film.
d. Roddy McDowall with Flicka in *My Friend Flicka* (1943). In the same year he starred in the archetypal boy-meets-dog film, *Lassie Come Home*, which also featured Elizabeth Taylor.

2.   a. Timothy Q. Mouse, a friend of *Dumbo* (1941), here

seen scrubbing the hero. Timothy later becomes Dumbo's business manager.

b. Napoleon, the dictatorial pig, from the Halas and Batchelor cartoon version of George Orwell's *Animal Farm*, a first-rate adaptation, and one of the very few non-American feature cartoons.

c. Gertie the Dinosaur, the star of a number of very early cartoons. Gertie's first appearance was in 1909, and she is reputed to be the first of the cartoon stars.

d. Flower, the amorous skunk, in *Bambi* (1943). He later settles down with his lady, and they subsequently have a son.

11 1. Mickey Rooney, from 1937 to 1947. There was also an unsuccessful comeback attempt (*Andy Hardy Comes Home*) in 1958.
The ladies were Fay Holden (his mother), Cecilia Parker (his sister) and Ann Rutherford, Lana Turner and Judy Garland. A purist might also include Sara Haden (his aunt).

2. Deanna Durbin, who made nineteen musicals in eleven years (from 1937), but who gradually dropped out as the musical began to change in the mid-forties. Her co-star was Leopold Stokowski and the 100 men were, of course, the members of a symphony orchestra.

3. The film was *Rebel Without a Cause*, and her co-stars were James Dean and Sal Mineo.

4. They were Jenny Agutter and David Gumpilil, accompanied by Lucien John.

5. All three have recently played teenage boys who have been involved with older women: Gary Grimes with Jennifer O'Neill in *Summer of '42* (1971), Leonard Whiting with Jean Simmons in *Say Hello to Yesterday* (1970), Timothy Bottoms with Cloris Leachman in *The Last Picture Show* (1971), and with Maggie Smith in *Love and Pain and The Whole Damn Thing* (1972).

12　1.　a. Laurence Olivier was the teacher accused of rape by Sarah Miles. Terence Stamp played her boyfriend and fellow-tormentor, and Simone Signoret was Olivier's doubting, mocking wife.

b. Glenn Ford was the threatened teacher in a slum high school in Brooklyn who rescued fellow-teacher Margaret Hayes from rape in the library. The local juvenile delinquents included Vic Morrow, Sidney Poitier and James Drury. Poitier was on the other side in *To Sir With Love* (1967).

c. David Hemmings was the new recruit with a passion to teach who was put in charge of the murderous Lower Five B. Michael Howe was Unman, Colin Barrie was Wittering and Zigo was absent.

d. Maggie Smith was the high-principled, undoubting, unseeing Miss Brodie who was eventually 'betrayed' to headmistress Celia Johnson by Pamela Franklin. The other girls of the 'Brodie Set' were Jane Carr, Diane Grayson and Shirley Steedman.

e. This adaptation of Lillian Hellman's play was first filmed as *These Three* by William Wyler in 1936. The story, about a charge of lesbianism levelled at two teachers who ran a private girls' school, was emasculated for the censors of the thirties, and given a happy ending. When Wyler re-made it in 1962, he stuck to the original story: Shirley MacLaine committed suicide and Audrey Hepburn didn't get James Garner. Miriam Hopkins, who played the Hepburn part in the original, was in the re-make, this time as the empty-headed aunt of Shirley MacLaine.

2.　The film was Lindsay Anderson's *If . . .* (1968). The 'Crusaders' were played by Malcolm McDowell, David Wood and Richard Warwick, assisted by Christine Noonan and Rupert Webster.

3. The film was *Lord of the Flies*. The boys who reversed the evolutionary process were Tom Chapin as Jack and Roger Elwin as Roger, resisted by James Aubrey (Ralph), Hugh Edwards (Piggy) and Tom Gorman (Simon).

Religion on the Screen

13 1. a. David Niven. The title role was played by Loretta Young.
   b. Humphrey Bogart
   c. Richard Dix
   d. Peter Sellers and Ian Carmichael
   e. Jean-Paul Belmondo
   f. Pat O'Brien
   g. Gregory Peck
   h. Robert Mitchum
   i. Bing Crosby

2.
a.	John Mills	*The Singer Not the Song*
b.	Frank Sinatra	*The Miracle of the Bells*
c.	Richard Burton	*The Night of the Iguana*
d.	Karl Malden	*On the Waterfront*
e.	Henry Fonda	*The Fugitive*
f.	Alec Guinness	*Father Brown*
g.	Spencer Tracy	*The Men of Boys' Town*
h.	Montgomery Clift	*I Confess*

3. a. Rex Harrison
   b. Orson Welles
   c. Donald Wolfit
   d. Anthony Quinn (described by one critic as Zorba the Pope).
   e. Richard Burton
   f. John Gielgud; as Louis VII of France, he intervened between Henry II and Becket.
   g. Tom Tryon, John Huston and Burgess Meredith

14
1. Deborah Kerr in *Heaven Knows, Mr Allison*
2. Debbie Reynolds
3. Jennifer Jones and Gladys Cooper
4. *The Nun's Story* (1956), with Edith Evans, Peggy Ashcroft, Mildred Dunnock, Patricia Collinge, Rosalie Crutchley, Ruth White, Barbara O'Neal and Margaret Phillips.
5. *The Devils* (1971)
6. Celeste Holm and Loretta Young, typical glamorous nuns of the forties.
7. Shirley MacLaine, in *Two Mules for Sister Sara* (1971)
8. Lilli Palmer and Sylvia Syms
9. Marni Nixon, who was one of the singing nuns in *The Sound of Music* (1965).
10. Rosalind Russell

Screen Biographies

15
1. Greer Garson as *Madame Curie* (1943). Walter Pidgeon played her husband Pierre.
2. John Gielgud as Benjamin Disraeli in *The Prime Minister* (1940).
3. Charles Laughton as *Rembrandt* (1936)
4. Montgomery Clift as *Freud* (1963)

16
1. Michelangelo, played by Charlton Heston.
2. Van Gogh, played by Kirk Douglas, *and* Gauguin, played by Anthony Quinn.
3. Gauguin again (in Somerset Maugham's fictionalized version), played by George Sanders.
4. Toulouse-Lautrec, played by Jose Ferrer.
5. Goya, played by Anthony Franciosa.
6. Modigliani, played by Gerard Philipe.

17
1. Wilfred Lawson, in *The Great Mr Handel*
2. Carl Boehm, in *The Magnificent Rebel*
3. Richard Tauber, in *Blossom Time*

4. Paul Henried and Katharine Hepburn, in *Song of Love*. Also represented were Liszt (Henry Daniell) and Brahms (Robert Walker).

5. Jean-Pierre Aumont, in *Song of Scheherezade*

6. Alan Badel, in *Magic Fire*

7. Dirk Bogarde, in *Song Without End*

18 1. In 1940, he played the title role in *Dr Ehrlich's Magic Bullet*, in a very daring (for the time) story about the first man to discover a cure for syphilis. In 1941, he played the founder of Reuters press service, in *Dispatch From Reuters*.

2. *Young Tom Edison*

3. *Edison the Man*, in the second part of MGM's two-part biography, as it were.

4. The title role in *The Story of Alexander Graham Bell*

5. The title role in *The Story of Louis Pasteur*

19 1. He was played by Robert Donat, in *The Young Mr Pitt*.

2. Ralph Richardson, in *Khartoum*

3. Cliff Robertson, in *PT 109*

4. Alexander Knox, in *Wilson*

5. In 1926, the silent film *Nelson* starred Cedric Hardwicke; in 1942, Laurence Olivier played him in *Lady Hamilton* [*That Hamilton Woman*], with Vivien Leigh in the title role. The 1968 German re-make of *Lady Hamilton* starred Richard Johnson.

6. Christopher Plummer, in *Waterloo*

7. Simon Ward, in *Young Winston*

8. Richard Basehart in *Hitler*. Several others have played him as well, including Richard Watson (*The Hitler Gang*, 1944), who made numerous walk-on appearances as the Führer (mostly as gags) in films made during the Second World War.

9. Fredric March, in *Inherit the Wind*. Spencer Tracy played Clarence Darrow, the famous trial lawyer, in the same film. Orson Welles also played Darrow, in *Compulsion* (1958).

10. Ralph Bellamy, in *Sunrise at Campobello*. Greer Garson played Eleanor Roosevelt.

11. Charlton Heston, in *The President's Lady*. Susan Hayward was in the title role.

20 1. F. Scott Fitzgerald, in *Beloved Infidel*. Deborah Kerr played Sheilah Graham.

2. Byron, in *The Bad Lord Byron*

3. Emile Zola, in *The Life of Emile Zola*, the film that began the late thirties/early forties spate of biopics.

4. *Oscar Wilde*

5. Wilde again, in *The Trials of Oscar Wilde* [*The Green Carnation*]

6. The three ladies played the Brontë sisters (Charlotte, Emily and Anne respectively), Arthur Kennedy was Branwell Brontë and Sidney Greenstreet played Thackeray in *Devotion*.

7. *Hans Christian Andersen*

8. Robert Browning and Elizabeth Barrett in *The Barretts of Wimpole Street*.

16 Movie-Makers

This section is about those involved in movie-making who are not usually seen on the screen.*

1 Charles Chaplin directed all his feature films and appeared in all but one of them (*A Woman of Paris*, 1923). Similarly, many of the silent stars (Keaton, Laurel, von Stroheim and Lloyd) directed themselves, usually performing their own scripts. Alfred Hitchcock's appearances in his own films have become a tradition. But these are exceptions, and most directors never appear on the screen. Some other exceptions are listed below: can you name the films in which these well-known directors have appeared, and the directors for whom they were acting?

1. George Marshall (1937)
2. Samuel Fuller (1955)
3. Nicholas Ray (1962)
4. Mitchell Leisen (1941)
5. John Huston (1947)
6. Preston Sturges (1958)
7. Sam Peckinpah (1956)
8. Jules Dassin (1954)
9. Tony Richardson (1963)
10. Cecil B. de Mille (1950)
11. Jean Renoir (1939)
12. King Vidor (1933)
13. Jean Cocteau (1959)
14. Ingmar Bergman (1952)
15. Robert Aldrich (1955)

* Answers on page 273.

16. Claude Chabrol (1968)
17. William Castle (1968)
18. Joseph Losey (1956)
19. Otto Preminger (1943)
20. Roman Polanski (1967)
21. Federico Fellini (1948)

2 Considering the central role of the camera in film-making, the accolades which cinematographers receive seem altogether insignificant. The films listed below have all won Academy Awards for cinematography: who was the cinematographer for each one?

1. *Wuthering Heights* (1939)
2. *Gone With the Wind* (1939)
3. *Great Expectations* (1946)
4. *The Naked City* (1948)
5. *A Place in the Sun* (1951)
6. *The Rose Tattoo* (1954)
7. *Lawrence of Arabia* (1962)
8. *Who's Afraid of Virginia Woolf?* (1966)
9. *Ben Hur* (1959)
10. *Cleopatra* (1934 and 1963)
11. *Bonnie and Clyde* (1967)
12. *My Fair Lady* (1964)
13. *She Wore a Yellow Ribbon* (1949)
14. *To Catch a Thief* (1955)

In addition to these Award winners, three others must be included in any list of outstanding cinematographers. Who photographed:

15. *Birth of a Nation* (1914)?
16. *Ivan the Terrible* (1942 and 1946)?
17. *Jules et Jim* (1961)?

3 John Grierson is credited with coining the term 'documentary' in 1929, but many films of this type had been made earlier: Ponting's *With Scott to the Antarctic* (1912),

267

Lowell Thomas's *With Allenby in Palestine* (1919), Turin's *Turksib* (1928) and Eisenstein's *The General Line* (1928). Today many films are described as documentaries, and the styles developed by the early documentarists are used by television, advertising and feature films, frequently perverting the ideals of the pioneers in the field.

1. Robert Flaherty was the great original documentary film-maker, one of the earliest proponents of an uncompromising personal style of cinema. Between *Nanook of the North* (1922) and *Louisiana Story* (1948), he made three films in the South Pacific and two in the British Isles. What were the five titles?

2. Can you name any of the documentaries made by these directors who are better known for their feature films?
   a. Ernest B. Schoedsack
   b. John Huston
   c. William Wyler
   d. Frank Capra
   e. John Schlesinger
   f. Carol Reed
   g. Roy Boulting
   h. René Clement
   i. Alain Resnais

3. Only a few, but highly influential, men were behind the triumphant achievements of the documentary production units.* Who were the directors who made:
   a. *Drifters* (1929)?
   b. *Housing Problems* (1935)?
   c. *Coal Face* (1936)?
   d. *Shipyard* (1935)?
   e. *The Plow that Broke the Plains* (1936)?

* Such as the Empire Marketing Board, the Crown Film Unit, the Resettlement Administration film unit, the Ceylon Tea Propaganda Board, the GPO Film Unit and the National Film Board of Canada.

f. *Fires Were Started* (1943)?

g. *Zoo* (1962)?

4   There have been only a handful of women directors, although many women are involved in most other aspects of movie-making. At present, there are probably more female movie-makers than ever before. Who directed these films?

1. *Mädchen in Uniform* (1931)
2. *Das Blaue Licht* (1932)
3. *Dance, Girl, Dance* (1940)
4. *Hard, Fast and Beautiful* (1951)
5. *The Connection* (1960)
6. *Cleo de 5 à 7* (1962)
7. *Loving Couples* (1964)
8. *Rattle of a Simple Man* (1964)
9. *La Fiancée du Pirate* [*Dirty Mary*] (1969)
10. *Wanda* (1970)
11. *Three Lives* (1970)
12. *Le Fruit du Paradis* (1971)
13. *The Lenin Gang* (1972)
14. *A New Leaf* (1972)

5   One of the most regrettable and disgraceful episodes in the history of film-making was the persecution of any actors, directors, writers and others in Hollywood who were thought to be sympathetic to, or connected with, the Communist Party. Had Hollywood stood firm, the whole affair would probably have blown over, but financial backers began to panic and the owner-producers came forward with the 'Waldorf Declaration', stating that they would not employ anyone who refused to testify to the Un-American Activities Committee, in spite of the constitutional right so to refuse. Those who did not testify were thus blacklisted by their own industry; some were fined, and a few served prison sentences. Hundreds of others immediately joined the ranks of the unemployed. Those who were loyal to them received the same treatment.

The ten writers, producers and directors who went to prison became known as 'The Hollywood Ten', and it was many years before all of them were able to work again under their own names.

1. Who were the Hollywood Ten?
2. Which one of them eventually recanted?
3. Who were Joseph Walton, Andrea Forzano, Robert Rich, Derek Frye, Nathan Douglas, Hugh Baker and Victor Hanbury?
4. Who were the uncredited writers of:
   The Bridge on the River Kwai (1957)?
   Friendly Persuasion (1956)?
   Lawrence of Arabia (1962)?
5. What do you know about a film called *The Execution of Private Slovik*?

6   Screenwriters seem to come in two varieties. Well-known writers contribute the occasional screenplay, either an adaptation of one of their own novels or plays, or an original work for the movies. Others, whose names are less well known, have written many successful screenplays.
Who were the writers of the screenplays for these films?

1. *Hangmen Also Die* (1943)
2. *Marty* (1955)
3. *Darling* (1965)
4. *The Chase* (1966)
5. *It Happened One Night* (1934)
6. *The Country Girl* (1954)
7. *The Hunchback of Notre Dame* (1940)
8. *The VIPs* (1963)
9. *The Ladykillers* (1955)
10. *Rebecca* (1940)
11. *Zee and Co [X, Y and Zee]* (1971)
12. *The Grapes of Wrath* (1940)
13. *Viva Zapata* (1952)
14. *Tom Jones* (1963)
15. *The Seven Year Itch* (1955)

16. *High Noon* (1952)
17. *Spellbound* (1945)
18. *Born Yesterday* (1951)
19. *King Rat* (1965)
20. *The Servant* (1963)

7 Broadly speaking, there are three types of composers of film music: 'serious' composers, whose principal musical contributions have been in other spheres; 'popular' composers, who from time to time have written film scores or individual songs for non-musicals; and professional film composers, most of whose work has been for the movies. Who composed the score of each film listed here?

1. *Alexander Nevsky* (1939)
2. *On the Waterfront* (1954)
3. *The Grapes of Wrath* (1940)
4. *Breakfast at Tiffany's* (1961)
5. *War and Peace* (1964)
6. *Around the World in 80 Days* (1956)
7. *Pygmalion* (1938)
8. *Paris Blues* (1961)
9. *Dangerous Moonlight* (1940)
10. *To Kill a Mockingbird* (1962)
11. *Our Town* (1940)
12. *Irma la Douce* (1963)
13. *High Noon* (1952)
14. *Far from the Madding Crowd* (1967)
15. *As You Like It* (1936)
16. *Tom Jones* (1963)
17. *Don Quixote* (1933)
18. *Jules et Jim* (1961)
19. *Caesar and Cleopatra* (1945)
20. *The Bridge on the River Kwai* (1957)

8 A number of well-known actors have turned director, with varying degrees of success. What films were directed by the following actors in the years indicated?

1. Gene Kelly (1956)
2. Clive Brook (1943)
3. Marlon Brando (1960)
4. Clint Eastwood (1971)
5. Charles Laughton (1955)
6. Leslie Howard (1938)
7. Nigel Patrick (1961)
8. Bob Fosse (1972)
9. John Cassavetes (1970)
10. John Wayne (1960)
11. Cornel Wilde (1965)
12. Albert Finney (1967)
13. Laurence Olivier (1958)
14. Lionel Jeffries (1970)
15. Richard Attenborough (1972)
16. Orson Welles (1942)
17. Peter Sellers (1961)
18. James Cagney (1958)
19. Paul Newman (1968)
20. Peter Ustinov (1946)

Movie-Makers – Answers

1 Unless stated otherwise, each of these directors was appearing in his own film.

1. George Marshall appeared in *The Crime of Dr Forbes* in 1937.

2. Samuel Fuller played a Japanese policeman in *House of Bamboo* (1955).

3. Nicholas Ray played the American Ambassador in *55 Days at Peking* (1962).

4. Mitchell Leisen appeared briefly in *Hold Back the Dawn* in 1941.

5. John Huston has made many appearances. His first was in *The Treasure of the Sierra Madre* (1947), in which his father, Walter Huston, also featured, winning an Academy Award as Best Supporting Actor. John Huston's name did not appear among the acting credits, as in his later film *The List of Adrian Messenger* (1963), where he also made a brief appearance. However, he has played larger, credited, roles in Otto Preminger's *The Cardinal* (1963) and in his own *The Bible* (1966).

6. Preston Sturges's last film credit was as an actor, when he appeared with Bob Hope and Fernandel in *Paris Holiday* (1958), directed by Gerd Oswald. He also appeared in his own *Sullivan's Travels* (1942).

7. Sam Peckinpah was in Don Siegel's *Invasion of the Body Snatchers* (1956).

8. Jules Dassin has played major roles in two of his own films: *Rififi* (1954) and *Never on Sunday* (1963).

9. Tony Richardson made a brief appearance in *Tom Jones* (1963).

10. De Mille made several film appearances: he was in Billy Wilder's *Sunset Boulevard* (1950), in which he played him-

self, a role he also played in *Star-Spangled Rhythm* (1943) and *Variety Girl* (1947), both directed by George Marshall, and in Frank Tashlin's *Son of Paleface* (1952).

11. Jean Renoir was seen in *La Règle du Jeu* (1939).

12. King Vidor was in *Our Daily Bread* (1933), which he wrote, produced and directed.

13. Jean Cocteau appeared in *Le Testament d'Orphée* (1959) and also in its predecessor *Orphée* (1949), in which he played an old woman. He narrated the film version of his novel *Les Enfants Terribles* (1950), for which he also wrote the screenplay.

14. Ingmar Bergman appeared in one of his early films, *Waiting Women* (1952).

15. Robert Aldrich was in *The Big Knife* (1955).

16. Claude Chabrol appeared in two of his own films, both in 1968: *Les Biches* and *The Road to Corinth*.

17. William Castle was in Roman Polanski's *Rosemary's Baby* (1968). The film was produced by Castle.

18. Joseph Losey was in *Intimate Stranger* [*Finger of Guilt*] (1956).

19. Otto Preminger's 1943 appearance in his own *Margin for Error* had been preceded by one in *They Got Me Covered* (1942) for director David Butler. His best-known screen appearance was in Billy Wilder's *Stalag 17* (1953).

20. Roman Polanski featured in *The Fearless Vampire Killers* [*Dance of the Vampires*] (1967), and was also in Andrzej Wajda's *A Generation* (1954) and Joseph McGrath's *The Magic Christian* (1969).

21. Federico Fellini appeared in Roberto Rossellini's *L'Amore II: Il Miracolo* (1948), in which he co-starred with Anna Magnani.

2   1. Gregg Toland (1904–48), best remembered for his pioneering deep-focus photography for *Citizen Kane* (1941). His other notable films included *Roman Scandals* (1933), *These Three* (1936), *Dead End* (1937), the re-make of *Intermezzo* (1939) and *The Grapes of Wrath* (1940).

2.   Ernest Haller (1896–1970) and Ray Rennahan (1898–).   Haller was also responsible for *Jezebel* (1938), GWTW's contemporary rival, as well as *Saratoga Trunk* (1943), *Mildred Pierce* (1945) and *Whatever Happened to Baby Jane?* (1962), among many others. Rennahan shared another Academy Award (with Ernest Palmer) for *Blood and Sand* (1942), and his other films included *For Whom the Bell Tolls* (1943), *The Perils of Pauline* (1947) and *The Paleface* (1948).

3.   Guy Green (1913–), who worked on other films for director David Lean (*In Which We Serve*, 1942; *Oliver Twist*, 1948), as well as for other directors (*Captain Horatio Hornblower*, 1950; *The Beggar's Opera*, 1952), before turning director himself, where his work was less distinguished, but included *The Angry Silence* (1959) and *A Patch of Blue* (1966).

4.   William Daniels (1895–1970), who first worked with von Stroheim (*Foolish Wives*, 1921; *Greed*, 1923), then on several of the Garbo films (*Grand Hotel*, 1932; *Camille*, 1936; *Ninotchka*, 1939, and others), and who certainly kept up with the changing times in the cinema, with *Winchester 73* (1950), *Harvey* (1950), *Cat on a Hot Tin Roof* (1958) and *Valley of the Dolls* (1967), among many others.

5.   William Mellor (1904–63), who also shot other notable films of the fifties such as *Bad Day at Black Rock* (1954), *Giant* (1956) and *The Diary of Anne Frank* (1959).

6.   James Wong Howe (1899–), one of Hollywood's busiest and most versatile cameramen, who began in 1917, and whose works ranged from *Trail of the Lonesome Pine* (1922) through films like *Fire Over England* (1936) and *King's Row* (1941) to *Come Back Little Sheba* (1952), *Hud* (1962) and *Hombre* (1967).

7.   Freddie Young (1902–), one of Britain's most distinguished cinematographers, responsible for films such as

Goodbye Mr Chips (1939), *Ivanhoe* (1952), *Invitation to the Dance* (1956), and best known recently for his three films with David Lean for which he has won Academy Awards: *Lawrence of Arabia* (1962), *Dr Zhivago* (1965) and *Ryan's Daughter* (1970).

8. Haskell Wexler (1926–   ), who also shot *The Best Man* (1964), *In the Heat of the Night* (1967) and *The Thomas Crown Affair* (1968), the latter two for director Norman Jewison. He turned director with *Medium Cool* (1969), a film which questions some of the moral attitudes and ambivalences of a news cameraman.

9. Robert Surtees (1906–   ), who also won Awards for *King Solomon's Mines* (1950) and *The Bad and the Beautiful* (1952), and who shot *Intruder in the Dust* (1949), *Quo Vadis* (1951), *Oklahoma!* (1955), *Raintree County* (1957), *Mutiny on the Bounty* (1962), *The Collector* (1965) and *The Graduate* (1967), among many others.

10. The 1934 version was shot by Victor Milner (1893–   ), Paramount's leading cameraman of the thirties, who shot seven other films for de Mille, including *The Crusades* (1935), as well as *Love Me Tonight* (1932) for Rouben Mamoulian and *The Palm Beach Story* (1942) for Preston Sturges.
The 1963 re-make also won an Award, surely the only such coincidence of its kind, this time for Leon Shamroy (1901–   ), who has also won Academy Awards for *The Black Swan* (1942), *Wilson* (1944) and *Leave Her to Heaven* (1945). His other films include *The Robe* (1953), the first Cinemascope film, *The King and I* (1956), *South Pacific* (1958), *The Cardinal* (1963), *The Agony and the Ecstasy* (1965) and *Planet of the Apes* (1967). He photographed and acted in *Caprice* (1967).

11. Burnett Guffey (1905–   ), who won an Award for *From Here to Eternity* (1953), and who also shot *Foreign Correspondent* (1940), *Cover Girl* (1944), *All the King's*

Men (1949), *Birdman of Alcatraz* (1962), *King Rat* (1965) and *The Madwoman of Chaillot* (1969), among others.

12. Harry Stradling (1910–   ), Award-winner for *The Picture of Dorian Gray* (1944), and cinematographer for *La Kermesse Heroïque* (1935), *Pygmalion* (1938), *The Pirate* (1948), *Guys and Dolls* (1955), *Funny Girl* (1968), *Hello Dolly* (1969), and many others.

13. Winton C. Hoch (1908–   ), also a winner for *Joan of Arc* (1948, with Joseph Valentine and William V. Scall), and for another John Ford film, *The Quiet Man* (1952). He also shot *Mr Roberts* (1955), *The Searchers* (1956) and *Robinson Crusoe on Mars* (1964).

14. Robert Burks (1910–68), who photographed *Arsenic and Old Lace* (1944), *The Fountainhead* (1949) and *A Patch of Blue* (1966), as well as a number of Hitchcock films, including *Strangers on a Train* (1951), *I Confess* (1953), *Vertigo* (1958), *North by Northwest* (1959), *The Birds* (1963) and *Marnie* (1964).

15. Billy Bitzer (1874–1944), who was cameraman for Griffith on nearly all his major films, including *Judith of Bethulia* (1913), *Intolerance* (1915), *Hearts of the World* (1918) and *Way Down East* (1921), and who is credited with many basic cinematographic developments.

16. Edouard Tissé (1897–1961), from 1924 cameraman for Eisenstein: *Strike* (1924), *Battleship Potemkin* (1925), *Que Viva Mexico* (1934), *Alexander Nevsky* (1939) and many others.

17. Raoul Coutard (1924–   ), whose contribution to France's *nouvelle vague* must be as great as those of its better-known directors, as he shot most of the films associated with the term, including *A Bout de Souffle* (1959), *Tirez sur le Pianiste* (1960), *Vivre sa Vie* (1961), *La Peau Douce* (1963) and many others, especially for Truffaut and Godard.

3   1. His three films in the South Pacific were:

Moana (1926), made for Famous Players-Lasky (Paramount) in Samoa. It was subtitled *The Love Story of a South Seas Siren*, and the company arranged to have live hula dancers in the cinemas in which the film was first shown.

White Shadows in the South Seas (1927) was made for MGM in Tahiti. During this film Flaherty finally became fed up with working for the major companies, and he quit. The film was completed by W. S. van Dyke.*

Tabu (1934) was another Tahitian film, this one a tragic love story. The making of this film was marked by another head-on clash, this time between Flaherty, the explorer and observer, and his collaborator F. W. Murnau (of *Nosferatu* fame), the German sophisticate and expressionist.

In the British Isles Flaherty made:

Industrial Britain (1933), for John Grierson's Empire Marketing Board. Grierson, in his book *Grierson on Documentary*, is curiously reticent about this film, although he comments that '. . . the workers' portraits in *Industrial Britain* were cheered in the West End of London . . .'

Man of Aran (1934) was one of his most successful films. It was made for another major enterprise, Michael Balcon's Gaumont British. Grierson called it '. . . a simple account of dignity and bravery through the years . . .', but in order to sell it, Flaherty resorted to publicity tactics which eventually had an excited Edgware Road crowd clamouring for a lock of leading player Tiger King's hair.

2. a. Schoedsack, in collaboration with Merian C Cooper, produced two classics: *Grass* (1925), shot in north-west Persia, and *Chang* (1927), made in Siam and complete with climactic elephant stampede.

b. John Huston, having written *Sergeant York* (1941 and directed *The Maltese Falcon* (1941), moved on to

---

* MGM producer Hunt Stromberg is reported to have said at a productio meeting for this film, 'Say, boys, I've got a great idea – let's fill the screen with tits!

the Army Pictorial Service and produced many documentaries. The best remembered of these are *Report from the Aleutians* (1943), *The Battle of San Pietro* (1945) and *Let There Be Light* (1945).

c. William Wyler made two notable documentaries about the Second World War: *Memphis Belle* (1943), made for the United States Air Force, which brought home the realities of bombing raids, and *Fighting Lady* (1944), about combat on aircraft carriers.

d. Frank Capra, first a major, then a lieutenant-colonel in the Orientation Branch of the U.S. War Department, was the man principally responsible for the *Why We Fight* series of documentaries. The best of this series included three films made in 1943: *Prelude to War*, *The Nazis Strike* and *Divide and Conquer*. The latter two were made in association with Major Anatole Litvak.

e. John Schlesinger, a former TV director and actor, moved into films with his documentary *Terminus* (1960), a film about Waterloo Station.

f. Carol Reed's major documentary was *The True Glory* (1945), a huge Anglo-American undertaking which told the story of the liberation of Europe. His collaborator on this highly successful film was Garson Kanin.

g. In 1943, Roy Boulting made *Desert Victory*, about the 8th Army in North Africa, which was shot by battle cameramen.

h. René Clement's international reputation dates from another war documentary, one he made about railway sabotage in occupied France: *La Bataille du Rail* (1943).

i. In 1955, Alain Resnais made *Nuit et Brouillard*, a cool, retrospective look at the concentration camps.

3. a. *Drifters* was made by John Grierson who founded the GPO Film Unit in 1933, was responsible for the formation of the National Film Board of Canada during the period that he was Canadian Film Commissioner, and helped to draw public attention to some of the best documentaries through his television series of the fifties and sixties.

b. *Housing Problems* was made by Edgar Anstey and Arthur Elton. Anstey, who also made *Enough to Eat* (1936), was for many years head of the film unit at British Transport. Elton was a producer for outstanding documentary production units like the GPO Film Unit and the Shell Film Unit.

c. *Coal Face* was made by Brazilian director Alberto Cavalcanti. He began in Paris, making 'realistic' films, then moved to Britain to join the GPO Film Unit in the late thirties, next directed several features for Ealing Studios in the forties, none of which were particularly notable, and then returned to Brazil to make films there, as well as making the occasional movie in Italy.

d. *Shipyard* was made by Paul Rotha, again for the GPO Film Unit. Rotha later went independent, but has continued to make documentaries, and has written several books and articles on documentary film.

e. *The Plow that Broke the Plains* was made by Pare Lorentz, an American documentarist who is best known for this film and for *The River*, made the following year.

f. *Fires Were Started* was made by yet another GPO Film Unit director, Humphrey Jennings. It was about the work of the Auxiliary Fire Service in London during the Blitz, and Jennings is remembered for his films of this period, including *The First Days* (1939), *London Can Take It* (1940), *Listen to Britain* (1941)

The Silent Village (1943) and *A Diary for Timothy* (1945).

g. *Zoo* is probably the best internationally-known documentary of Dutch director Bert Haanstra, although some of his other documentaries have received attention abroad, including *Rembrandt, Painter of Man* (1956) and *The Human Dutch* (1964). He also directs feature films.

4

1. Leontine Sagan (1889–) grew up in Vienna and Johannesburg before going to Germany to study theatre. During the latter period she made this film about the conflict between affection and brutal discipline in a girls' school. She directed *Men of Tomorrow* (1932) in Britain, and then returned to South Africa to found its National Theatre.

2. Leni Riefenstahl (1902–) studied in Berlin, and became known as an actress, dancer and choreographer after studying with Max Reinhardt. She first appeared in films in 1926; this was her first film as director, and she acted in it as well. She is best remembered for her *Olympische Spiele* (1936), a documentary about the 1936 Olympic Games in Berlin, and for *Triumph of the Will* (1934).

3. Dorothy Arzner (1900–) began in the movie world as a waitress in her father's Hollywood café, which was frequented by the stars. She was an ambulance driver during the First World War, following which she got her first break when William de Mille gave her a job as a stenographer at Paramount. She worked her way up through the cutting rooms (*Blood and Sand*, 1922; *Covered Wagon*, 1923) to directing her first feature, *Fashions for Women*, in 1927. She was Hollywood's only woman director in the thirties, and her films included *The Wild Party* (1929), *Nana* (1935) and *The Bride Wore Red* (1937). She seems to have done little in the movies since the early forties.

4.   Ida Lupino (1918–   ) came from a London theatrical family; her father was comedian Stanley Lupino, and she was the cousin of comedian Lupino Lane. Allan Dwan gave her her first lead in 1932 (*Her First Affair*). She made four other films in England before going to Hollywood in 1934, where she made many films, including *Come On Marines* (1935), *They Drive by Night* (1940), *The Sea Wolf* (1941), *High Sierra* (1941) and *The Man I Love* (1946). She began writing and directing in 1950 with *The Outrage*, as well as continuing to act in other people's films (*The Big Knife*, 1955), and since the fifties has been Hollywood's almost only woman director. Her films include *The Hitch Hiker* (1953) and *The Trouble with Angels* (1966), and well as many films for TV.

5.   Shirley Clarke (1925–   ) was a dancer and choreographer, president of the National Dance Association of America, until going into the movies in 1953 (*Dance of the Sun*). *The Connection* was her first feature, and in the same year she founded (with Jonas Mekas) the New York Film Maker's Co-operative. Since then she has been principally involved in non-mainstream projects like an eleven-screen film for Expo 67 (*Man and the Polar Regions*) and underground features such as *Cool World* (1963) and *Portrait of Jason* (1967).

6.   Agnes Varda (1928–   ) was a professional photographer until she made *La Pointe Courte* (1954) with Alain Resnais. Since then she has made several features, including *Cleo*, *Le Bonheur* (1964) and *Lion's Love* (1969), and documentaries like *Salut les Cubains* (1963) and *Black Panthers* (1968).

7.   Mai Zetterling (1925–   ) first received attention as a director with the surprising debauchery of *Night Games* (1965), although it was her seventh film. *Loving Couples*, *The War Game* (1963) and four documentaries for the BBC had preceded it. She is probably best known as an actress.

She began in Swedish films and theatre in 1941, moving to Britain in 1947 where she appeared in many films including *The Bad Lord Byron* (1948), *Quartet* (1948), *The Ringer* (1953), *Knock on Wood* (1955) and *Only Two Can Play* (1961).

8. Muriel Box (1905–), wife of writer-producer-director Sidney Box and sister-in-law of producer Betty Box, is the principal British exponent of 'magazine fiction of the screen'. She began as Anthony Asquith's script girl in the twenties. She directed Service Training Films (with her husband) and graduated to writing (*The Seventh Veil*, 1947). Her other films include *Happy Family* (1952), *To Dorothy a Son* (1954), *The Passionate Stranger* (1956) and *Subway in the Sky* (1958).

9. Nelly Kaplan (1932–), originally from Argentina, works in France. Her varied career has embraced writing erotic novels (under the pseudonym 'Belène'), working with Abel Gance on the development of Polyvision and Magirama and making controversial shorts: *Gustave Moreau* (1963), *André Masson* (1964) and *Victor Hugo* (1966). Her latest feature is *Papa les Petits Bateaux* (1971).

10. Barbara Loden (1936–) worked hard at sorting herself out and becoming an actress, and was rewarded by being spotted by Arthur Miller when he was auditioning for the Broadway production of his *After the Fall*. The play was directed by Elia Kazan, who subsequently featured her in two of his films: *Wild River* (1960) and *Splendour in the Grass* (1961). She is now married to Kazan. Although she has certainly been influenced by his attitudes and style, *Wanda* (in which she also played the title role) is very much her own creation.

11. Kate Millett (1934–), scion of the American section of the Women's Liberation Movement, shot this documentary with active political purposes very much in mind, using an all-woman crew. This is her only film to date: she is

better known as the author of the best-selling *Sexual Politics*.

12. Vera Chytilova (1929–) is a graduate of the Czech film school FAMU, where she made *The Ceiling* (1960), an autobiographical film based on her experiences as a model. Since then she has directed some startling films about women, including *Something Different* (1963), a comparison of the stresses in the lives of an ordinary housewife and an Olympic lady gymnast, and the prizewinning *Daisies* (1965).

13. Kirsten Stenbaek (1922–) was a painter and theatre designer in her native Denmark (where she developed the idea of 'collage theatre') before turning to film directing in 1966 with *The Dreamers*. Noted for her freshness and anarchy, her other films include *Le Danois Extravagant* (1968) and *Do You Believe in Witches?* (1969). *The Lenin Gang* was a parody of Russia's October Revolution.

14. Elaine May, wife and former partner of Mike Nichols, also starred in this, her first film, a gentle comedy and a considerable achievement. Her second, *The Heartbreak Kid* (1972), is even better.

5

1. The Hollywood Ten were Alvah Bessie, Herbert Bieberman, Lester Cole, Edward Dmytryk, Ring Lardner Jr, John Howard Lawson, Albert Maltz, Sam Ornitz, Adrian Scott and Dalton Trumbo.

2. Edward Dmytryk was one of several names given to the Committee by director Sam Wood, then president of the right-wing Motion Picture Alliance for the Preservation of American Ideals. Dmytryk refused to testify, was cited for contempt of Congress and fired by RKO. He left the United States for England, where he made three pictures (*So Well Remembered*, 1947; *Obsession*, 1948; *Give Us This Day*, 1949), but was forced to return to America for passport renewal. While there he was formally charged, tried, fined

$1,000 and sentenced to six months in prison. In 1951, he appeared before the Committee once again, and this time he did testify about his former political affiliations.

3. All were pseudonyms used by various blacklisted directors and writers, which allowed them to continue to work, although not in the United States for some time.

'Joseph Walton' was the name used by Joseph Losey when he made *The Intimate Stranger* [*Finger of Guilt*] in 1956. He made several other films in Britain in the fifties (*Stranger on the Prowl*, 1953; *The Sleeping Tiger*, 1954; *Blind Date*, 1959), and in spite of the lifting of the Hollywood restrictions, has remained there and made several outstanding films, among them *The Servant* (1963), *King and Country* (1964), *Accident* (1967), *Figures in a Landscape* (1970) and *The Go-Between* (1971).

'Andrea Forzano' was really Ben Barzman, another writer who left the United States and moved to Europe. *Stranger on the Prowl* (1952) was the first film to use this pseudonym. His earlier collaboration with Losey (*The Boy with Green Hair*, 1948) was continued with *Time Without Pity* (1957) and *Blind Date* (1959); he also wrote *He Who Must Die* (1956) for fellow exile Jules Dassin. His subsequent scripts, including *The Fall of the Roman Empire* (1963), on which he collaborated, *The Heroes of Telemark* (1965) and *The Blue Max* (1966) were released with his own name on the credits.

'Robert Rich' was the winner of an Academy Award in 1956 for the script of *The Brave One*. In fact the writer was Dalton Trumbo. The blacklist began to lose its force in the late fifties, as the power of the studios declined and independent producers began to control their own work. One of the first major blows against it was Otto Preminger's hiring of Trumbo to write the script of *Exodus* (1960), for which Trumbo also received screen credit. His other scripts have included *Spartacus* (1960), *The Sandpiper* (1965), *Hawaii* (1966) and *The Fixer* (1968).

'Derek Frye' was really Carl Foreman, another blacklisted writer-director. He had previously collaborated with Stanley Kubrick, but Kubrick repudiated him at the time of his blacklisting. Foreman went to Britain, where he worked with Losey on *The Sleeping Tiger* (1954). In the sixties he began to produce and direct, as well as continuing to write screenplays. In 1968 he was elected president of the Writer's Guild of Great Britain, was awarded a CBE in 1970, and is a former governor of the British Film Institute.

'Nathan Douglas' was the nom-de-film of blacklisted actor-writer Ned Young. In 1958 he won an Academy Award (as Nathan Douglas) for his script of *The Defiant Ones*, which he wrote with Harold Jacob Smith.

'Hugh Baker' was the pseudonym used by director Cy Endfield, another to move to Britain in the fifties. He was also known as Cyril Endfield and C. Raker Endfield. Most of his output was not particularly notable (*Tarzan's Savage Fury*, 1952; *Hell Drivers*, 1957; *Mysterious Island*, 1961) until he formed a production company with actor-director Stanley Baker, which was responsible for *Zulu* (1964) and *Sands of the Kalahari* (1965).

'Victor Hanbury' was another of Joseph Losey's pseudonyms, used for *The Sleeping Tiger* (1954), scripted by 'Derek Frye'.

4.   All three of these films are connected with Michael Wilson, another writer who appeared before the Committee and who was subsequently blacklisted. Previously he had scripted *Five Fingers* (1952) and had won an Academy Award for *A Place in the Sun* (1952). He received no credit for his work on *Friendly Persuasion*, and neither he nor

collaborator Carl Foreman received any credit for *The Bridge on the River Kwai*; in fact the credits for the latter implied that Pierre Boule, author of the original story, had written the screenplay; Boule subsequently accepted an Academy Award for it. Wilson also collaborated on the script for *Lawrence of Arabia*, but again was not credited for his work. More recently, he has received credit for his work on *The Sandpiper* (1965), *Planet of the Apes* (1968) and *Che* (1969), all collaborative ventures.

5.   In 1960, Frank Sinatra announced his intention to produce *The Execution of Private Slovik*. He hired black-listed writer Albert Maltz to write the screenplay, about the only American GI to be shot for desertion during the Second World War. Right-wing America, notably the Hearst press, John Wayne and Ward Bond, denounced Sinatra, who stood his ground and maintained his right to hire the best man for the job. The pressure on Sinatra increased, and several of Sinatra's friends lost their television sponsors. Finally, he was forced to back down, and made a financial settlement with Maltz. The picture never got made, but two years later, Sinatra's recording of 'Have Yourself a Merry Little Christmas' was used as background music for the execution of an American deserter during the Second World War in *The Victors* (1962), written, produced and directed by Carl Foreman.

6   1.   Bertolt Brecht wrote it, and Fritz Lang directed it. Earlier, Pabst had filmed Brecht's own adaptation of his *Threepenny Opera* (1931), and two of Brecht's stage plays have been filmed: *The Mother* (1958) and *Mother Courage* (1960); both of these were records of stage productions by the Berliner Ensemble, the company which Brecht founded.

2.   Paddy Chayefsky, who won an Academy Award for this adaptation of his own play for television. His other works for the screen include *The Goddess* (1957), *A Catered Affair* (1959, with Gore Vidal), *The*

Americanization of Emily (1964), *Paint Your Wagon* (1969) and *The Hospital* (1972).

3. Frederic Raphael, another screenplay which won an Academy Award. His other scripts include *Nothing but the Best* (1964), *Two for the Road* (1967) and *Far from the Madding Crowd* (1967).

4. Lillian Hellman, better known for her adaptations of her own stage plays (*These Three*, 1936, and its re-make *The Children's Hour* [*The Loudest Whisper*] 1962; *Toys in the Attic*, 1963). Her other original screenplays include *Watch on the Rhine* (1943), *North Star* (1943) and *Another Part of the Forest* (1948).

5. Robert Riskin, who also wrote *Lady for a Day* (1933), re-made as *Pocketful of Miracles* (1961), *Mr Deeds Goes to Town* (1936), *Lost Horizon* (1937) and *You Can't Take It With You* (1938).

6. Clifford Odets adapted his own play for the screen, as he had done with *Golden Boy* (1939). He also wrote *The Big Knife* (1955) and wrote and directed *The Story on Page One* (1960).

7. Sonja Levine, one of the few women writers in Hollywood, who wrote screenplays for *State Fair* (1933), *Rhapsody in Blue* (1945), *Quo Vadis* (1951) and *Interrupted Melody* (1955, for which she received an Academy Award).

8. Terence Rattigan, whose other original screen works include [*Breaking*] *The Sound Barrier* (1952) and *The Yellow Rolls Royce* (1964). Most of his stage plays have been filmed, including *The Winslow Boy* (1948), *The Browning Version* (1951) and *Separate Tables* (1958).

9. William Rose, an American writer who was also responsible for *Genevieve* (1953), *The Smallest Show on Earth* (1957), *The Russians Are Coming, The Russians Are*

Coming (1966), and *Guess Who's Coming to Dinner* (1967, another Academy Award winner).

10. Robert Sherwood, an American playwright who wrote original screenplays (*Waterloo Bridge*, 1932; *The Best Years of Our Lives*, 1945) as well as adaptations such as *Rebecca* (in collaboration), and who had several of his works filmed (*Reunion in Vienna*, 1932; *The Petrified Forest*, 1936; *Abe Lincoln in Illinois* (1939), and others).

11. Edna O'Brien, an Irish novelist who wrote another original screenplay for *I Was Happy Here* (1966), and whose *Girl With Green Eyes* (1964) was filmed. She also wrote *Three into Two Won't Go* (1969).

12. Nunnally Johnson, screenwriter (*Tobacco Road*, 1941; *The Keys of the Kingdom*, 1944), writer and producer (*The Gunfighter*, 1950; *The Mudlark*, 1951; *The Desert Fox*, 1953), writer and director (*The Man in the Grey Flannel Suit*, 1956) and writer-producer-director (*The Three Faces of Eve*, 1959).

13. John Steinbeck. This is his only screenplay, but many of his novels have been filmed, including *Of Mice and Men* (1939), *The Grapes of Wrath* (1940), *Tortilla Flat* (1942), *The Red Pony* (1948), *East of Eden* (1954) and *The Wayward Bus* (1957).

14. John Osborne, better known for the film versions of his own plays: *Look Back in Anger* (1959), *The Entertainer* (1960) and *Inadmissible Evidence* (1968).

15. George Axelrod adapted his own play. He wrote the screenplays for *Breakfast at Tiffany's* (1961), *The Manchurian Candidate* (1962), and wrote, produced and directed *Lord Love a Duck* (1966) and *The Secret Life of an American Wife* (1968).

16. Carl Foreman, whose other screenplays include *Home of the Brave* (1949), *Cyrano de Bergerac* (1950), and *The*

Bridge on the River Kwai (1957). He wrote and produced *The Guns of Navarone* (1961) and *Young Winston* (1972), and wrote, produced and directed *The Victors* (1962).

17. Ben Hecht, who also wrote the screenplays for *Scarface* (1932), *Nothing Sacred* (1937), *Comrade X* (1940) and *Notorious* (1946). He is also well known for his collaborations with Charles MacArthur (*The Front Page*, 1931, and its re-make *His Girl Friday*, 1940; *Gunga Din*, 1938; *Wuthering Heights*, 1939), especially for the Academy Award-winning *The Scoundrel* (1934), which they wrote, produced and directed.

18. Garson Kanin, stage and screen writer-producer-director, and his wife Ruth Gordon (better known as an actress: *Rosemary's Baby*, 1968; *Harold and Maude*, 1972), whose other joint screenplays are *A Double Life* (1947), *Adam's Rib* (1949), *The Marrying Kind* (1952) and *Pat and Mike* (1952).

19. Bryan Forbes, an actor turned writer (*Cockleshell Heroes*, 1955; *The Angry Silence*, 1959), writer-director (*The L-Shaped Room*, 1962; *Seance on a Wet Afternoon*, 1964; *King Rat*, 1965; *The Whisperers*, 1966; *The Raging Moon*, 1970), and more recently a director and producer.

20. Harold Pinter. This was the first of his three screenplays for Joseph Losey (*Accident*, 1966, and *The Go-Between*, 1971, were the others). He also adapted his play *The Caretaker* [*The Guest*] (1963), and wrote the screenplays for *The Pumpkin Eater* (1964) and *The Quiller Memorandum* (1966).

7

1. Sergei Prokoviev, who subsequently turned the score into a cantata, and whose other film scores include *Lermontov* (1942) and Eisenstein's two-part *Ivan the Terrible* (1942, 1946).

2. Leonard Bernstein, better known in films for his two musicals, *On the Town* (1949) and *West Side Story* (1961).

3.   Alfred Newman, composer of more than 250 film scores, winner of six Academy Awards for musical direction (*Alexander's Ragtime Band*, 1938; *Tin Pan Alley*, 1940; *Mother Wore Tights*, 1947; *With a Song in My Heart*, 1952; *Call Me Madam*, 1953; *The King and I*, 1956), whose two brothers, Lionel and Emil, were also musical directors of note.

4.   Henry Mancini, for which he won an Academy Award. He has been arranger (*The Glenn Miller Story*, 1954) and musical director (*Rock Pretty Baby*, 1957; *High Time*, 1960) of films, but he is best known as a composer of scores (*The Pink Panther*, 1963; *Charade*, 1963; *Two for the Road*, 1967) and of title songs (*Days of Wine and Roses*, 1962, another Academy Award winner).

5.   Dmitri Shostakovich, whose other film work has included *The Fall of Berlin* (1947), *Hamlet* (1964) and *King Lear* (1971).

6.   Victor Young. He won a posthumous Academy Award for this score, the last of several hundred that he composed between 1935 and 1956.

7.   Arthur Honneger, whose film compositions included *Crime and Punishment* (1935), *Mayerling* (1936), *Regain* (1937) and *Un Revenant* (1946).

8.   Duke Ellington, whose band also played the score. This is the only film for which he has composed, although he and his band appeared in several minor musicals of the thirties and forties.

9.   Richard Addinsell. For this film he wrote his famous 'Warsaw Concerto', and his other film scores include *Goodbye Mr Chips* (1939), *Gaslight* (1940), *Blithe Spirit* (1945), *The Prince and the Showgirl* (1958) and *The Waltz of the Toreadors* (1962).

10. Elmer Bernstein, a reliable and prolific composer of film scores, whose best-known works include *The Man with*

the Golden Arm (1955), *The Magnificent Seven* (1960), *A Walk on the Wild Side* (1962), and who won an Academy Award (for musical direction) for *Thoroughly Modern Millie* (1967).

11. Aaron Copland, who also wrote the scores for *Of Mice and Men* (1939), *The Red Pony* (1948) and *The Heiress* (1949), for which he won an Academy Award.

12. André Previn, for which he won an Academy Award. He has written scores for many films (including *Bad Day at Black Rock*, 1954; *Elmer Gantry*, 1960) and has won Academy Awards as musical director of several films: *Gigi* (1958); *Porgy and Bess* (1959); *My Fair Lady* (1964) and *Throughly Modern Millie* (1967, with Elmer Bernstein).

13. Dmitri Tiomkin. This was one of his Academy Award scores, the others being *The High and the Mighty* (1954) and *The Old Man and the Sea* (1958). His many other scores include *Lost Horizon* (1937), *Duel in the Sun* (1946), *Giant* (1956) and *The Fall of the Roman Empire* (1964).

14. Richard Rodney Bennett, who has also written scores for *Only Two Can Play* (1961), *Billy Liar* (1963) and *Lady Caroline Lamb* (1972).

15. William Walton. He wrote the scores for the three Shakespeare–Olivier films as well: *Henry V* (1944), *Hamlet* (1948) and *Richard III* (1956).

16. John Addison. For this score he won an Academy Award; his other scores include *Look Back in Anger* (1959), *The Entertainer* (1960), *A Taste of Honey* (1961), *The Loneliness of the Long Distance Runner* (1962) and *Torn Curtain* (1966).

17. Jacques Ibert, who also wrote the music for Orson Welles's *Macbeth* (1948), and for one of the sequences (*The Circus*) in Gene Kelly's *Invitation to the Dance* (1956).

18. Georges Delerue. He also wrote the music for *Hiroshima mon Amour* (1958), *La Peau Douce* (1963), *The Pumpkin Eater* (1964) and *Viva Maria* (1965).

19. Georges Auric, who wrote scores for several notable films, including most of Cocteau's films (*Le Sang d'un Poète*, 1930; *La Belle et la Bête*, 1946; *Orphée*, 1949) and for others such as *Dead of Night* (1945), *Roman Holiday* (1953), *Rififi* (1954) and *Bonjour Tristesse* (1959).

20. Malcolm Arnold, for which he won an Academy Award. His other scores include [*Breaking*] *The Sound Barrier* (1952), *Island in the Sun* (1956), *The Inn of the Sixth Happiness* (1958) and *Tunes of Glory* (1960).

8

1.   Gene Kelly directed two films in 1956: his experimental but unsuccessful *Invitation to the Dance*, and *The Happy Road*, which he also produced. Previously he had co-directed (with Stanley Donen) three of the musicals in which he starred: *On the Town* (1949), *Singin' in the Rain* (1952) and *It's Always Fair Weather* (1955). Since 1956 he has directed *The Tunnel of Love* (1958), *Gigot* (1963), *A Guide for the Married Man* (1967), *Hello Dolly* (1969, probably his most successful directorial effort) and produced and directed *The Cheyenne Social Club* (1970).

2.   Clive Brook has directed only one film, *On Approval* (1943), which he also produced. He has made only one film appearance since 1944, in John Huston's *The List of Adrian Messenger* (1963).

3.   Marlon Brando has directed only one film: *One-Eyed Jacks* (1960), in which he also starred.

4.   To date, Clint Eastwood has directed one film, *Play Misty For Me* (1971), in which he starred as well. In it, director Don Siegel played a small part (the bartender);

Siegel has directed Eastwood in some of his best films: *Coogan's Bluff* (1968), *Two Mules for Sister Sara* (1969), *The Beguiled* (1971) and *Dirty Harry* (1972).

5.   Charles Laughton had only one directorial credit: *The Night of the Hunter* (1955), a promising début.

6.   In 1938, Leslie Howard co-directed *Pygmalion* with Anthony Asquith. His last two films were ones which he produced: *The Gentle Sex* (1942) and *The Lamp Still Burns* (1943).

7.   Nigel Patrick directed *Johnny Nobody* in 1961. Previously he had directed *How to Murder a Rich Uncle* (1957).

8.   Bob Fosse directed *Cabaret* in 1972. He began in films as a dancer (*Give a Girl a Break*, 1952), moved on to dancer-choreographer (*Kiss Me Kate*, 1953; *Damn Yankees*, 1958) to choreographer (*How to Succeed in Business Without Really Trying*, 1966) to choreographer-director (*Sweet Charity*, 1968, and *Cabaret*).

9.   In 1970, John Cassavetes directed *Husbands*, in which he also starred. His other films as director are *Shadows* (1960), *Too Late Blues* (1961), *Faces* (1968) and *Minnie and Moscowitz* (1972).

10. John Wayne has been credited with directing *The Alamo*, although it is said that John Ford had a hand in it as well. His other director-star effort was *The Green Berets* (1968), about which the less said the better.

11. Cornel Wilde directed and starred in *The Naked Prey* (1965). He has also been the director-star of *Storm Fear* (1956) and the producer-director-star of *The Devil's Hairpin* (1957), *Maracaibo* (1958), *Lancelot and Guinevere* (1963) and *Beach Red* (1967).

12. Albert Finney has only one film as director to date: the underrated and unseen *Charlie Bubbles* (1967).

13. Laurence Olivier directed and starred in *The Prince and the Showgirl* (1958), in which his co-star was Marilyn Monroe. He has also directed and starred in his three Shakespeare films: *Henry V* (1944), *Hamlet* (1948) and *Richard III* (1956). In 1970, he directed *Three Sisters*.

14. Lionel Jeffries's first directional effort was *The Railway Children* (1970), followed by *The Amazing Mr Blunden* (1972).

15. Richard Attenborough directed *Young Winston* (1972), his second film as a director. His first, which he also co-produced, was *Oh! What a Lovely War* (1969).

16. Orson Welles's second film as director was *The Magnificent Ambersons* in 1942. In the previous year he had starred in *Citizen Kane* (1941), the Academy Award-winning film which he directed and co-scripted. His other actor-writer-director films are *Journey into Fear* (1942, completed by Nórman Foster), *The Stranger* (1946, which he did not write), *Macbeth* (1948), *Othello* (1951), *Confidential Report* (1955), *Touch of Evil* (1958), *The Trial* (1962), *Chimes at Midnight* (1966) and *The Immortal Story* (1968). He has made almost forty films for other directors.

17. Peter Sellers's sole directorial venture has been *Mr Topaze* (1961).

18. James Cagney has also directed only one film: *Short Cut to Hell* (1958).

19. So far, Paul Newman has directed two films: *Rachel Rachel* (1968) and *Sometimes a Great Notion* [*Never Give an Inch*] (1971).

20. Peter Ustinov's first film as a writer-director was *School for Secrets* in 1946. He was also writer-director for *Vice-Versa* (1948) and was actor-writer-director for *Private Angelo* (1949), *Romanoff and Juliet* (1961), *Billy Budd* (1962) and *Lady L* (1965). He is also the director-star of *Hammersmith is Out* (1972).

Bibliography

Anderson, Lindsay and Sherwin, David: *If . . .*, Lorrimer Publishing, London, 1969.

Baxter, John: *The Gangster Film*, Tantivy Press, London, 1970.

Baxter, John: *Hollywood in the Thirties*, Paperback Library, New York, 1970.

Baxter, John: *Science Fiction in the Cinema*, Tantivy Press, New York, 1970.

Bentley, Eric: *Thirty Years of Treason: Excerpts from Hearings before the House Committee on Un-American Activities, 1938–1968*, The Viking Press, New York, 1971.

Bessie, Alvah: *Inquisition in Eden*, Macmillan, New York, 1965.

Blum, Daniel: *A Pictorial History of the Silent Screen*, Spring Books, London, 1962.

Blum, Daniel: *A Pictorial History of the Talkies*, Spring Books, London, 1958.

Blum, Daniel: *A Pictorial History of the Talkies* (revised edition), Spring Books, London, 1968.

Bogdanovitch, Peter: *Allan Dwan, The Last Pioneer*, Studio Vista, London, 1971.

Brownlow, Kevin: *The Parade's Gone By*, Secker & Warburg, London, 1968.

Boussinot, Roger (ed.): *L'Encyclopédie du Cinéma*, Bordas, Paris, 1967.

Cameron, Ian and Elisabeth: *Broads*, Studio Vista, London, 1969.

Cameron, Ian and Elisabeth: *Heavies*, Studio Vista, London, 1967.

Chaplin, Charles: *My Autobiography*, Penguin Books, Harmondsworth, 1966.

Cogley, John: *Report on Blacklisting: 1. Movies*, Fund for the Republic, New York, 1956.

Essoe, Gabe and Lee, Ray: *Gable: A Complete Gallery of his Screen Portraits*, Wolfe Publishing, London, 1967.

Everson, William K.: *The Bad Guys*, Bonanza Books, New York, 1964.

Eyles, Allen: *Horror Film Album*, Ian Allen, London, 1971.

Bibliography

Eyles, Allen: *Westerns Film Album*, Ian Allen, London, 1971.

Franklin, Joe: *Classics of the Silent Screen*, Citadel Press, New York, 1959.

French, Philip: The Movie Moguls: An Informal History of the Hollywood Tycoons, Penguin Books, Harmondsworth, 1971.

Furhammar, Leif and Isaksson, Folke: *Politics and Film*, Studio Vista, London, 1971.

Goodman, Walter: *The Committee: The Extraordinary Career of the House Committee on Un-American Activities*, Secker & Warburg, London, 1969.

Grierson, John: *Grierson on Documentary* (ed. Forsythe Hardy), Collins, London, 1966.

Griffith, Richard and Mayer, Arthur: *The Movies*, Simon & Schuster, New York, 1970.

Guarner, Jose Luis: *Roberto Rossellini*, Studio Vista, London, 1970.

Halliwell, Leslie: *The Filmgoer's Companion* (3rd edition), MacGibbon & Kee, London, 1969.

Higham, Charles and Greenberg, Joel: *Hollywood in the Forties*, Paperback Library, New York, 1968.

Lawson, John Howard: *Film: The Creative Process*, Hill & Wang, New York, 1964.

McCarty, Clifford: *Bogey: The Films of Humphrey Bogart*, Bonanza Books, New York, 1965.

Manvell, Roger: *New Cinema in Britain*, Studio Vista, London, 1969.

Mayersberg, Paul: *Hollywood, the Haunted House*, Allen Lane The Penguin Press, London, 1967.

Pickard, Roy: *A Companion to the Movies*, Lutterworth Press, London, 1972.

Pinter, Harold: *The Caretaker* (2nd edition), Methuen, London, 1962.

Preview, 1950, World Film Publications, London, 1950.

Robinson, David: *Hollywood in the Twenties*, Paperback Library, New York, 1968.

Rotha, Paul, Road, Sinclair and Griffith, Richard: *Documentary Film*, Faber & Faber, London, 1952.

Sarris, Andrew: *The American Cinema: Directors and Directions 1929–1968*, E. P. Dutton & Co., New York, 1968.

Smith, John M. and Cawkwell, Tim: *The World Encyclopedia of Film*, Studio Vista, London, 1972.

Stephenson, Ralph and Debrix, J. R.: *The Cinema as Art*, Penguin Books, Harmondsworth, 1965.

Taylor, John Russell and Jackson, Arthur: *The Hollywood Musical*, Secker & Warburg, London, 1971.

Truffaut, François: *Hitchcock*, Panther Books, London, 1968.

Vallance, Tom: *The American Musical*, A. Zwemmer & Co., New York, 1970.

Wiseman, Thomas: *Cinema*, Cassell, London, 1964.

Who's Who 1971, Adam & Charles Black, London, 1971.

Acknowledgements

The stills reproduced in this book come from the following films, and acknowledgements are due to:

ALLIED ARTISTS INTERNATIONAL
Al Capone (1958)
55 Days at Peking (1962)

ANGLO — EMI
Kind Hearts and Coronets (1949)
School for Scoundrels (1960)

BRITISH LION FILMS
The Belles of St Trinians (1954)
The Lady with the Lamp (1951)

COLUMBIA PICTURES
The Big Heat (1954)
Born Yesterday (1951)
Comanche Station (1960)
Don't Knock the Rock (1957)
It Happened One Night (1934)
Me and the Colonel (1957)
The Professionals (1966)
Rock Around the Clock (1956)
Salome (1953)
3.10 to Yuma (1957)
Underworld USA (1960) (Globe Enterprises/Columbia)
Zarak (1956)

METRO-GOLDWYN-MAYER
Act of Violence (1948)
Bohemian Girl (1936)
Escape from Fort Bravo (1953)
Forbidden Planet (1956)

A Free Soul (1931)
Gone with the Wind (1939)
Good News (1947)
The Haunting (1963)
High School Confidential (1960)
Honky Tonk (1941)
Ivanhoe (1952)
Johnny Eager (1941)
Knights of the Round Table (1954)
Laugh, Clown, Laugh (1928)
Love Me or Leave Me (1955)
Love on the Run (1937)
Madame Curie (1943)
Mrs Miniver (1942)
National Velvet (1944)
Night Train to Munich (1940)
The Prodigal (1955)
Quentin Durward (1956)
Romeo and Juliet (1936)
Royal Wedding (1948)
The Sheepman (1958)
2001; A Space Odyssey (1969)
The Unknown (1927)
West of Zanzibar (1928)

PARAMOUNT
Cleopatra (1934)
City Streets (1932)
The Conquest of Space (1955)
Golden Earrings (1947)
I Walk Alone (1947)
It Started in Naples (1959)
Lucky Jordan (1942)
The Man from Laramie (1953)
Morocco (1930)
On the Double (1962)
One-Eyed Jacks (1960)
Psycho (1960)
Rosemary's Baby (1968)
Seconds (1966)
When Worlds Collide (1955)

Acknowledgements

RANK FILMS
The Captain's Table (1958)
49th Parallel (1941)
Great Expectations (1946)
Waterloo Road (1944)

TWENTIETH-CENTURY FOX
The Black Rose (1950)
Blood and Sand (1941)
Captain from Castille (1947)
Charley's American Aunt (1941)
Cleopatra (1962)
Cry of the City (1949)
David and Bathsheba (1951)
The Day the Earth Stood Still (1952)
The Girl Can't Help It (1957)
The Innocents (1961)
Journey to the Centre of the Earth (1959)
Monte Walsh (1970)
Music is Magic (1935)
My Darling Clementine (1946)
My Friend Flicka (1943)
Planet of the Apes (1969)
The Prince of Foxes (1949)
The St Valentine's Day Massacre (1967)
Ziegfeld Follies (1944)

UNITED ARTISTS
Baby Face Nelson (1957)
The Garden of Allah (1936)
In Which We Serve (1942) (Gainsborough)
Knight without Armour (1937)
Kes (1970) (Woodfall Films and Kestrel Productions)
The Long Wait (1954)
Satyricon (1971)
Scarface (1932)
Sergeant York (1941) (United Artists TV)
Suddenly (1954)
The Unforgiven (1960)

UNIVERSAL
Frenzy (1972)

Freud (1963)
Guns in the Afternoon (1962)
The Invisible Ray (1935)
The Invisible Woman (1940)
Mirage (1965)
Phantom of the Opera (1925)
Rough Night in Jericho (1967)
Tarantula (1955)
Where the River Bends (1952)

WALT DISNEY
Bambi (1943)
Dumbo (1941)
Old Yeller (1957)
Treasure Island (1950)

WARNER BROTHERS
Dames (1934)
Don Juan (1926)
Fashions of 1934
Gold Diggers of 1935 (First National/Vitaphone)
Gold Diggers of 1937 (First National)
The Great Dictator (1940)
The Prime Minister (1940)
The Roaring Twenties (1939)
The Scarface Mob (1960)
Shalako (1968)